I.B.TAURIS SHORT HISTORIES

I.B.Tauris Short Histories is an authoritative and elegantly written new series which puts a fresh perspective on the way history is taught and understood in the twenty-first century. Designed to have strong appeal to university students and their teachers, as well as to general readers and history enthusiasts, *I.B.Tauris Short Histories* comprises a novel attempt to bring informed interpretation, as well as factual reportage, to historical debate. Addressing key subjects and topics in the fields of history, the history of ideas, religion, classical studies, politics, philosophy and Middle East studies, the series seeks intentionally to move beyond the bland, neutral 'introduction' that so often serves as the primary undergraduate teaching tool. While always providing students and generalists with the core facts that they need to get to grips with the essentials of any particular subject, *I.B.Tauris Short Histories* goes further. It offers new insights into how a topic has been understood in the past, and what different social and cultural factors might have been at work. It brings original perspectives to bear on the manner of its current interpretation. It raises questions and – in its extensive bibliographies – points to further study, even as it suggests answers. Addressing a variety of subjects in a greater degree of depth than is often found in comparable series, yet at the same time in concise and compact handbook form, *I.B.Tauris Short Histories* aims to be 'introductions with an edge'. In combining questioning and searching analysis with informed history writing, it brings history up-to-date for an increasingly complex and globalized digital age.

www.short-histories.com

'Mark Woolmer has given us a new and up-to-date introduction to Phoenician history and culture that will also act as a useful reference work for scholars and students looking for discussion of the most recent excavations, discoveries and ideas in the field. He challenges the traditional chronological limitations of the Phoenician period in the Levant as well as academic preconceptions of religion in the Phoenician cities, and he brings the social position of women to the fore for the first time. He additionally tackles the western Phoenicians, cutting through much scholarly verbiage on the varied motivations that lay behind Phoenician expansion in the Mediterranean, and on the different kinds of settlements they established there.'

– Josephine Crawley Quinn, Associate Professor in Ancient History, University of Oxford and Martin Frederiksen Fellow and Tutor in Ancient History, Worcester College, Oxford

'It is not often that specialists can make information simple and accessible to the wider public. Mark Woolmer has very successfully, and in a clear and attractive way, met the challenge of presenting to both specialist and layman the complex historical and archaeological documentation on the Phoenicians. His book succeeds in being both an informative and an enjoyable read.'

– Hélène Sader, Professor of Archaeology, American University of Beirut

'Students, teachers and other interested readers will find here accurate information, insightful interpretation, and a comprehensive discussion, briefly presented. The author is internationally recognised as an expert on the Phoenician civilisation, and this excellent and readable short history does his reputation full justice.'

– Philip C. Schmitz, Professor of History, Eastern Michigan University

A Short History of . . .

A SHORT HISTORY OF THE PHOENICIANS

Mark Woolmer

I.B. TAURIS

LONDON · NEW YORK

Published in 2017 by
I.B.Tauris & Co. Ltd
London • New York
www.ibtauris.com

Copyright © 2017 Mark Woolmer

ISBN: 978 1 78076 617 1 (HB)
ISBN: 978 1 78076 618 8 (PB)
eISBN: 978 1 78672 217 1
ePDF: 978 1 78673 217 0

A full CIP record for this book is available from the British Library
A full CIP record is available from the Library of Congress

Library of Congress Catalog Card Number: available

Typeset by Free Range Book Design & Production Limited
Printed and bound by T.J. International, Padstow, Cornwall

Contents

List of Maps and Illustrations

MAPS

FIGURES

Acknowledgements

In the preparation of this book I am indebted to a great number of friends, family and colleagues who have offered encouragement, assisted in the acquisition of illustrations, provided scholarly input, generously made available their time and recent research, or acted as guides around Lebanon and the Middle East. None should be supposed to agree with my arguments, let alone share responsibility for any errors. Thanks go to Anne-Marie Afeiche, Craig Barclay, Rachel Barclay, Barney Chesterton, Claude Doumet-Serhal, Jennifer Ingleheart, Ted Kaizer, Desiree Karam, Joe Khalife, Sian Lewis, Lloyd Llewellyn-Jones, Jonathan Prag, Andrej Petrovic, Ivana Petrovic, Josephine Quinn, Hélène Sader, Clemence Schultze, Kathryn Stevens, Jonathon Tubb, Rana Yaacoub and Rashed Zarka. Particular thanks are owed to Mr Srkis El Khoury (Director General of Antiquities – Ministry of Culture of Lebanon) for kindly granting me permission to include images of the items held in the National Museum of Beirut, and to Luke Evans and Justine Wolfenden who took the time and effort to improve the structure and expression of this volume. I am also grateful for the enthusiasm and ideas of the many students who have helped to guide and shape this work, in particular those who took my 'World of the Phoenicians' module or participated in the Daily Life in Ancient Lebanon exhibition at Durham University. Special mention goes to Savana Armitage, Hannah Bash, Claire Cosset, Nicole Di-Cicco, Ankaret El-Haj, Cally Horobin, Ben Kolbeck, Molly Sadler, Zenia Selby, April Stephenson and Eris Williams-Reed. Finally, I am grateful to Alex Wright for having invited me to write this book and for having proved such a patient, supportive and encouraging editor.

Mark Woolmer

This volume is dedicated to my very own Phoenician queen, Reine El Fata, to whom I owe the greatest debt of appreciation, and to the memory of Glenn Markoe, a true gentleman and scholar who I hope would have approved of this work.

Abbreviations

ANET   Pritchard, J.B. (ed.), *Ancient Near Eastern Texts Relating to the Old Testament* (Princeton, NJ: Princeton University Press, 1969).

EA   The El-Amarna tablets numbered according to: Knudton, J.A., *Die El-Amarna-Tafeln, mit Einleitung und Erläuterungen* (VAB 2) (Leipzig: Hinrichs, 1915). English translations of these texts can be found in: Moran, W.L., *The Amarna Letters* (Baltimore, MD: Johns Hopkins University Press, 1992).

IG II²   Kirchner, J. (ed.), *Inscriptiones Graecae II et III: Inscriptiones Atticae Euclidis anno posteriores* (Berlin: De Gruyter, 1913–40).

IGLS VII   Rey-Coquais, J.-P. (ed.), *Inscriptions grecques et latines de la Syrie, VII. Arados et régions voisines* (Beirut: Bibliothèque archéologique et historique, 1970).

KAI   Donner, H. and Röllig, W., *Kanaanäische und aramäische Inschriften* (I⁵ 200; II² 1968; III² 1969) (Wiesbaden: Harrassowitz, 1968–2002).

Saggs   Saggs, H., 'Numrud Letters, 1952 – Part II', *Iraq*, vol. 17 (1955), pp. 126–60.

SEG   *Supplementum Epigraphicum Graecum*

TSSI   Gibson, J.C.L., *Textbook of Syrian Semitic Inscriptions III: Phoenician Inscriptions* (Oxford: Clarendon Press, 1975).

Preface

Of all the peoples of the ancient Near East, it was the Phoenicians who conceivably had the greatest impact on the history of the Mediterranean, and yet they are also the least understood. Occupying a narrow strip of land along the coast of modern-day Lebanon, Syria and northern Israel, the Phoenicians were pre-eminent merchants who, unlike their Syrian and Canaanite neighbours, never sought to create a unified empire or kingdom but instead coalesced into a number of fiercely independent city states (the most important of which were Arwad, Byblos, Beirut, Sidon, Sarepta and Tyre). Though politically independent from one another, these city states nevertheless had a common language and script, shared several cultural traits, and were united by their maritime and trading interests, thus allowing us to think in terms of a Phoenician civilisation.

However, despite being famed in antiquity as learned scribes who transmitted the alphabet to the West, as skilled artisans who produced objects of unrivalled quality and beauty, as navigators and mariners *par excellence* who helped expand and define the boundaries of the ancient world, and as exceptional businessmen who revolutionised long-distance exchange, outside of Lebanon the Phoenicians have failed to capture the public's interest or imagination in quite the same way as the Assyrians, Egyptians or Greeks. This can largely be explained by the lack of systematic excavations at Phoenician sites prior to the mid-twentieth century and by the relative mundanity of Phoenician material culture when compared to the monumental stone reliefs of Assyria, the mummies and royal tombs of Egypt, and the exquisite pottery and statuary of Archaic and Classical Greece. Consequentially, whereas the objects recovered during the late eighteenth and early nineteenth centuries at sites in Greece (Knossos, Mycenae), Egypt (the Valley of the Kings, Karnak) and Iraq (Nimrud, Nineveh) garnered much public attention throughout Western Europe, Phoenician items were generally considered to be of little interest and thus largely absent from museum collections and exhibitions (a situation that continued until the late 1980s).

Further compounding matters was the fact that, in a supremely ironic twist of fate, the civilisation responsible for disseminating the alphabet to the West has left virtually no written legacy of its own. With no Phoenician histories, mythologies, liturgies or business documents on which to draw, and with a dearth of material remains, early scholars considered the Phoenicians to be a lost civilisation. Although knowledge of Phoenician society and culture has improved greatly in the past 40 years, the Phoenicians have nevertheless largely remained an enigma outside of academic circles.

By drawing together information that is either scattered in a multitude of academic journal articles, written in foreign languages, in books that are out of print, or in conference proceedings that are difficult to obtain for the non-specialist reader, this volume seeks to provide an accessible and engaging introduction to the Phoenician civilisation. It therefore includes a schematic overview of Phoenician culture and history (between *c.*1550 to *c.*300 BCE), an examination of the present state of archaeological investigation, and several case studies which are used to highlight topics of particular interest or significance. To cover such a broad array of themes I have inevitably had to be selective; however, important items of modern scholarship are referenced so that those wishing to learn more about certain topics should find it relatively easy to do so. As with all studies of the Phoenicians, this book should be considered a work in progress as new archaeological discoveries from Phoenician sites around the Mediterranean will undoubtedly disprove or modify the interpretations it presents. Finally, by promoting the rich cultural heritage of Lebanon at a time when perceptions of the country in the Western world are often distorted by politics, I hope to encourage intellectual dialogue and to promote greater cultural understanding and awareness.

Timeline

All dates BCE unless otherwise stated.

7000	First human settlement at the site which would become Byblos.
c.4000	Founding of the city of Sidon.
c.4000–3000	First trade contact between Byblos and Egypt.
2900	The Egyptian king Sneferu sends a maritime expedition to Phoenicia in search of cedar wood.
c.2700	The Temple of The Lady of Byblos is constructed.
2750	Traditional date for the founding of Tyre.
c.2500	Regular trade links are established between Egypt and Phoenicia.
2100	The conquest of Byblos by the Amorites.
c.1800	Emergence of the alphabetic script known as 'proto-Canaanite'.
c.1500	The Phoenicians take the first steps towards developing a phonetic alphabet.
1479–1425	The reign of Thutmosis III who becomes the first Egyptian pharaoh to fully subjugate the Phoenician cities and extract tribute from them.
c.1332–1292	The Amarna Dynasty rules in Egypt.
c.1200–800	First wave of Phoenician migration during which small settlements and trading posts are established throughout the Mediterranean.
c.1200	Tyre and Sidon replace Byblos as the most influential Phoenician cities. Outbreak of the Trojan War.

1115–1076	Reign of Tiglath-Pilesar I of Assyria who conquers Phoenicia and incorporates it into the Assyrian Empire.
1100	Earliest appearance of the Phoenician alphabet. Phoenician mariners begin to navigate by use of the Pole Star.
*c.*1056	The Phoenician cities regain their independence as the Assyrian Empire collapses.
1000	Death of Ahriam of Byblos, whose sarcophagus bears the oldest inscription written using the Phoenician alphabet.
*c.*969–939	Hiram ascends to the throne of Tyre and forms a close bond of friendship with the Israelite kings David and Solomon.
*c.*876–854	Ashurbanipal II demands tribute from the Phoenician cities and asserts Assyrian dominance over the region. During his reign the Phoenician cities are eventually incorporated into the Neo-Assyrian Empire.
*c.*860	Jezebel, a princess of Tyre, marries Ahab, King of Israel.
*c.*830	The city of Kition is founded in Cyprus.
814	Traditional date for the founding of Carthage in Tunisia.
*c.*800–600	Second wave of Phoenician migration during which trading-posts are converted into colonies and a number of new, larger settlements are founded.
*c.*800–750	The Phoenicians begin to settle in Sicily.
*c.*770–760	The city of Gadir (Cádiz) is founded in Spain.
*c.*750	The city of Motya is founded in Spain.
727	King Luli of Tyre attempts to break free of Assyrian rule but is quickly defeated.
701	Following a second unsuccessful rebellion, King Luli flees to Cyprus where he eventually dies in exile.
678–675	Sidon rebels against Assyrian rule and is completely destroyed following a three-year siege.
636	The Phoenicians regain their independence following the collapse of the Neo-Assyrian Empire.
*c.*600	The Phoenicians undertake the first circum-navigation of Africa.

588–587	Destruction of Tyre by the Babylonian king Nebuchadnezzar following a 13-year siege. Sidon replaces Tyre as the most influential Phoenician city.
528	The Phoenician cities willingly accept their absorption into the Persian Empire following the defeat of Babylon.
333	Alexander the Great sacks Sidon.
332	Alexander the Great besieges and conquers Tyre.
c.301–83	Control of Phoenicia passes back and forth between the Seleucid and Egyptian empires.
64 CE	The Roman general Pompey subdues the last remains of the Seleucid Empire and assimilates Phoenicia into the Roman province of Syria.

Map 1: The principal cities, and
approximate extent, of Phoenicia during the Iron Age

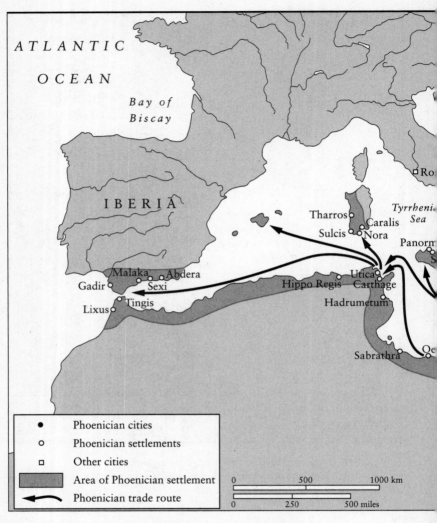

Map 2: The Phoenicians' principal Mediterranean settlements and trade routes

Black Sea

THRACE

MACEDONIA

Troy

Aegean
GREECE *Sea* Sardis

ANATOLIA

Athens Ephesus

Sparta

Tarsus

Ugarit
Latakia
Arwad
Byblos
Berytus
Sidon
Tyre

Kition

Mediterranean Sea

is Magna

Dor

Alexandria Joppa Jerusalem

Memphis

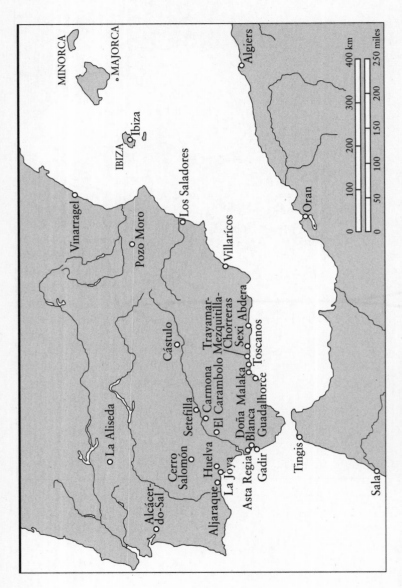

Map 3: The principal Phoenician colonies and settlements in southern Iberia

Introduction

WHO WERE THE 'PHOENICIANS'?

We begin with perhaps the most contentious question faced by those studying ancient Phoenicia: just who were the 'Phoenicians'? Although this may appear to be a relatively simple and straightforward question, providing anything close to a satisfactory answer requires engagement with a number of complex theories and models. In fact, this question has proved so contentious that it has led some scholars to question the very existence of a 'Phoenician' civilisation (a somewhat shocking proposal considering this volume is intended as an introduction to this very people).[1] Perhaps the best explanation as to why there is no easy answer to what should be a relatively straightforward question is that the identity and history of the 'Phoenicians' have long been defined by outsiders (most prominently the Egyptians, Israelites and Greeks).

The earliest appearance of a word that is even approximately analogous to the modern term 'Phoenician' is the ancient Greek Φοινίκη (Phoiníkē), which first appears in the Iliad (an epic poem written in the late eighth or early seventh century BCE). The poem's author, Homer, does not use 'Phoenician' as an ethnic demonstrative (ethnonym) as might be expected but rather as a term to denote people from one of the coastal cities of the Levant who were on or over the sea. At the funeral games of Patroclus, for example, the prize bestowed to the victor of the foot race was an ornate silver mixing bowl which was said to have been made by Sidonian craftsmen and then conveyed to Greece by 'Phoenician men' (Iliad, 23.74–5). Significantly, the artisans responsible for making the bowl are

1

identified according to their city state whilst the men who shipped it to Greece are simply given the generic label 'Phoenician'. Similarly Odysseus, when masquerading as a fugitive from Crete, recounts that he had paid some 'lordly Phoenicians' to transport him to Ithaca, men who had subsequently returned home to 'well-peopled Sidon' (*Odyssey*, 13.271–86). The implication from these two passages is that individuals from Sidon could be referred to as either 'Phoenician' or 'Sidonian' depending on the context in which they are found (the former being employed when they are on or over the sea, the latter when they are at home).

The same is also true of people from the other Levantine coastal cities, thus, for instance, an individual from Tyre was referred to as 'Phoenician' when abroad and 'Tyrian' when at home. A recent investigation into the use of the term 'Phoenician' by Greek and Roman authors has in fact shown that it was almost exclusively employed to denote people from one of the Levantine coastal cities who were on or over the sea and rarely, if ever, as an ethnonym.[2] Although cognisant of the fact that the Levantine coastal cities had markedly different cultures and were politically independent of one another, the Greeks, and subsequently the Romans, could justify grouping these populations together under the generic label 'Phoenician' due to the distinctive Semitic dialect they were all perceived to speak (although each of the city states had slightly different vernaculars – see Chapter 2 – to an outsider they must have sounded almost identical). Thus, despite the term 'Phoenician' being widely employed by Greek and Roman authors, it was never used as a form of self- or group-identification by the 'Phoenicians' themselves.

The other appellation commonly associated with the Phoenicians is Canʿani (Canaanites) which, like *Phoiníkē*, appears to have been bestowed upon them by outsiders, firstly by the Egyptians and then by the Israelites. The earliest reference to the Canaanites, found in an eighteenth-century BCE letter from the king of Mari to one of his generals, merely records that a group of men referred to as Canaanites were living in a region (or town) known as Raḫiṣum. The brevity of the reference means that it is impossible to determine whether the term was being used as an ethnonym or to designate a social or occupational group. From the sixteenth to the twelfth centuries BCE, the term Canaan was used to denote a large geographic area of the Levant controlled by Egypt; the precise boundaries of this region are unknown but they must have fluctuated in response to the changing political and military fortunes of Egypt. Although it is still unclear whether the term referred to a formal Egyptian province or administrative district, it undoubtedly had political connotations as attested by its use in the Amarna Letters. To complicate matters, however, the term is also occasionally employed as a social or occupational designation during this period.

Following Egypt's withdrawal from the Levant at the end of the Bronze Age, the terms 'Canaan' and 'Canaanite' completely vanish from the historical record and only reappear in the context of the Old Testament. In the Old Testament 'Canaan' is used to denote a large area of land west of the River Jordon in which the inhabitants all spoke North-West Semitic dialects, whilst 'Canaanite' could simply mean 'merchant'.[3] Although including the Phoenician cities, the biblical Canaan was not limited to the coast and thus encompassed a variety of tribes and nations including the Hittites, Girgashites, Amorites, Canaanites, Perizzites, Hivites and Jebusites (it is not until the late Classical or early Hellenistic Period that the term is used solely to denote the cities now referred to as 'Phoenician'). Moreover, whereas during the Bronze Age the terms 'Canaan' and 'Canaanite' had been used as political or social demonstratives, they now acquired a number of theological or ideological connotations (for instance, the Israelites often used the Canaanites as a convenient religious or social 'other'). Consequently, care must be taken not to confuse 'Canaan' of the Late Bronze Age with that found in the Old Testament as there are significant differences between the two. Significantly, as 'Canaanite', like the Greek *Phoinikē*, was neither an ethnic demonstrative nor indigenous to the city states of the Levantine coast, the hypothesis that the 'Phoenicians' self-identified using this term can be dismissed.

So what did the 'Phoenicians' call themselves? There is no clear indication that the inhabitants of the Levantine coastal cities ever considered themselves to be a cultural or political collective and thus the populations which others referred to as 'Phoenician' or 'Canaanite' self-identified according to city-based affiliations or family groups. For instance, the indigenous epigraphic sources reveal that the Phoenicians considered their cities to be physical spaces rather than communities and thus individuals typically used toponyms rather than ethnonyms when self-identifying (e.g. citizens of Sidon tend to record that they are 'from the city of Sidon' in preference to calling themselves 'Sidonian'). This way of self-identifying may well originate from the royal practice of claiming rule over a particular city rather than over a particular group or people (i.e. the title 'King of Byblos' is used in preference to 'King of the Byblians').

Furthermore, in contrast to Greece, where civic identities could be subsumed into wider regional ones (for instance, citizens of Athens could define themselves by their deme, city or nationality – e.g. Archarnian, Athenian, Greek), in Phoenicia there was no concept of a common or shared identity beyond the level of the city state. Consequently, instead of developing any notion of a national identity, the Phoenicians retained a fierce sense of independence and individuality resulting in an unwillingness to co-operate or come together as a unified political entity. This independence is perhaps most prominently emphasised by the Greek historian Herodotus in his account of the Persian Wars. Although highlighting the strength and superiority of Phoenician warships within the Persian navy, Herodotus records that each of the city states sent its own contingent and commander. Consequently, this so-called 'Phoenician' fleet should not be viewed as a collective effort but rather as the sum of each city state's separate contribution. The lack of a national identity also meant that the Phoenicians placed a much greater importance on ancestry, leading many to cite multiple generations of their immediate or extended family when constructing their identity (most commonly in epitaphs). Therefore, in answer to the question posed above, as the Phoenicians never considered themselves as having a shared ethnic identity, they typically defined themselves according to the city state in which they held citizenship (i.e. 'I am a man of Byblos' or 'I am from Tyre' rather than 'I am a Phoenician' or 'I am a Canaanite' for which there are no equivalents in the Phoenician language).

Phoenician Ethnicity

If the Phoenicians self-identified according to city-based affiliations and if these city states never achieved, or even desired, political unity, why then are they studied in conjunction with one another? The answer lies in the belief that the citizens of these city states were ethnically similar. Ethnicity is created by the attributing of marked cultural characteristics to a particular group and can occur as the result of self-ascription or ascription by others. These cultural characteristics include language (both written and oral), ritual behaviour, mortuary practices, physical features, cuisine, dining practices and various facets of material culture such as manufacturing techniques, architectural forms, artistic traditions and clothing styles.[4] It is clear that the Greeks, Romans, and the Israelite authors of the Old Testament, considered the city states between Akko and Arwad as sharing some of these cultural characteristics (although which ones is often unclear). This view was to have a profound influence on scholarship, so much so that in 1646 Samuel Bochart (a French biblical scholar) fully embraced the idea that the Phoenician cities shared a common ethnicity – a conclusion which is directly attributable to the fact that he relied solely on the classical and biblical texts when composing his history.

Although Bochart's work was not the first to depend exclusively on these sources, it was certainly the most influential. Therefore, by the mid-nineteenth century, when linguistic, archaeological, historical and anthropological research on the Levant and North Africa came into fashion, there were already several centuries of scholarship devoted to 'Phoenicia' and the 'Phoenicians'. Hence, despite utilising revolutionary new models, methods and theories, the academic works produced at this time were founded on long-established, and indeed long-accepted, scholarly traditions, and so generally tried to prove rather than challenge pre-existing views concerning the nature and ethnicity of the 'Phoenicians'. Consequently, most nineteenth-century academics readily accepted that the 'Phoenicians' had a shared ethnicity which justified studying the various 'Phoenician' city states in conjunction with one another.

It was not until the 1980s that scholars first began to question the extent to which this assumption was correct. In 1983 Wolfgang Röllig criticised the vagueness of the term 'Phoenician', querying the appropriateness of using it to denote a hypothetical ethnic group.[5] This was a view also championed by the renowned Italian archaeologist Sabatino Moscati who concluded that the lack of an acknowledged territory, homogeneous language and shared historical and cultural traditions meant that the Phoenicians cannot be thought of as an ethnic group.[6] Since the work of Röllig and Moscati it has become customary to acknowledge the city-based allegiances of the Phoenicians whilst emphasising a number of co-occurring cultural features that made their civilisation distinct from those of their neighbours (although it must be noted that these shared cultural features are not evidence for the 'Phoenicians' ever considering *themselves* as sharing a common ethnicity). In recent years, however, even the notion of shared cultural characteristics has been called into question as many of the supposedly 'Phoenician' traits have turned out to be limited to one or two city states or were shared with other groups or peoples (for instance, the so-called 'Phoenician' bichrome ceramic ware is now known to have been produced in cities all along the Levantine coast, both in Phoenicia and Palestine, and on Cyprus).

So where does this leave us? In this volume, the term 'Phoenician' will be used as short-hand to denote a specific group of Levantine city states that were connected by their geographic location, had a common interest in seafaring and maritime commerce, and shared a small number of cultural characteristics. It will be used sparingly and only on those occasions when it is appropriate to talk in general terms rather than specifying an individual city or groups of cities. Additionally, the term 'Phoenicia' will be used to denote the combined area controlled or administered by the various 'Phoenician' city states.

Defining Phoenicia

There is a general consensus regarding the approximate geographic limits of the Phoenician homeland both in the classical sources and in modern histories of Phoenicia. It is therefore widely accepted that the Phoenician homeland (i.e. the territory in which the Phoenician cities first arose or distinguished themselves) roughly adhered to a narrow coastal strip stretching from northern Israel, through Lebanon, and into southern Syria. This was a territory that was squeezed between the Mediterranean to the west and the formidable Lebanon mountain range to the east, a position that limited the opportunities for cultural and political expansion, and which was instrumental in determining the maritime persuasion of its inhabitants (see Map 1). Although scholars are in broad agreement regarding the northernmost limits of Phoenicia (with the majority advocating the island of Arwad situated just off the coast of western Syria) there is a slight divergence of views when it comes to defining the region's southern limits (proposals include Tyre in southern Lebanon, Akko and Mount Carmel in northern Israel, and even as far south as Ashkelon near the northern border of the Gaza Strip). These conflicting opinions result from the differing importance that has been given to the textual and archaeological evidence. Those who endorse a more southerly location generally accept the view propagated by the classical authors that the Phoenicians occupied almost the entirety of the Levantine coast. Whilst those who favour a more northerly border place a much greater emphasis on the archaeological evidence which suggests that those cities with a predominantly 'Phoenician' material culture were generally situated to the north of Akko.

In order to avoid confusion or controversy, this present study will adopt the position that the Phoenician homeland encompassed a narrow coastal fringe along the Levantine coast from Akko in the south to Arwad in the north. Although recognising that the extent of these borders could fluctuate (for instance, Tyre regularly attempted to extend its sphere of influence southwards), the territory between Akko and Arwad will be considered as comprising the core of the Phoenician homeland. The primary focus of this volume will therefore be the cities of Arwad (or Arad), Berytus (or Beirut), Byblos (or Jebail, Jebeil, Jubail, Gebal), Sarepta, Sidon (or Ṣaydā) and Tyre. In contrast to previous scholarship which has tended to draw an arbitrary distinction between the inhabitants of this region prior to and post 1200 BCE (with the former being known as 'Canaanite' and the latter 'Phoenician'), this volume will refer to the inhabitants of the cities listed above as 'Phoenician' throughout. This decision is justified on two counts: firstly, it will help avoid unnecessary confusion and, secondly, neither the literary nor archaeological evidence indicates that the cultural and social changes that occurred at the end of the Bronze Age were significant enough to warrant such a distinction.

Geographic Terminology

Historians use a bewildering array of terminology to describe different regions of the ancient Near East. The most commonly encountered are:

Levant: an imprecise geographical term that is used to refer to a large area in the Middle East covered by Israel, Lebanon, parts of Syria and western Jordan. The Levant is bordered by the Taurus Mountains to the north, the Zagros Mountains to the east, the Sinai Peninsula to the south and the Mediterranean to the west.

Canaan: an area encompassing the land between the Jordan River and the Mediterranean as well as much of present-day Lebanon, Israel, Palestine,

Jordan and parts of western Syria (in Biblical usage the name was conferred to the region west of the Jordan River).

Syro-Palestine: a region of the ancient Near East which incorporated parts of southern-central Syria and Palestine. In modern terms this region comprises Israel, the West Bank, the Gaza Strip, Jordan, Lebanon and southern Syria.

Phoenicia: from 1200 BCE it is customary to distinguish the coastal inhabitants of Canaan from those dwelling further inland. Consequently, from this point on, the narrow coastal fringe stretching from northern Israel, through Lebanon and into Syria becomes known as Phoenicia.

Mesopotamia: the name for the area of the Tigris–Euphrates river system that roughly equates to modern-day Iraq, Kuwait, the north-eastern part of Syria and areas of south-eastern Turkey and south-western Iran.

THE CLIMATE AND LANDSCAPE OF PHOENICIA

The paleo-environmental evidence, provided by pollen cores and dendroclimatological analysis (the study of tree rings), indicates that the climate of ancient Phoenicia was generally comparable with that of modern Lebanon. The temperature and weather conditions of the region are determined by its position between the subtropical aridity of the African continent and the subtropical humidity of the eastern Mediterranean region. Phoenicia is thus considered to have had a temperate Mediterranean climate which was characterised by long, hot summers (June–September), during which there was virtually no rain, and cool, wet winters (December–March), which received about 60 per cent of the region's annual rainfall. Autumn (October–November) was a transitional season which saw a gradual lowering of temperatures and little rain, whilst spring (April–May) saw the ceasing of the winter rains and the beginning of the growing season. As is still true today, rainfall varied from year to year and precipitation was often concentrated in violent storms resulting in erosion and flooding, especially during the winter months. The mean temperature on the coastal plains was about 27° C in summer and 10° C in winter. January would have been the coldest month with an average temperature of 7–8° C, whilst the warmest was August with an average temperature of around 28° C (when the Sirocco – a hot, dry, southerly wind – was blowing, temperatures could reach well in excess of 40° C).[7] However, the influence of the Mediterranean Sea, the diverse topography of the region, and the Syrian desert to the north helped to create a variety of micro-climates within the borders of ancient Phoenicia and thus it is possible to identify four distinct topographic/climatic zones:[8]

A narrow coastal plain: this was a small strip of land (only 6.5 kilometres at its widest point) situated between the Mediterranean to the west and mountains to the east. Most of the major Phoenician cities such as Berytus, Byblos, Sidon, Tyre, Sarepta and Arwad were founded in this region and thus from the tenth century it housed the majority of Phoenicia's population. The region had a typical Mediterranean climate and was blessed with fertile soil that was enriched by the minerals and nutrients washed down from the mountains.

The Lebanon Mountains: adjacent to the narrow coastal plain was a chain of mountains, modern Mount Lebanon, which ran parallel to the sea from north to south and reached over 3,000 metres at its highest point. On average the distance between the mountains and the coast was 30 kilometres. This region experienced a typically alpine climate, with plenty of snow and sub-zero temperatures on the peaks during winter. During spring the melting snow created fast-flowing rivers which provided the Phoenicians with one of the best supplies of fresh water in the ancient Near East. The famous cedar trees grew high in the mountains, while the lower slopes were ideally suited for the cultivation of grapes, figs, olives and even barley.

The Bekaa Valley: an inland plateau, situated 1,000 metres above sea level, and located 30 kilometres to the east of Beirut. In antiquity the region received less precipitation than the rest of Phoenicia and had more dramatic climatic extremes: summers were intensely hot and dry, while winters were cold and frosty. However, as the Bekaa Valley was watered by two rivers (the Orontes and the Litani) it was ideally suited to agriculture and thus coveted by many of the Phoenician cities.

The Anti-Lebanon Mountains: these formed Phoenicia's most easterly topographical zone running north–south in parallel with the Bekaa Valley. The range's highest peak is Mount Hermon at 2,814 metres, making it a formidable barrier for would-be invaders and creating a natural boundary with neighbouring Syria. The peaks of the Anti-Lebanon, like those of the Lebanon Mountains, were snow-covered for much of the year. However, the Anti-Lebanon was far more arid than the Lebanon Mountains, especially in its northern parts, meaning it was less productive and more thinly populated.

Despite Phoenicia's compact dimensions, what it lacked in size it certainly made up for in geographical diversity. The mountainous landscape of Phoenicia, at least half of which was situated at over 900 metres, was extremely complex and diverse, with landforms, soils and vegetation varying considerably within short distances. Although Phoenicia's coastline was abrupt, rocky and lacking deep estuaries, the calmness of the eastern Mediterranean combined with the region's generally mild and predictable weather and abundance of natural harbours meant it was well suited for commercial shipping. By situating their cities either directly on the coast, on mainland promontories that dominated a bay, in small natural inlets, or occasionally on islands lying just offshore (Tyre and Arwad), the Phoenicians were able to control the most lucrative sea routes between the eastern and western Mediterranean and thereby became important commercial centres. In order to protect and expand their burgeoning maritime interests, many of the Phoenician cities (particularly Sidon, Tyre, Byblos and Arwad) sought to become regional thalassocracies and so invested heavily in their navies. The profits acquired from maritime trade also helped ensure that the Phoenician cities retained some level of commercial and political independence even when subjugated by more powerful empires such as Egypt, Assyria and Babylon. As they could afford to pay high levels of tribute, most empires found it advantageous to allow the Phoenician cities to retain some degree of autonomy so as not to disrupt their lucrative trading operations which could be heavily taxed. The coastal positioning of the major Phoenician cities can therefore be identified as having a profound impact not only on their economic prosperity, but also on their political power, prestige and influence for much of the first millennium. The coastal location of their cities also enabled the Phoenicians to harvest a variety of marine resources including various fish, molluscs and salt.

The coastal cities were also positioned so that they could exploit the fertile low-lying agricultural regions situated just inland. Due to the numerous streams and rivers which flowed through the coastal plains, the soil was rich in nutrients and well irrigated, making it particularly suited to the growing of wheat, vines, fruit (such as figs) and olives. Significantly, although these regions contained an abundance of watercourses, none of them was navigable and so could not be harnessed for transport. Moreover, because these rivers and streams had such steep gradients, which meant they were very fast flowing, they tended to be erosive instead of depository in nature and so carved the landscape into segments. The foothills and spurs of the Lebanon Mountain range, which further broke up the landscape, provided the Phoenician cities with a number of other valuable resources, the most important of which were the vast forests of cedars, pines and cypresses. The dearth of forests in much of the rest of the Near East meant that there was a great demand for Phoenician timber as it was ideally suited for the construction of buildings and ships. The famous cedars of Lebanon, an example of which can be found on the Lebanese national flag, were particularly prized and could thus command high prices. These forests were also home to wild game, panthers, bears, hyenas, wolves and jackals, all of which were excellent sources of meat. The Lebanon and Anti-Lebanon mountain ranges also provided the Phoenicians with an array of mineral resources, albeit in limited quantities. Recent archaeological excavations have shown that Phoenician mining techniques were surprisingly advanced, enabling them to extract a number of valuable minerals including iron, lignite, marble, limestone and a fine-grained sand that was used to manufacture high-quality glass. Like the coastal plains, the Bekaa Valley, which was sandwiched between the Lebanon and Anti-Lebanon mountain ranges, also had a temperate climate that made it ideally suited to agriculture. From the first century BCE, the region, which had been subsumed into the Roman Empire, served as a source of grain for the Roman provinces of the Levant. The southern half of the valley, which was irrigated by the Orontes and Litani rivers, could support a variety of crops including wheat, corn, vegetables and fruit, whilst the northern half, which received a lower annual rainfall and had less fertile soil, was used primarily as grazing land by pastoral nomads. On the whole, the landscape of Phoenicia provided the inhabitants with excellent resources.

However, the geographical diversity and topography of the region could also be a hindrance. For instance, although Phoenicia was one of the most fertile regions of the Levant, the amount of cultivable land which could sustain high-yield crops such as wheat or barley was small. Therefore, as the population of Phoenicia increased, demand quickly outstripped production and thus the Phoenicians never achieved self-sufficiency in terms of foodstuffs. Moreover, the numerous streams and rivers that were so important for irrigating the land, and the numerous rocky spurs jutting out from Mount Lebanon, created a divided and segmented landscape. The topography of Phoenicia therefore favoured political individualism and isolation, and encouraged the emergence of competing city states rather than a unified nation. A further obstacle to political unification was the intense commercial rivalry that resulted from a shared reliance on inter-regional trade to secure much-needed foodstuffs, mineral resources and revenues. Therefore, as has already been suggested, the Phoenicians rarely aspired to political unity and strongly resisted any move towards becoming a unified state.

SOURCES FOR THE STUDY OF ANCIENT PHOENICIA

Before examining the history and culture(s) of ancient Phoenicia, it is worth commenting briefly on the sources that historians have at their disposal. Any study of the ancient past is hampered by the fact that all eyewitnesses are long dead, the extant evidence is fragmentary, and the cultural assumptions shared by the people in question have long since vanished. The loss of cultural assumptions is particularly frustrating as they gave meaning to everything an individual said or thought: without a detailed knowledge of these, the task of reconstructing any ancient society becomes infinitely more difficult. Thus, without knowing the cultural values that made a document or artefact significant, historians are often unable to fully comprehend their meaning and importance.[9] The challenge facing historians studying ancient Phoenicia is particularly daunting as, aside from a small number of inscriptions, little remains of the Phoenicians' own literary tradition. The great libraries of the Levant have long since disappeared, meaning that the numerous histories and mythologies which were diligently recorded on papyrus scrolls (as attested by the *Report of Wenamun*, 5 and 40, and Josephus, *Antiquities of the Jews*, 1.107–8) have all but vanished, a fate which is shared by the vast majority of indigenous epigraphic material. Scholars are therefore generally reliant on the scattered testimony produced by other cultures and the slowly increasing body of archaeological evidence when reconstructing the history of Phoenicia. The following sections provide an overview of the strengths and weaknesses of each type of evidence and an assessment of their usefulness to the study of ancient Phoenicia. Keeping in mind the caveats outlined below, this volume will utilise all available evidence so as to present as comprehensive and nuanced an introduction to Phoenician history, culture and society as possible.

Literary Texts: An Overview

In general, there are four main groups of texts which scholars utilise when studying ancient Phoenicia: the classical sources (those written by Greek and Roman authors); the biblical texts; the literary outputs of contemporary societies such as Egypt, Assyria and Ugarit; and the scant epigraphic tradition created by the Phoenicians themselves. Aside from the small number of Phoenician inscriptions, the majority of sources either pre- or post-date the traditional period of Phoenician history (such as the Ugaritic archives of *c*.1400–1200 BCE or the writings of Josephus which date to the late first century CE) or are written by non-Phoenician authors and thus present an outsider's view of Phoenician history and culture (such as the Old Testament or the classical texts). Although non-contemporary and non-indigenous texts are a vital source of evidence, they must nevertheless be treated with caution. In the case of the former, although it is tempting to transpose non-contemporary data in order to overcome the extensive gaps in our knowledge, when doing so it is important to keep in mind the fluctuating cultural, political and economic circumstances experienced by the Phoenicians throughout their history. On the other hand, non-indigenous sources are frequently tainted by biases and preconceptions resulting from political rivalry, religious intolerance, conflicting ideologies or the simple misunderstanding of cultural differences. One further point that needs to be kept in mind is that literature was the exclusive domain of a small, highly educated group of elite men. Scribes, priests and a few aristocrats were the producers and target audience for most ancient literature and so the sources only reflect the values and opinions of a very narrow cross-section of the societies in which they were produced. Even so, the importance of these literary sources is considerable so long as they are read critically.

The Classical Texts

The classical texts have long been the preferred source of information for scholars seeking to reconstruct the history and culture of ancient Phoenicia. This trend can clearly be identified in the work of George Rawlinson, a nineteenth-century English scholar, historian and Christian theologian, who addressed the use of classical texts when reconstructing Phoenician history in his volume *The History of Phoenicia* published in 1889. Despite more than a century of scholarship since Rawlinson, the classical texts are still often considered as the pre-eminent sources for reconstructing Phoenician history. These texts have been accorded such importance as they provide information that is otherwise undocumented in the archaeological, numismatic and epigraphic records and, aside from the biblical texts, they offer the most detailed and coherent narrative accounts of Phoenician history. However, we must be careful not to allow the apparent thoroughness of the classical sources blind us to the fact that they, like any other historical text, are tainted by bias and are influenced by the cultural and political ideology prevalent at the time of their composition. The classical sources that include information pertaining to Phoenicia are tremendously diverse as they were written at disparate times and in disparate places, and belong to a number of different literary genres; consequently, scholars have often struggled to categorise this eclectic mix of material. Those studying ancient Phoenicia have therefore adopted one of four approaches when dealing with the classical texts. These can be broadly defined as: genre-based, thematic, chronological and ideological.

The first approach divides the classical sources into several genre-based, literary categories including, but not limited to, historiography, drama, philosophy, oratory, poetry, ethnography and travel literature. The advantage of this method is that it enables a finer distinction to be drawn between the different categories of literature and their respective historical reliability. Thus, for instance, evidence contained in the philosophical texts is analysed and considered in vastly different ways from that which is included in the historiographic works. The primary problem with such an approach is that not every text can be easily assigned to a particular category. A further criticism is that many texts actually provide a richer historical narrative when examined in isolation from the literary genres to which they are assigned. In contrast, scholars adopting a thematic approach have attempted to reconstruct Phoenician history by exploring the various themes that permeate the classical sources. Although this method allows for a more detailed investigation of certain aspects of Phoenician society, there are many others which are universally ignored by the classical authors: the result is the emergence of an incomplete or distorted picture of Phoenician culture and society.

Scholars utilising a chronological approach have sought to chart the diachronic changes in attitudes displayed by classical authors in relation to Phoenicia and the Phoenicians throughout the first millennium BCE. The strength of this method is that it examines the classical sources within their historical context, thereby allowing connections to be drawn between changing economic and political circumstances and the attitude displayed towards the Phoenicians. However, it has a considerable drawback in the sense that the picture it produces is often too simplistic or overly generalised. A methodology that is closely related to the chronological approach is ideological criticism, which seeks to identify common ideological and cultural attitudes towards the Phoenicians. Scholars adopting this approach have generally concluded that the classical texts present a consistent view of the Phoenicians, which, on the one hand, grudgingly recognises their cultural and economic advances whilst, on the other, condemns them as robbers, pirates, liars, thieves, abductors of women and children, and prone to the worst kinds of atrocities. According to ideological critics, it is the latter of these two views which prevailed for much of the first millennium. Despite this uniformity of opinion, however, the justification for this pejorative view shifted and changed according to the economic and political circumstances of the times. Consequently, at different times, the collision of cultures, conflicting economic interests, political animosity and imperial agendas have all been identified as underpinning the generally negative portrayal of the Phoenicians in the classical texts.

The methodology adopted by this present study combines elements from the genre-based, thematic and ideological approaches. It therefore acknowledges distinctions between different genres of literature (for example, recognising that Herodotus' *Histories* should not be casually grouped together with Demosthenes' oratory) whilst maintaining awareness of the diachronic change in the way that the classical authors thought about the Phoenicians. If considered critically and, where possible, in conjunction with other sources of evidence, the classical texts are still a vitally important resource for anyone studying ancient Phoenicia.

The Biblical Texts

The Bible is perhaps the single most comprehensive literary source for Phoenician history, providing both direct and indirect evidence for Phoenician culture and religion, and containing first-hand documentation relating to the political and economic interactions between Israel and the Phoenician city states, in particular Sidon and Tyre. However, the value of the Old Testament is severely undermined by the hostile view it takes of non-Israelite customs and beliefs: consequently, the usefulness of the more 'historical' books such as *Kings* and *Chronicles* is counterbalanced by the damning prophecies and invectives delivered by Isaiah and Ezekiel. It is important to note that the Old Testament should not be considered 'history' even in the sense of the *historia* found in Greece and Rome (i.e. a pseudo-scientific enquiry). Although some minor similarities can be noted between the narrative stories of the Old Testament and *historia* (most prominently *Chronicles*), the differences are still vast. In essence, the Old Testament is an anthology of stories which were strung together using a chronological framework. The purpose of compiling these stories was not to interpret the past but rather to record events which were considered to be significant in some way. When necessary, new stories could be incorporated into the framework like adding links to a metaphorical chain. On occasion these stories may be grounded in historical tradition or composed using now-lost sources (such as king lists or regional genealogies) but they are not 'history' *per se*. Rather, the biblical books most closely resemble the epic narratives found in other contemporary societies such as Mesopotamia, Egypt and Canaan. It is thus important to avoid labelling the Old Testament as a 'historical' text as in so doing there is the danger of introducing a set of expectations that the biblical narratives were not designed to fulfil. Therefore, when using the biblical texts to reconstruct Phoenician history, rather than asking 'is the Bible accurate?' a more pertinent question is, 'why does the Bible construct this particular vision of the past?'. As with the classical sources, as long as the data from the Old Testament is analysed critically, it can still be of considerable use when reconstructing the history of Phoenicia.

Texts from Other Contemporary Societies (e.g. Ugarit, Assyria and Egypt)

Aside from the classical and biblical texts, scholars also rely heavily on the literary works produced in other contemporaneous cultures when reconstructing the history of Phoenicia. The use of this evidence is beset by many of the same problems as have already been encountered – i.e. these texts are often tainted by bias or influenced by the cultural and political ideology prevalent at the time of their composition (e.g. the Assyrian annals), are not intended as a factual historical account (e.g. Egyptian and Canaanite epic poetry), or were written many centuries before or after the main period of Phoenician history (i.e. *c*.1200–*c*.300 BCE) and thus do not reflect the cultural, political or economic circumstances of the first millennium (e.g. the Ugaritic texts and the Amarna Letters). Nevertheless, as with the classical and biblical texts, provided these sources are used critically they can be of great benefit. For example, the Assyrian annals, which were primarily intended as royal propaganda to extol the virtues of the reigning monarch, offer unique insights into the payments and tributes imposed on the vassal kings of the Phoenician coast. In turn, this information sheds light on the volume of commercial transactions and the types of commodity that flowed through the Phoenician cities.

Similarly, the Ugaritic documents (which predate the traditional period of Phoenician history by approximately 200 years) provide some insights into Phoenician religious beliefs and practices at the start of the first millennium. For instance, a study of the theophoric names (personal names that contain the title or name of a deity) recorded in the Ugaritic texts reveals that there was a common pantheon of deities throughout the Levant at the end of the Bronze Age. However, what these texts cannot confirm is whether these 'universal' deities were worshipped or venerated equally in every location. For instance, the storm deity Ba'al may have been afforded more or less respect in Ugarit than he was in Tyre or Byblos. Furthermore, it is only appropriate to use the Ugaritic evidence as a point of comparison for the very early years of the Iron Age so as to avoid unwarranted anachronisms.

The same warnings also hold true for the letters contained in the Egyptian archive at Tell El-Amarna. These documents, known collectively as the Amarna Letters, date to the middle of the fourteenth century BCE and are mostly diplomatic correspondences between the Egyptian administration and its vassals in Canaan and Amurru. As the archive includes a number of letters from the kings of Byblos, Tyre and Sidon it is an attractive source of evidence for those studying Phoenicia. Nevertheless, as with the Ugaritic texts, although these documents are useful for reconstructing the origins of Phoenician social, political and economic institutions, they can only be used as a point of comparison for the very early years of the Iron Age.

Phoenician Epigraphic Sources

In contrast to the sources discussed above (all of which provide an outsider's assessment that is often tainted by bias and misconception) indigenous inscriptions present an insider's view of prevailing social, political, economic and religious concerns.[10] Recent works have thus highlighted the unique insights that the epigraphic evidence provides in regard to Phoenician ethnicity and identity, economy, power relations, and social compositions and conventions.[11] Traditional epigraphy is particularly interested in monumental inscriptions – i.e. those that are erected on a stone medium, are of substantial length and concern a person who held a special rank in society (for example, royal or civic announcements, votive offerings or funerary inscriptions) – as they often provide insights into the social, political or economic circumstance at a given point in time. However, these inscriptions need to be used with caution as they were often created to glorify an important individual or to propagate a particular political message.

In contrast to inscriptions recovered in neighbouring cultures (which are written in a diverse range of languages, genres and styles) the Phoenician monumental inscriptions of the first millennium tend to be stylistically, linguistically and thematically monotonous. This uniformity combined with the small number of extant examples means that scholars are often reliant on non-monumental inscriptions when reconstructing Phoenician culture and society. These less grandiose inscriptions (including *ostraca*, monetary inscriptions, countermarks, graffiti, etchings or markings on ceramic objects, and various stamps and markers) are useful as they often include testimonies from sections of society not otherwise documented in the monumental inscriptions. *Ostraca*, which can be seen as analogous to modern notebooks, are particularly important as they often record mundane snippets of daily life which would otherwise have been lost. This information is particularly valued as it is less likely to be distorted by literary pretensions or ideological objective on account of the fact that *ostraca* were intended for private use and were not written with posterity in mind. Although many of the non-monumental inscriptions are only a few words, or at best a few lines, long, they nevertheless aid our understanding of Phoenician culture and society. For instance, votive inscriptions, the majority of which simply record the name of the dedicator and the deity being praised, help to reveal the relative popularity and influence of different gods and goddesses.

Finally, by studying the different scripts and languages utilised in both monumental and non-monumental inscriptions, it is possible to gain invaluable insights into the nature and extent of intercultural contact and communication. For instance, the use of loanwords (i.e. words which are borrowed from a donor language and incorporated into a recipient language without translation) is clear evidence for cultural contact and thus improves our understanding of interconnectivity between states and regions.[12] The study of writing has also led scholars to conclude that, from the eighth century onwards, there was a high degree of literacy amongst the populations of the coastal cities of Phoenicia. As the epigraphic evidence provides the most direct insights into the views and opinions of the indigenous populations of Phoenicia, these texts will, where possible, be the starting point for all subsequent discussion.

Archaeology

There has been a long history of archaeological excavation in Lebanon stretching back to at least the middle of the eighteenth century when R. Wood and J. Dawkins jointly published their work on Palmyra (in Syria) and Baalbek (in Lebanon). However, it was during the middle of the nineteenth century that the first extensive excavations of Phoenician sites were conducted. These excavations were carried out under the auspices of the French archaeologist Joseph Ernest Renan who oversaw digs at four Phoenician sites, three of which he supervised himself (Amrit, Byblos and Tyre) whilst the fourth (Sidon) was entrusted to a colleague. The excavations and the extensive publications which accompanied them were considered a huge success, leading Renan to claim that he could now establish the history of Phoenicia through archaeology.[13] Renan's work, which was well respected by his peers, led to European scholars acknowledging him as the founder of Phoenician studies.

Although there have been sporadic excavations since those of Renan, and despite Lebanon's wealth of ancient settlements, there is still a dearth of evidence. One of the primary reasons for this was the disruption caused by Lebanon's civil war (1975–91) and the brief but destructive conflict with Israel in 2006. These two wars not only caused archaeological fieldwork to come to a complete standstill but also led to the destruction of a number of ancient settlements.[14] With government funds necessarily being prioritised for rebuilding and development, the excavation at Tell-el-Burak under the auspices of the American University of Beirut is one of only a handful of ongoing projects. Furthermore, as many of the most important sites (including Byblos, Beirut, Tyre and Sidon) have been continuously occupied since antiquity, very few traces of the Phoenician settlements remain. Consequently, the archaeological data available to those studying ancient Phoenicia is considerably less than is available to those interested in other ancient cultures such as Egypt, Greece and Rome.

It is also worth stressing the random nature of archaeological discoveries. People do not generally bury their possessions so that archaeologists might unearth them in the future and so the dataset provided by archaeology is incomplete and presents only a partial picture. It must also be kept in mind that, as with all methods of research, archaeology has its limitations. For instance, although able to refute hypotheses, archaeology can never prove them. Moreover, archaeological evidence rarely reveals: what ideas and beliefs were held by ancient societies; the individual roles of men and women within these societies; or even the prevailing social organisations. Thus, despite two centuries of excavations in Lebanon which have unearthed considerable quantities of pottery, metalwork, tools, jewellery and the remains of numerous buildings, there are still sizeable gaps in current knowledge.

Due to the fragmentary nature of the material record it is imperative that archaeologists and historians work together in order to produce a more comprehensive understanding of Phoenician history. However, even when the archaeological and literary evidence does occasionally overlap, the two datasets are often at odds with one another. When this occurs, scholars must make a choice from four options: (1) accept that the bulk of the information in the literary texts is credible and attempt to manipulate the archaeological data to fit these accounts; (2) dismiss the majority of the literary texts as corrupt or distorted and thus focus on the archaeological record; (3) use the archaeological and textual evidence in a manipulative way, reconstructing processes, phenomena and events imaginatively; (4) accept that the literary texts contain kernels of truth (even if composed a long time after the events they report) and use the archaeological evidence to assess critically the merits of each. It is the last of these approaches which has been adopted in this volume. Thus, for instance, although accepting that the biblical texts are the product of an oral tradition intended to ensure that culturally significant folk tales were not forgotten, it is recognised that they nevertheless retain some important historical information which can be critically evaluated through study of the material record.

1

HISTORICAL OVERVIEW

Although the region of the Levant which became known as Phoenicia has a long history of human occupation which dates back at least as far as the tenth millennium BCE, scholars are generally of the opinion that it was during the Early Iron Age, in around 1200 BCE, that the Phoenicians first emerged as a distinct cultural entity. Two main hypotheses have been put forward to explain why cultural differentiation occurs at this time: the first proposes that the coastal cities of the Levant were far less affected by the socio-political turmoil which occurred at the end of the Bronze Age (see below) than those situated further inland and so were better able to retain their established social, economic and political structures;[1] whilst the second posits that the distinction in material culture results from the coastal cities being quickest to adapt to the newly emerging social and political conditions.[2]

The discrepancies between these opposing opinions are primarily attributable to the different ways in which scholars have interpreted the archaeological record (in particular, the destruction levels found at numerous Early Iron Age sites). Despite scholars agreeing that the damage at these sites must have been caused by military conflicts rather than natural disasters, interpretations vary with regard to the extent and duration of the disruption these conflicts caused. Significantly, despite this divergence of views, there is still a general consensus that 1200 BCE marked the dawn of 'Phoenician' history. In a slight departure from the majority of earlier studies, this volume

22

Chronological Chart*

Palaeolithic	before *c.*18000
Mesolithic	*c.*18000–8000
Neolithic	*c.*8000–4500
Chalcolithic	*c.*4500–3500
Early Bronze Age (EB)	3500–2000
Middle Bronze Age (MB)	2000–1550
Late Bronze Age (LB)	1550–1200
Iron Age I (IA I)	1200–900
Iron Age II (IA II)	900–586
Babylonian Period	586–539
Persian Period	539–332
Alexander the Great	336–323
Hellenistic Period	323 BCE–63 CE
Roman Period	63–324 CE

*All dates BCE unless otherwise stated.

adopts the position that the emergence of distinctly Phoenician cultural, religious and political traditions was a far more gradual process which began during the early decades of the Late Bronze Age (a time when many of the coastal cities first became true urban entities) and culminated in the Early Iron Age. Consequently, in order to provide a more complete and nuanced picture of Phoenician society at the dawn of the Iron Age, it is important to examine the key events and developments that occurred during the Bronze Age. It is from this perspective that the material in the initial sections of this chapter is presented. All dates from hereon are BCE (Before Common Era) unless otherwise stated.

THE BRONZE AGE (*c.*3500–1200)

The Bronze Age in Lebanon was a period of almost continuous development that gave rise to a plethora of cultural and technological advances (perhaps the most significant of which were the social processes that resulted in the emergence of the first cities). However, a lack of systematic, large-scale excavations at Early Bronze Age settlements means that scholars are poorly informed about this early period of Lebanon's history (to make matters worse, much of the data which has been collected is as yet unpublished). As a result, little can be said with any degree of confidence about the size, layout or organisation of Early Bronze Age settlements. However, thanks to the excavations at Sidon-Dakerman and Byblos, which unearthed the remains of a number of Early Bronze Age food offerings, it has been possible to identify that the three most important economic activities during this period were the harvesting of marine resources, agriculture and animal husbandry. Although the use of metals is attested at a number of sites, the majority of tools were still constructed from flint (in particular the Canaanean sickle blades, tabular scrapers and axes). Pottery was still entirely handmade, although the Early Bronze Age does see the emergence of ceramic objects adorned with incised decoration and red or reddish-brown 'slip' (a liquefied suspension of clay particles which is often coloured with oxides and used in the decoration of ceramic objects).

Jar burials, which involved the interment of human remains in a large earthenware vessel, were widely employed during the first half of the Early Bronze Age. The jars were buried either under the floors of domestic structures or in the open spaces between buildings. Although the majority of jar burials excavated at Byblos were devoid of lavish grave goods, at least 20 contained rich inventories of gold and silver jewellery and copper weapons, thus suggesting a socially stratified society. Social stratification was to be a consistent feature of Phoenician culture and can be identified in all of the major cities and overseas settlements (see Chapter 2). By the middle of the Early Bronze Age, burial customs seem to have changed considerably and there is a move towards rock-cut chamber tombs which were located outside of settlements. The grave goods recovered from these new types of tomb reveal other cultural changes and innovations. For instance, pottery vessels such as bowls and cups, jars, jugs, juglets, hole-mouth cooking pots and four-spouted lamps begin to appear in significant quantities. These objects also bear witness to new modes of production such as the potter's wheel and the use of kilns for firing wet clay.

The discovery of similar pottery styles throughout the Levant reveals the existence of developed inter-regional and international commercial networks. Byblos appears to have particularly benefited from the creation of stable trade links. Due to its favourable geographic location at the centre of the main trade routes between Syro-Palestine and Egypt, Byblos was able to absorb and assimilate the innovations that were being made in Mesopotamia, northern Syria and the Nile Delta. Thus, for much of the Early Bronze Age, Byblos was the wealthiest, and arguably most powerful, city in ancient Lebanon. Significantly, most of the city's power and wealth was derived from its relationship with Egypt. From the beginning of the third millennium it is possible to identify sustained political and economic contact between the two, a situation which is attested by: the numerous inscribed Egyptian objects recovered from Byblos; the presence of an Egyptian temple in Byblos; and the mention of Byblos in a number of Egyptian sources. The Egyptians were keen to foster closer relations with Byblos as they coveted the timber resources and tree products (such as the resin used in the mummification process) which the city controlled. Although Byblos was evidently Egypt's primary commercial partner in Lebanon, occasional finds of Egyptian objects from sites such as Tyre and Sidon suggest that other cities may also have been part of this trading network. Another important Byblian trade partner was the city of Ebla. A number of texts recovered from Ebla have revealed that Byblos maintained close commercial ties with the city, importing a number of commodities including textiles, foodstuffs, livestock, raw metals and manufactured goods such as jewellery, fine-quality linen and pottery. The marriage of a Byblian king to an Eblaite princess during the last quarter of the 23rd century indicates that the relationship between the two cities was based on equality.

By the Middle Bronze Age (*c.*2000–1550) towns and villages had been established every 15–20 kilometres along the coastline of ancient Lebanon. Many of these settlements were established near natural bays or inlets where trading ships would anchor, thus allowing them to prosper and flourish. A few settlements were situated further inland but these were nearly always established in close proximity to estuaries or rivers, thereby enabling them to maintain a connection to the sea. The end of the Middle Bronze Age witnessed a steady increase in cultic construction with Byblos housing the largest concentration of temples and sanctuaries. The best preserved was the so-called 'Temple of Obelisks' which was built over the remains of a

Fig. 1: The Temple of Obelisks in Byblos

much older sanctuary that had been destroyed by fire at the end of the third millennium (see Figure 1).

Cultic activity is also evinced in contemporary burial rites and practices, with the Middle and Late Bronze Ages witnessing the emergence of four new tomb types: the shaft tomb, the earthen pit burial, the cist burial and the built tomb.[3] Adults were generally interred in rock-cut, shaft or built tombs whilst infants and children were usually buried in ceramic storage jars. The presence of several pins and needles in the majority of adult burials indicates that the bodies would have been shrouded in cloth before interment. Other funerary goods included pottery, jewellery, weaponry, scarabs and cosmetic boxes that were either locally made or imported from Egypt, Crete or Cyprus. When considered in conjunction with the general inclusion of food offerings, the emergence at Arqa of a standardised funerary kit comprised of globular pots, juglets and platters hints at a nascent belief in an afterlife.

The recovery of grave goods and other deposited or discarded items has shown that a number of crafts flourished during the

Middle Bronze Age. Metalworking is particularly well represented and appears to have been largely influenced by Egyptian and Syrian art. Due to the stable political conditions of the Middle Bronze Age, inter-regional trade flourished, enabling the coastal cities to establish and maintain complex trade networks and commercial relationships with cities located throughout Mesopotamia, the Levant, Egypt and Anatolia. The larger of these coastal cities specialised in exporting highly sought-after commodities (such as olive oil, wine and wood) whilst importing foreign commodities such as fish and wheat from Cyprus, gems and precious stones from Egypt, and silver from Anatolia. The abundance of silver objects recovered from Sidonian tombs indicates that there was extensive and sustained trade with Anatolia, especially the Taurus Mountain region where the ore would have been mined (see Chapter 5). During the final years of the Middle Bronze Age, the Hyksos (a people of mixed origin from Western Asia) settled in the Nile Delta and in so doing reduced Egypt's influence over the Levant. Quick to take advantage of their newly gained independence, the Phoenician city states extended their commercial networks and spheres of influence, thus enabling them to increase their wealth significantly during this period.

The Late Bronze Age (*c.*1550–1200) is characterised by the emergence of 'great kings' (i.e. the rulers of powerful empires such as Egypt, Mitanni, Hatti and later Assyria) and 'lesser kings' (i.e. the rulers of a multitude of smaller city states and kingdoms). This period of Levantine history is therefore dominated by the political machinations of the larger empires which regularly sought to establish hegemony over the less powerful states that lay on their peripheries. Egypt was the first of the great empires which sought political dominance over the Levant under the leadership of Thutmosis III (1479–1425), the sixth pharaoh of the 18th Dynasty. Although Thutmosis I (1506–1493) had previously campaigned against the cities of Syria-Palestine, even extracting tribute from a number of them, it was his grandson Thutmosis III who was to subjugate the region entirely, forcing many of its cities and states to become Egyptian vassals. In the 22nd year of his reign Thutmosis was faced with a coalition of rulers from Palestine, Lebanon and Syria who were opposed to Egyptian claims to political and economic control of their territories. The ensuing battle, fought in close proximity to the important city of Megiddo, was an abject disaster for the coalition and laid the foundations for

Egypt's annexing of Canaan. After a further 16 campaigns (some of which involved serious fighting and others of which were parades of strength), Thutmosis had succeeded in expanding Egypt's sphere of influence to include the whole of southern Lebanon, the Lebanese coast, the Bekaa Valley and southern Syria as far as Damascus. The subjugation of Canaan not only allowed the Egyptians to regulate and tax the lucrative maritime and overland trade networks which converged in the region, it also provided them with access to a wide range of commodities which could either be purchased or acquired through tribute.

The annals of Thutmosis's military campaigns (carved on the walls of the Temple of Karnak in recognition of the fact that the God Amen-Re had provided the victory) list the commodities desired by Egypt; in particular they highlight the importance of Levantine timber (*ANET*, p. 143). With Egypt being relatively devoid of any wide-circumference trees suitable for large construction projects, the Egyptians were keen to secure regular shipments of high-quality timber. The extensive forests of Lebanon were therefore highly attractive to Thutmosis and thus it was no surprise that he required the coastal cities to provide Egypt with annual shipments of wood (*ANET*, p. 241). His account of the on-site construction of cedar boats at Byblos and their overland transport to the Euphrates reveals the size and complexity of these operations (*ANET*, p. 240).

The success of Thutmosis's campaigns meant that by the middle of the fourteenth century the Egyptian Empire stretched as far north as the borders of the Hurrian kingdom of Mitanni. Evidence contained in the Amarna tablets reveals that the Egyptians, for the purposes of administration, divided the region of Syria-Palestine into three distinct districts: Canaan (encompassing the entire Levantine coast from the Egyptian border at Sinai in the south to Berytus in the north); Apu (encompassing the inland regions of modern-day Israel and Lebanon); and Amurru (encompassing the northern coastal plain from Byblos to Arwad and the inland cities and villages of the Akkar plain). The Amarna tablets also reveal that, despite being vassals of Egypt, the kings of Byblos, Berytus, Tyre and Sidon retained a considerable amount of autonomy in their inter-regional dealings. This led to fierce political and commercial rivalries (in particular between Tyre and Sidon) with Pharaoh often being asked to intervene and settle local disputes.

Due to their diversified economies which enabled them to exploit a variety of revenue streams (see Chapter 2), the period between the invasions of Thutmosis III and the death of Amenhotep III (*c.*1352) was to be a prosperous one for Byblos, Tyre, Sidon and Berytus. According to the Egyptian historical records the most lucrative source of income was the trade in timber and metals – an assessment which is supported by the huge profits that Byblos is known to have made from trading in tin and copper (at its height, the Byblian trade network encompassed Afghanistan, North Africa and numerous sites around the western Mediterranean). However, the Phoenician cities also generated substantial incomes from their various craft industries. For instance, a number of Ugaritic documents reveal that Tyre and Byblos were particularly active in the textiles trade, whilst excavations at Akko and Sarepta have unearthed facilities for the large-scale production of purple dye. There was also an extensive trade in glass and faience wares, with items produced in Tyre being known for their vivid colours and quality. The discovery of a late fourteenth-/early thirteenth-century shipwreck at Ulu Burun (located just off the coast of modern Turkey) provided physical proof of the diverse range of commodities that were being traded during this period. The vessel's varied cargo, much of which had been remarkably well preserved, included: Canaanite amphorae, Cypriot ceramic ware, carved ivories, ornate metal items, boxwood writing tablets and a large quantity of copper and tin ingots.[4]

This era of prosperity was to come to an abrupt end with the death of the Egyptian Pharaoh Amenhotep III and the accession of his son, Akhenaton (*c.* 1353–1336). Although the kingdom of Mitanni and the more remote political powers, like Assyria and Babylon, had generally maintained cordial relations with Egypt, during the latter half of the fourteenth century another dominant power, the Hittites, had begun to threaten the northern borders of the Egyptian Empire. Whereas Amenhotep III had managed to temper Hittite interest in Canaan, Akhenaton's religious preoccupation and indifference to military matters was to prove disastrous. With Egypt's attention now focused inwards, its Canaanite and Levantine vassals began to argue and fight amongst themselves. The Hittite king Shubiluliuma was to take full advantage of this turmoil. Wary of provoking a direct military confrontation, Shubiluliuma instead sought to make territorial gains via political subterfuge (primarily by offering support and encouragement to any state or kingdom which wished to break free of Egyptian rule). His most notable success was in persuading the Amorite king, Abdi-Ashirta, to renounce his allegiance to Egypt and agitate on the Hittites' behalf. Although Abdi-Ashirta and his son Aziru tirelessly promoted the Hittite cause, they managed to convince only a small number of states to switch their allegiance and so, with political machination having failed, and recognising Akhenaton's reluctance to undertake an extensive military campaign, they began openly to attack any city which remained loyal to Egypt. To complicate matters further, Canaan was also subject to a number of incursions by the Ḥapiru. There is great uncertainty as to who these Ḥapiru were and where they originated from as they are variously described as nomadic, or semi-nomadic, rebels, outlaws, raiders, mercenaries, bowmen, servants, slaves and migrant labourers. What is certain is that during this period they were enemies of Egypt who allied themselves with Abdi-Ashirta and who helped besiege and destroy a number of cities that had remained loyal to Akhenaton.

The Amarna correspondences of the Byblian king Rib-Addi provide a vivid picture of the political situation in Canaan during this turbulent period, documenting the shift in the balance of power between the Egyptian and Hittite empires. The loss of the coastal cities north of Byblos dealt Egypt a serious economic blow which not only limited its access to a number of lucrative trade networks, but also served to weaken its administrative control over the southern Phoenician coast. Consequently, the coastal cities of southern Lebanon and Palestine appear to have enjoyed a much greater degree of independence than they had previously. This political autonomy, however, quickly ended with the dawning of the Ramesside Dynasty. One of Seti I's (1306–1290) primary objectives upon ascending the Egyptian throne was to restore Egypt's hegemony over the southern coastal cities. Thus, in the first year of his reign, Seti undertook a successful military campaign that reaffirmed Egyptian dominance over the Phoenician coast from Akko to just north of Tyre (a clear demonstration of the economic importance of this region). Despite numerous attempts by Seti I and his successor Ramesses II (c. 1279–1213), the northern coastal cities and the Akkar plain remained within the Hittite sphere of influence until the Empire's demise during the late twelfth century.

In fact, the division of political control over Phoenicia was confirmed by a peace treaty signed by the Egyptians and Hittites in

1269 (*ANET*, p. 199). The agreement not to encroach upon each other's land essentially fixed the northernmost limit of Egyptian, and the southernmost limit of Hittite, influence. A stone stele erected on location by Ramesses II suggests that the boundary between the two empires was the Nahr el-Kelb, or River Dog, situated between Berytus and Byblos. This status quo was to continue until the end of the Bronze Age, allowing the Phoenician cities once again to prosper. Those in the north, such as Arwad, now exploited their trading connections with the Hittite Empire whilst those in the south, such as Tyre, continued to profit from their relationship with Egypt. Byblos occupied the middle ground geographically, commercially and politically, fostering connections with both the Egyptians and the Hittites.

THE END OF THE BRONZE AGE

The end of the Bronze Age was heralded by a series of disruptive and destabilising crises that were to adversely affect the entire region. A number of these crises were the direct result of environmental and climatic changes which brought about a gradual rise in both temperature and sea level. Significantly, modern geological surveys have shown these climatic changes would not only have affected the types and volume of crops that could be sustained, but also when and where they could be grown. These climatic changes are also believed to have caused a series of droughts which, in the years leading up to 1200, led to the transformation of regional agricultural practices and the emergence of new growing seasons. Although in the mid- to long term Phoenician farmers were able to adapt to these climatic changes (as seen by their innovation in irrigation technology), in the short term they played havoc with traditional farming practices, resulting in significant food shortages. Environmental changes are also believed to be responsible for the series of devastating floods and epidemics that afflicted the region during this period.

Further instability was generated by a number of internal crises that resulted from political tensions, social inequality (i.e. an ever-widening gulf between the affluence and rights of the ruling and productive classes), and economic weakness due to an over-dependency on inter-regional trade to meet subsistence needs. Arguably the most disruptive crisis was the invasion of the Sea-Peoples in *c.*1200

31

Fig. 2: A group of defeated Sea-People warriors as depicted on a wall relief adorning the mortuary temple of Ramesses III at Medinet Habu

(commonly described as the 'Sea-People Catastrophe') which marked the end of the Bronze Age in the eastern Mediterranean, led to the downfall of many prosperous civilisations in the Aegean, Anatolia, and the Levant, and even affected the mighty Egyptian Empire (see Figure 2). Despite the invasion being well documented in the literary and archaeological records of contemporary cultures, there is a dearth of evidence from Phoenicia itself and thus little is known about its impact on the Phoenician city states. What can be ascertained, however, is that for many of the Phoenician city states the effects of this event were predominantly short- rather than long-term (though, as previously noted, whether this was due to these cities being the least affected or the quickest to recover is still debated).[5]

IRON AGE I (1200–900)

Little is known about the early years of Phoenicia's recovery during the Early Iron Age as the period is poorly represented in the archaeological record and, in contrast to the Amarna Age, there are no detailed documentary sources. The earliest textual source is an inscription of the Assyrian king Tiglath-Pilesar I (1114–1076) which recounts his 'military' campaigns against the Phoenician city states during the fifth year of his reign. Like Thutmosis III before him, Tiglath-Pilesar coveted the cedar forests of Lebanon and thus one of the primary objectives of his campaign was to obtain timber for the renovation of the temple of Anu-Adad at Ashur (*ANET*, p. 275). Having 'subjugated' the region, Tiglath-Pilesar demanded tribute from Byblos, Sidon and Arwad. Despite the military hyperbole in the king's report, the tribute seems to have been arranged by means of a peaceful agreement, albeit one that was secured by the threat of Assyrian military intervention.

The reign of Tiglath-Pilesar I marked the beginning of Assyrian ascendancy in the Near East; Egypt, in contrast, was entering a period of decline. The political and economic situation along the Phoenician coast during the early eleventh century is vividly recorded in an Egyptian document known as the *Report of Wenamun* (*ANET*, pp. 25–9). The document recounts the journey of Wenamun, a senior official in the Theban Temple of Amon-Ra, who was assigned the task of travelling to Byblos to acquire cedar wood for the construction of a new sacred barge (although likely to be fictitious, the account is nevertheless thought to present an accurate picture of prevailing social and political conditions at the time of its composition). Following a series of calamitous events, Wenamun arrives in Byblos without money and without his official retinue and so is refused an audience with the Byblian king (Zakar-Baal). Wenamun spends 29 days in Byblos before eventually being granted a royal audience. Even then, Zakar-Baal still refuses his request for wood until a partial payment is dispatched from Egypt.

The indifferent treatment that Wenamun receives reflects the changed economic and political circumstances of Egypt which was now forced to negotiate for the timber it had previously exacted in tribute. It is clear from this account that the Byblian king no longer considered himself subservient to Egypt; instead his somewhat arrogant and brash manner is indicative of the burgeoning political and economic independence of Byblos. The story of Wenamun therefore reveals the almost complete collapse of Egyptian prestige abroad and highlights the rapidity at which this once powerful empire had declined under the weak successors of Ramesses III (1186–1155). It also reveals that trade, which during the Late Bronze Age had been under Egyptian or Hittite control, was now at the initiative of, and organised by, the Phoenicians themselves.

The account also suggests that the various commercial centres of the eastern Mediterranean (in particular those of Palestine, Phoenicia and Cyprus) maintained strong commercial ties, an assertion supported by the archaeological record. Shared elements in the material and cultural assemblages of these commercial centres suggest that the contacts between them were not only extensive but also sustained, and that their development and prosperity were in many ways interconnected. The wide distribution of Phoenician bichrome (two-colour) pottery reveals that these interactions led to the emergence of far-reaching commercial networks that encompassed Egypt, Cyprus, the Levant and parts of southern Anatolia. The Early Iron Age was therefore a period of commercial expansion for the coastal cities of Phoenicia, both at home and overseas. This period of prosperity also resulted in the emergence of urbanisation, an important innovation that would come to be synonymous with the Phoenicians. At Tyre and Sarepta, for instance, architectural innovation and a move towards urbanism led both cities to alter their layout significantly during this period. There is also evidence for urban expansion and development at inland sites such as Tell-Kesian and Tell-Dan, where substantial town planning and domestic construction are attested.

In contrast to the fourteenth and thirteenth centuries, during which Byblos and Tyre had been dominant, the twelfth and eleventh centuries saw Sidon emerge as the most powerful of the Phoenician cities. In the biblical accounts dating to this period it is Sidon which is depicted as holding hegemony over a large territory. This territory included the access routes into the fertile southern Bekaa Valley, thus allowing Sidon to control the lucrative overland trade routes that ran southwards from Syria to the Upper Jordan Valley. This gave the Sidonians significant political power and influence and enabled them to subsume other Phoenician cities (most notably Tyre) into their sphere of control. In fact, due to the pre-eminence of Sidon at this time, the term 'Sidonian' was often used as a generic designation for Canaanites or Phoenicians.

Sidon's pre-eminence and Tyre's decline in the early years of the Iron Age were clearly the result of their differing geopolitical circumstances. Due to its southerly location Tyre enjoyed close political and commercial relationships with Egypt: however, Tyre's reliance on Egypt meant that when the latter experienced a rapid economic and political decline under the weak leadership of the Tanite Dynasty, the former also suffered. By contrast, Sidon's political and commercial alliances appear to have been focused northwards, in particular towards the cities and states of southern Anatolia and Assyria, and thus the decline of Egypt caused minimal disruption to the Sidonians. Following the death of Tiglath-Pilesar I in 1076, Assyria was ruled by a succession of weak and ineffectual kings whose poor governance and lack of political acumen led to a significant deterioration in Assyrian power and influence. This sustained period of political infirmity enabled the Phoenician cities to break free of Assyrian control and meant that by the beginning of the tenth century Assyria had been reduced to a small state whose influence was largely confined to the upper valley of the Tigris and Euphrates. The Phoenicians, particularly Tyre, also benefited from the defeat of the Philistines at the hands of King David in 975, the political unification of Israel and the disruption in Syria caused by the Aramaeans. Consequently, by the end of the first quarter of the tenth century, the Phoenician cities were once again free to pursue their own political and commercial agendas.

The end of the eleventh and beginning of the tenth centuries also witnessed a shift in the balance of power between Tyre and Sidon. Tyre, which was no longer subservient to one of the major empires, began to actively exploit, and profit from, the diverse commercial and political opportunities which arose from the unique geopolitical landscape of the Levant. The accession of King Hiram I (969–936) marked the beginning of Tyre's so-called 'golden age', and resulted in considerable economic, social and political innovation. There can be little doubt that Tyre's dramatic change in fortune was the product of its deliberate and systematic exploitation of the pan-Mediterranean trade routes. For instance, the biblical book of II Chronicles (8:18) credits Hiram with utilising his navy to achieve a monopoly over maritime trade in the Levant and by so doing gain supremacy over the other Phoenician cities (a particularly frustrating situation for Byblos and Sidon). Hiram's position was strengthened by the close commercial and political relationships he fostered with the nascent state of Israel, specifically during the reign of Solomon (*c.*960–930).

The particularly close relationship between Tyre and Israel is most clearly attested in the famous commercial treaty signed by Hiram and Solomon (I Kings 5:1–18). At the heart of this treaty was a reciprocal agreement which saw Hiram supplying Solomon with advanced construction technology, high-quality building materials, specialist technical assistance and services, and luxury goods; in return, Solomon provided Tyre with silver, agricultural products and food for the royal household.[6] As Tyre had been founded on a small island, the city was dependent on its mainland territories to provide it with natural resources (most importantly food, water and wood). Although controlling an extensive and exceptionally fertile plain, the population density of Tyre (which averaged 520 inhabitants per hectare) meant that the city rarely achieved self-sufficiency with regard to foodstuffs. Solomon's provision of both cereals and fine foods would therefore have been especially welcomed by Hiram. This alliance with Israel also provided Tyre with unrestricted access to the overland trade routes leading to the Euphrates, Mesopotamia and Arabia, thereby further expanding the city's commercial horizons. Although there has been considerable debate over the precise nature of the political and commercial relationship between Tyre and Israel during the tenth century, with some arguing that Israel was the dominant party, the evidence points towards a more equitable alliance that was founded on the concept of reciprocity to ensure that both parties benefited.

The second aspect of the commercial relationship was the undertaking of joint maritime enterprises with the aim of identifying new markets in Africa and Asia in which gold, silver, ivory and precious stones could be acquired (e.g. I Kings 9). These joint enterprises demonstrate that during the tenth century, the Tyrians were already capable of organising long-distance maritime ventures and, due to their high level of naval technological sophistication, could reach distant markets without having to rely on intermediaries. From the biblical accounts, and the writings of Flavius Josephus (*Antiquities of the Jews*, 8.7.2.), we know that Hiram and Solomon profited greatly from these joint ventures, enabling them to spend lavishly on monumental construction projects. Solomon built the temple in Jerusalem, whilst Hiram rebuilt Tyre's harbour, constructed a number of large shipyards, extended the city by joining together the two islands on which it was founded, built a royal palace and public market, and renovated and erected a number of temples.

For much of the tenth century Byblos had found itself marginalised both politically and economically due to its schism with Egypt and because of Tyre's ascendency. In an effort to rectify this situation, the Byblian kings Abibaal and Elibaal sought to re-establish close political and commercial links with Egypt: a policy which may also have been a pragmatic response to the military expedition of Pharaoh Sheshonk I (*c*.943–922) which had once again brought Egyptian forces back into the southern Levant. As in the past, Byblos favoured a policy of co-operation and conciliation and so made no effort to resist the Egyptian incursions. Furthermore, rather than agitating for greater independence, Byblos allied itself with Egypt and remained faithful irrespective of the latter's changing political circumstances. As a result, Byblos did not become an Egyptian province nor was it governed or administered by an Egyptian official. In the true spirit of a mercantile nation, Byblos preferred the advantages resulting from an alliance with a more powerful empire rather than complete independence and the dangers that came with it. The decision to ingratiate itself with Egypt was perhaps also partially taken because Byblos was apprehensive of the renewed military threat posed by Assyria under the leadership of Adad-Nirari II (*c*.911–891).

The political upheavals that occurred during the final decades of the tenth century, including the division of Solomon's kingdom into two states (Judah and Israel), the rise to prominence of the Aramaic states in the north (an amalgam of West Semitic pastoralist tribes who now occupied large tracts of Syria and central Mesopotamia), a resurgent Egypt in the south, and a rejuvenated Assyrian Empire to the east, not only profoundly affected Byblos but also forced Tyre to rethink and revise its economic and political alliances.

IRON AGE II (900–586)

The principal strategies that had driven Tyrian foreign policy during the reign of Hiram I were largely adhered to by his successors in the ninth and eighth centuries. The reign of Ithobaal I (or Ethbaal, *c*.887–856) marked a further growth in Tyre's commercial empire and instigated a period of territorial expansion, initially in the Levant and then at sites throughout the Mediterranean. Ithobaal

37

was to succeed in re-establishing Tyre's hegemony over the cities of southern Phoenicia, creating a state that appears to have subsumed the previously powerful city of Sidon. Consequently, Ithobaal was the first Tyrian monarch to use the title 'king of the Sidonians', although exactly how this term should be understood is still unclear.[7] The absence of Sidon in the Assyrian inscriptions of this period is a further indication of the city's political subservience to Tyre, as is the fact that subsequent Tyrian monarchs appear to have dictated Sidon's domestic and foreign policies, a situation that continued until the end of the eighth century. Tyre also renewed and strengthened its relations with Israel via the diplomatic marriage of Ithobaal's daughter, Jezebel, to the Israelite king Ahab (c.874–853). By offering his daughter in marriage, the Tyrian king hoped to secure favourable commercial concessions from the flourishing Israelite kingdom and to gain access to the profitable trade routes that cut through the interior of Palestine.

The discovery that a significant number of Phoenician craftsmen, architects and merchants were living and working in Israel at this time (in particular in the cities of Samaria, Hazor and Megiddo) suggests that Ithobaal's policy was successful. Although unproven, it is likely that Ithobaal also sought an alliance with Aram-Damascus, the most powerful of the central Syrian Aramaean states. In antiquity, the north of Syria, in particular the coastal territory on the Gulf of Alexandretta, was the point at which a number of important communication and trade routes converged and thus it was vital for Tyre to remain on cordial terms with those who controlled it.

Tyre's economic and commercial advances under Ithobaal also found clear expression in the city's initial efforts at colonisation. According to Menander of Ephesus (Josephus, *Antiquities of the Jews*, 8.324) Ithobaal founded two colonies, the first (Azuza) in Libya and the second (Batroun) just to the north of Byblos on the Lebanese coast. Ithobaal is also believed to have established a colony on Cyprus (Kition) in an effort to gain access to the island's lucrative copper trade (see Chapter 5). The founding of 'Phoenician' Kition reflects a change in Tyrian commercial strategy as, for the first time, the city considered it necessary to try and cultivate a more direct form of control over an overseas territory in order to ensure continued economic benefits. The ninth century also witnessed Tyre expanding its commercial horizons by initiating trading relations with the islands of the Aegean and the Greek mainland. The distribution of the first Phoenician imports in Greece indicates sporadic rather than organised trade at this point (as is reflected in the Homeric epics, e.g. *Iliad*, 23.74–5; *Odyssey*, 13:272–7); however, by the end of the ninth century, Tyrian ships were regularly visiting Crete and the Islands of the Dodecanese, resulting in the creation of a permanent and regularly traversed trade route between Greece and the Levant.

Tyre was not to have everything its own way, however, as a resurgent Assyria was once again beginning to involve itself in the affairs of the Phoenician cities. In *c.*870, Ashurnasirpal II (883–859) was to be the first Assyrian king to visit Phoenicia in nearly 200 years. Although Ashurnasirpal claims to have extracted tribute from the Phoenician cities, it is more likely that these payments were voluntary gifts that were offered in order to secure trade concessions. These gifts – including prized metals (gold, silver, copper and tin), fine linen garments, various types of wood, ivory and even a monkey – were clearly intended to impress the Assyrian monarch. That Phoenician diplomacy had achieved its purpose is evinced by the inclusion of both Tyrians and Sidonians amongst the list of dignitaries invited to the inauguration of Ashurnasirpal's new palace at Nimrud in 879 (*ANET*, pp. 558–60). Aside from his visiting Phoenicia as part of his 'grand tour', Ashurnasirpal was content to leave the Phoenician cities to govern themselves so long as they swore loyalty to Assyria. Tyre was therefore able to remain on the fringes of any armed conflict between Assyria and the states of western Asia, preferring to pay tribute rather than attempt to break free of Assyrian rule. In fact, Tyre was often in a position to benefit from any Assyrian campaign as it could provide Assyria with much-needed food and arms.

The political situation in the Levant was to change dramatically with the accession of Ashurnasirpal's son and heir Shalmaneser III (858–824). Fearing an uprising, Shalmaneser abandoned his father's non-interventionist policy and undertook an aggressive campaign against northern Syria and southern Anatolia which terminated at the Mediterranean. Although not invading Phoenicia, Shalmaneser nevertheless demanded tribute from the 'kings of the sea coast', a mysterious group which probably included the rulers of Arwad, Batroun, Berytus, Byblos, Sidon and Tyre. The bronze gates adorning Shalmaneser's palace at Dur-sharrukin (Khorsabad) depict Tyrian tribute being transported into the presence of the Assyrian monarch.

Fig. 3: The Kurkh Stele recording the military achievements of Shalmaneser III, including his campaign against Arwad

Significantly, when the Aramean and Syrian confederation rose up against Shalmaneser in *c*.853, the only Phoenician cities to join the rebellion were Arwad and Arqa (see Figure 3). This perhaps indicates that Sidon and Tyre enjoyed a special protected tributary position within the Assyrian Empire which they had no desire to jeopardise. Although Shalmaneser increased the level of tribute it was expected to pay and more closely monitored its foreign and domestic policies, Arwad retained many of the previous freedoms it had enjoyed (perhaps due to the close economic ties that it had maintained with Ashurnasirpal II). Overall, the growing power of the Assyrian Empire actually served to amplify the geopolitical importance of the Phoenician cities, thus enabling them to play a more prominent role in inter-regional politics and diplomacy. Their strategic importance meant that they were a valuable resource which needed to be controlled and protected in order to prevent them from aligning themselves with Assyria's great rival, Egypt. However, it was also vital that any political interference did not curtail Phoenician trading ventures which were a lucrative source of tribute and so vitally important for the provisioning of the Assyrian Empire. As a result, Shalmaneser's successors were content to collect tribute from the Phoenician cities while avoiding any form of direct interference which may have negatively impacted upon their commercial operations.

This period of relative political freedom and independence was brought to an abrupt end by the accession of Tiglath-Pilesar III (744–727) in 744. Soon after his inauguration, Tiglath-Pilesar initiated a series of aggressive military ventures aimed at subjugating the Levant and assimilating it into the Assyrian provincial system. The final defeat of the north Syrian coastal kingdom of Unqi in around 738 gave rise to Assyrian dominance over the Levant and marked the end of Phoenician political independence. Following Tiglath-Pilesar's initial campaign, the cities north of Byblos were directly annexed by Assyria and formed into a new province centred on the Phoenician city of Simyra. To the south, Tyre and Byblos were reaffirmed with tributary status, which permitted them to retain some degree of political self-determination.

However, the following year whilst Tiglath-Pilesar was campaigning in the north, the Tyrian king, Hiram II (739–730), joined Arwad, Syria, Israel and Philistia in their revolt against Assyrian rule. Tiglath-Pilesar responded immediately to this nascent threat to his empire: abandoning his campaign in the north, he turned his army southwards and swept violently down the Phoenician coast. Tyre, following the lead of Arwad, quickly abandoned the coalition and offered its unconditional surrender to the Assyrian king. Significantly, despite being one of the main protagonists of the revolt, Hiram was offered fairly favourable terms: the city would be stripped of some of its hinterland, pay an increased level of tribute (Hiram's successor, Mattan II (730–729 BCE), would pay a record sum of 150 talents of gold), and would allow Assyrian inspectors and customs officials to be stationed in the city's harbours and markets.[8] However, the city would survive and would not be incorporated into an Assyrian province: moreover, its citizens would not share the fate of their allies who were deported to Assyria in large numbers.

The favourable treatment that Tyre received can only be explained by the city's position at the head of a maritime empire. Recognising that Assyria was in no position to assume control of Tyre's lucrative maritime trading operations, the ever-pragmatic Tiglath-Pilesar realised that the partial domination of Tyre would better serve the economic and trading interests of the Assyrian Empire than any form of punitive retribution. That Assyria coveted the revenues and resources procured by Tyre's maritime commerce is clearly evinced by the subsequent actions of Sargon II (721–705), who secured the submission of Cyprus and in so doing stripped Tyre of its lucrative copper trade.

The early reign of the Tyrian king Luli (or Elulaios, 729–694), brought about a short period of respite from the conflicts that had seen the Phoenician cities set in opposition to the Assyrians. However, having suppressed uprisings within the cities of Kition, Ushu, Sidon and Akko, King Luli appears to have pursued an anti-Assyrian policy which led to successive conflicts with Salmanasar V (727–722), Sargon II (722–705), and lastly with Sennacherib (705–681). During the reigns of Sargon II and Sennacherib, perhaps as a result of Luli's agitating, Assyrian policy towards Phoenicia changed significantly. Whereas the Phoenician cities and their territories had previously been left alone so long as they intermittently offered tribute, maintained a submissive posture towards Assyria and regularly paid taxes, tribute payments were now to be made annually as a sign of fealty towards Assyria. Moreover, Sargon no longer merely pressurised or annexed territories but instead introduced a deliberate policy of destruction, devastation and mass deportations in order to quell dissent amongst his Levantine vassal.[9] Although Salamanasar V and Sargon II shied away from the complete destruction of Tyre, a particularly striking fact considering Salamanasar spent five years besieging the city, King Luli's luck finally ran out when in 701 he rebelled against the rule of Sennacherib. With the Assyrian king closing in on the city, Luli fled to Cyprus where he would die in exile.

In order to diminish the threat posed by Tyre, Sennacherib deported a large percentage of the city's inhabitants to Nineveh and awarded the Tyrian throne, and all of the city's mainland holdings, to a pro-Assyrian monarch named Tubalu (Ithobaal). This was a shrewd move

– by separating Tyre from its mainland dependencies Sennacherib severely diminished the city's powerbase, thereby forcing it to rely on its overseas territories for its economic survival. In the short term the damage to the city's economy must have been devastating and it is this weakened and humbled Tyre that the Israelite prophet Isaiah (23:1–17) sings about in his great oracle against the city.

In contrast, Sidon had profited greatly from Assyrian support and from its acquisition of Tyre's mainland dependencies.[10] Sidon's supremacy was not to last long, however: encouraged by its flourishing economy and bolstered by an alliance with the Cilician king Sanduari, Sidon took advantage of the assassination of Sennacherib to renounce Assyrian suzerainty and declare its independence. This was an unusually bold move that was ultimately to prove disastrous for the city. In 677, less than three years after ascending the Assyrian throne, Sennacherib's youngest son and successor Esarhaddon (c.680–669) sought retribution for the affront. Having suppressed any potential domestic opposition to his rule, Esarhaddon undertook a brief but bloody military campaign which re-established Assyria's control over Sidon and its surrounding territories. The annals of Esarhaddon's reign reveal that his retribution for Sidonian sedition was both quick and brutal: after a short siege the city and its walls were razed to the ground, the imperial palace and treasuries were ransacked and their contents appropriated by the Assyrian king, the royal family and court (alongside the city's other inhabitants) were exiled to Nineveh and, in the following year, the Sidonian king, Abdi-Milkuti (c. 685–677), was captured and beheaded (*ANET*, p. 90). The city was subsequently rebuilt by the Assyrians, who renamed it Kar Esarhaddon ('Port Esarhaddon'), and repopulated it with foreign immigrants.

Due to Tyre's recent displays of loyalty, Esarhaddon awarded control of Sidon's southern territories to the Tyrian king Baal I (680–660), who had already asserted his influence over Tyre's former coastal holdings in the Akko Plain. However, Tyre's display of fealty appears to have been a smokescreen that masked the city's true intention (to free itself from Assyrian rule) whilst it rebuilt its commercial and political powerbases. By the end of the first quarter of the seventh century Tyre stood at the head of a league of independent Levantine kingdoms known in the Assyrian annals as the 'twenty-two kings of Hatti [Syria], the seashore, and the islands'. Allying itself with the resurgent Egyptian Empire, now ruled by a dynasty of Nubian pharaohs known as the Kushites, Tyre and its western collation were soon drawn into Pharaoh Taharqa's (*c.*690–664) war with Assyria.

Having already clashed with the Kushite Dynasty, Esarhaddon undertook a second campaign against Egypt in 671. The campaign, which had the dual aim of diminishing Egyptian power and punishing Tyre for its treachery, was to be a resounding victory for the Assyrians. Having captured the Egyptian capital of Memphis and forced Taharqa to flee to Nubia, Esarhaddon turned his attentions to Tyre which, faced with the full might of the Assyrian army and isolated from its allies, prudently capitulated and agreed to pay a heavy tribute and accept the loss of its mainland territories. The treaty between Baal I of Tyre and the Assyrian king Esarhaddon (most likely signed in 671), although granting the Tyrians complete freedom of trade with the north and west, was nevertheless humiliating for a city which had once dominated the Mediterranean and Levantine trade routes. That the Tyrian king's authority was significantly reduced at this time is highlighted by the clause allowing Assyrian representatives to involve themselves in the running of Tyre's port and the limiting of commercial shipping under threat of confiscation (*ANET*, pp. 533–4).[11]

Remarkably, Tyre was once again spared from destruction, a fate it must have expected after Esarhaddon's annihilation of Sidon, and, although stripped of its mainland territories, was allowed to retain some commercial autonomy within the Assyrian Empire. Upon Ashurbarnipal's (668–631) accession to the Assyrian throne in 668, Tyre, Byblos and Arwad reaffirmed their alliance to Assyria by providing tribute and naval assistance for the king's first campaign against Egypt. Once again, Tyre's submission appears to have been a political charade. With Assyria distracted by its military operations, Tyre, along with Arwad and a number of states which had previously been part of its western alliance, went into rebellion. In 662, having successfully captured the Egyptian city of Thebes, thereby neutralising the threat from Egypt, the Assyrians instigated a land blockade of Tyre which eventually forced the city to surrender. Once more Ashurbarnipal showed leniency by sparing the city from destruction and allowing Baal to remain as monarch: however, the city was again forced to pay a heavy tribute and accept the loss of much of its mainland territory.

Although by 640 Tyre and its remaining mainland dependencies had become an Assyrian province, Assyria's hegemony over the Levant was slowly disintegrating due to a sustained period of civil unrest and an enervating war with Elam (a war which would ultimately prove to be a Pyrrhic victory for Assyria). With Assyrian control over the Levant weakening, the Phoenician cities once again came under the thrall of Egypt, with many willingly becoming Egyptian dependents. However, worried by the nascent threat posed by the newly emerging Babylonian Empire, Egypt took the drastic step of allying itself with its arch-enemy Assyria. This ill-fated alliance was to be short-lived as the Babylonian crown prince Nebuchadnezzar II succeeded in routing the combined forces of Assyria and Egypt at the battle of Carchemish in 605. This victory heralded a period of Babylonian hegemony of the Levant.

THE BABYLONIAN PERIOD (586–539)

With Assyria and Egypt's defeat at the hands of the Babylonians, the Phoenician cities regained their independence without the need for military action. However, they soon found that their newly gained freedom was precarious at best. In the first year of his reign, Nebuchadnezzar II (604–562) undertook an extensive military campaign in Syria which led to the kings of 'Hatti' (which included the rulers of the Phoenician coastal cities) swearing allegiance and loyalty to Babylon and offering tribute. Despite this, and probably as a direct result of Egyptian agitation, a number of Levantine states (including the Phoenician cities and the kingdom of Judah) rose up against Babylonian rule. For the first time, the Phoenician cities appear to have put aside their political rivalries and worked together for a common good (although whether this co-operation was military or economic is uncertain).

Nebuchadnezzar's immediate response was to besiege and destroy Jerusalem in 587, a decision which was perhaps influenced by Israel's control of the lucrative southern overland trade routes. The next stage of the campaign involved subjugating the Phoenician coastal cities, and thus in c.585 Nebuchadnezzar began his famous 13-year siege of Tyre (Josephus, *Antiquities of the Jews*, 10.228; *Against Apion*, 1.156). This drawn-out operation, which probably comprised a land rather than naval blockade, was intended to contain the city without the need for a military assault. With neither the Babylonians nor Tyrians willing to gamble on the outcome of a decisive military operation, the blockade was finally ended by mutual consent. Although Nebuchadnezzar allowed Tyre to retain its commercial autonomy and some degree of self-governance in return for recognising Babylonian suzerainty, the reigning Tyrian monarch, Ithobaal III (591/0–573/2), was exiled to Babylon and replaced by a more pro-Babylonian king, Baal II (573–564). Baal's death in 564 marked a constitutional change as institutional monarchy was abandoned in favour of governance by a body of annually appointed judges (*suffetes*); whether this change was introduced due to Tyrian initiative or Babylonian insistence is still open to debate. Although monarchical rule was reintroduced seven years later, by this stage Tyre had been assimilated into the Babylonian province of Kadesh and thus the title of king was largely symbolic.

The reign of Nebuchadnezzar and his successor was to have a severely detrimental impact on Phoenician commercial ventures. Babylon's annexation of southern Palestine, Trans-Jordon and Cilicia denied the Phoenicians access to the highly lucrative south Arabian and southern Anatolian trade networks, whilst commercial interactions with Egypt and Israel had been significantly curtailed. Moreover, like Egypt and Assyria before it, the Babylonian Empire coveted the forests of Lebanon and so Nebuchadnezzar immediately initiated extensive logging operations, thereby eliminating another of the Phoenicians' revenue streams (*ANET*, p. 307). Although a number of administrative documents refer to Phoenician craftsmen living and working in Babylon (*ANET*, p. 308), the money they sent home did little to alleviate the economic pressures faced by their compatriots. There is scant information pertaining to the relationship between the Phoenician cities and Babylon following the death of Nebuchadnezzar in 562; however, as Babylonian control weakened during the Empire's final years under the leadership of Nabonidus (556–539), the Phoenician cities tentatively began to reassert their political independence. Beset by social unrest at home, and dragged into simultaneous conflicts against Arabia and the recently established Median kingdom, the Babylonians gradually loosened their administrative grip over the Levant – a situation perhaps evinced by the reinstating of the exiled ruling families of Tyre, Sidon, Arwad and Byblos, a policy which appears to have been intended to placate these cities and ensure their future loyalty. To a certain degree this strategy was effective as all four cities remained tacitly loyal to Babylon despite the mounting internal and external pressures that threatened its existence.

THE PERSIAN PERIOD (539–332)

The end of Babylon came swiftly: in October 539 the Persian army, under the command of Cyrus the Great (559–530), swept through the Babylonian Empire, capturing Sippur and Babylon in quick succession. The final defeat of Nabonidus opened the way for Cyrus to assume control of the Levant and ushered in a period of Persian rule that was to last for more than 200 years.[12] None of the extant sources record the precise political status of the Phoenician cities during the early years of the Persian Empire but it seems likely that their transition from subjects of Babylon to subjects of Persia was a smooth and voluntary one. It is widely believed that the kings of the Phoenician cities were included among the monarchs of the Upper Sea (Mediterranean) who willingly offered loyalty and tribute to Cyrus in 539.[13] By the end of the sixth century, the Phoenician cities were part of a large satrapy (a type of administrative district) known as Athura ('Assyria'), which encompassed all of Mesopotamia and Syria-Palestine.

In the early decades of the fifth century, however, Darius I (522–486) reorganised the Persian provincial system, creating a new satrapy known as Abarnahara ('Beyond the River') which included the Levantine cities west of the Euphrates and Cyprus (Herodotus 3.61). The Phoenicians were included amongst the most privileged tributary states and were permitted to retain their institutions and their autonomy.[14] Like the Egyptians, Assyrians and Babylonians before them, the Persians treated the Phoenician cities favourably as they recognised their commercial and geostrategic importance. In essence, the Persians' relationship with the Phoenician cities appears to have been one of 'managed autonomy', whereby the Phoenicians were allowed to run their own affairs largely unhindered so long as they collaborated on imperial projects and paid their tribute in a timely fashion. As Persia's westerly imperial desires required a powerful navy, the Phoenicians were able to use their galleys as diplomatic bargaining chips with which to extract generous concessions from the Persian king. The first demonstration of the crucial role that the

Phoenician navies would play in Persia's military campaigns can be identified in Cambyses II's (530–522) invasion of Egypt in 525. According to Herodotus's account of the campaign, Tyre's fleet played a critical role in supporting and provisioning the Persian army, thus ensuring Cambyses's eventual success.

Persia's hegemony over Mesopotamia, Egypt and the Levant brought political stability, whilst its efficient communications networks and infrastructures, such as the great Royal Highway, helped facilitate trade (Herodotus 5.52–4). The construction of roads not only aided transportation but also helped to ensure the safety of travellers due to the placement of regular staging posts and checkpoints. The Phoenicians sought to take full advantage of the opportunities offered by Persian suzerainty and so, during the last quarter of the sixth century, they re-established trade connections with the interior of Mesopotamia, created new commercial networks throughout the Persian heartland and took a more active (and indeed aggressive) stance when it came to competing with the Greeks for control of markets in Egypt and throughout the Mediterranean. In the previous two centuries, having been weakened and distracted first by Assyrian and then Babylonian rule, the Phoenicians had faced increasing opposition from the Greeks who were vying for control of the Mediterranean markets and trade routes. By providing naval assistance for Persian aggression against the Ionian and mainland Greeks, the Phoenicians were in reality advancing their own agenda as these campaigns diminished their rivals' ability to challenge them for commercial supremacy. For instance, the destruction of Miletus at the hands of the Persians in 547 removed one of Phoenicia's greatest commercial rivals and opened up new markets in the Aegean.

For the first time during the early Persian Period, the Phoenician city states were encouraged to create federal bonds with one another and to establish a common council in an effort to try and limit political and economic competition. Diodorus Siculus (16.41.1) records that in the fourth century this council (comprising officials from Tyre, Sidon and Arwad) took the decision to found the city of Tripolis (i.e. the city of three cities). Although Tyre desperately sought to regain its supremacy, it was Sidon which was to profit most from Persian rule as is apparent from: the city's role as a regional administrative headquarters which housed the residence of a Persian satrap throughout the Achaemenid era; the presence of a sizeable

Fig. 4: Marble bull protome from the Sidonian royal palace (now housed in the National Museum, Beirut). The artistic style demonstrates a clear Persian influence

Persian garrison; the Persian king's decision to construct a royal garden (*paradeisos*) close to the city (Diodorus 16.41.5); and the incorporation of Persian symbols and iconography into Sidonian artistic traditions (see Figure 4).

Sidon's coinage also bears testimony to the city's elevated status within the Persian hierarchy as it alone was given royal permission to depict the Great King on its coins and to issue the double-stater (a heavy coin which had considerable political prestige as well as financial value). By including Persian imperial imagery on their coinage, Sidonian kings were able to publicise their status within the Persian Empire and thus maintain their economic, religious and political supremacy within Phoenicia.[15] The distribution of Sidonian coinage provides strong evidence for the city's commercial dominance during the Persian Period, with studies showing that it was more widely circulated than any other Phoenician currency. Sidon also maintained particularly close commercial ties with Athens, with this relationship intensifying during the first quarter of the fourth century. In 364, during the reign of the philhellene king Straton I (= Abd'ashtart I, c.376–361), the commercial relationship between the two cities was to reach its zenith when the Athenians exempted all persons who resided and exercised their political rights in Sidon from paying a variety of taxes and from performing public liturgies (i.e. public services) when trading in Athens (*IG II*² 141). The fifth and early fourth centuries were clearly a period of prosperity for Sidon as reflected in the city's urban expansion, the monumental remodelling and extension of the Eshmun temple complex, and the lavish royal burials of Sidonian monarchs. Despite Sidon's commercial pre-eminence, the other Phoenician cities were still able to pursue their own economic interests and agendas and thus many of them also flourished during the first 150 years of Persian rule.

The final years of the fifth century witnessed increasing political unrest and weakness within Persia (in particular, in the western regions of the Empire). Although Darius II's (423–404) early reign had been a period of relative peace and stability which had enabled the consolidation of Persian satrapal power, the latter part of his rule was characterised by a series of successive civil disturbances and unrest which would continue into the fourth century. The first major disturbance of this period occurred in 420 when Pissuthnes (satrap of Lydia) attempted to secede from Persian rule. Although the reasons for this revolt are unrecorded, what is certain is that he was supported in his efforts by the Athenians. The defeat and execution of Pissuthnes in 415 was not to bring about the peace that Darius desired as Pissuthnes's bastard son, Amorges, fled to Caria and continued his father's insurrection. Again, Athens lent its support to this rebellion, thereby enabling Amorges to continue his agitations against the Persians until his eventual capture and execution in 411.

A further significant blow to Persia's power and prestige was the loss of Egypt: by 405, the entire region of the Nile Delta was in open revolt under the leadership of Amyrtaeus (who is thought to be related to the Egyptian royal family that had previously been replaced by Cambyses II). Within five years the indigenous royal dynasty had re-established control of upper Egypt, thereby bringing an end to more than 100 years of Persian rule. By *c.*385, this new dynasty of Egyptian pharaohs had successfully re-established Egypt's military and political power and was thus able to defend itself against tentative Persian advances. The marked deterioration of Persian control in the west and the growing influence of Egypt, Asia Minor and Greece were of considerable concern to the commercially minded Phoenician city states. Whereas in the fifth century, a time when Persia had been in firm control of the eastern Mediterranean, they had been content to remain loyal, once Persian power began to wane, many of the Phoenician cities calculated that their political and commercial priorities were best served by independent action.

A case in point was Tyre's decision to aid Evagoras, the Greek tyrant of Cyprian Salamis, in his unsuccessful efforts to wrest control of Cyprus from the Persian king Artaxerxes II (404–358) during the 380s. Despite successfully quelling the rebellion, Artaxerxes's next major campaign was to prove disastrous. In 373, having achieved temporary respite from the revolts that had previously demanded his attention, Artaxerxes decided it was finally time to restore Persian control in Egypt. However, in contrast to their shambolic attempt to defend themselves against Cambyses II's invasion 150 years earlier, this time the Egyptians were able to blockade the Pelusiac entrance to the Nile Delta, thereby stalling the Persian advance. The Egyptian defenders held out long enough that the Persians became trapped by the annual inundation of the Nile and so were forced to withdraw after suffering heavy losses.

Persia's failure to regain control of Egypt was to have long-lasting consequences and served as a direct catalyst for the Great Satrapal Revolt that broke out in 363. The role that the Phoenicians played in this revolt is unclear and divides scholarly opinion. Although many of the Phoenician cities appear to have remained loyal to Persia, at least initially, in 360 the Sidonian king Abd'ashtart I (*c.*365–352) decided to rebel against Persian rule. Sidon's seditious tendencies are evident in the city's coinage, which now displayed the crowned portrait of the Sidonian monarch rather than Persian imperial symbols. Having established alliances with Athens, Egypt and Cyprian-Salamis, and by timing his rebellion to coincide with an invasion of Phoenicia by the Egyptian pharaoh Tachos (362–360), Abd'ashtart was confident of victory. His confidence, however, was unjustified, and thus, despite some initial successes, his rebellion was eventually quelled in 355. The revolt proved to be a grave political error: although the Persian king, Artaxerxes III (358–338), allowed him to retain his throne, large numbers of Sidonian citizens were exiled to Susa and Babylon, whilst the city was stripped of large swathes of its mainland territories, was prevented from minting coins, no longer held a privileged position within the Persian hierarchy and so was cut off from the political and commercial benefits it had previously been afforded, and, finally, was now garrisoned with a considerable number of Persian troops.

A year after Abd'ashtart's death in 358, Sidon reaffirmed its fealty to Persia and was granted autonomy: keen to ensure the city's unwavering loyalty, Artaxerxes handpicked the new Sidonian king, Tabnit II (or Tennes, 358–345). However, Tabnit's pro-Persian sympathies were not as strong as Artaxerxes had hoped and thus in 351, less than six years after his coronation, the Sidonian king was leading another rebellion against Persian rule. Sidon's disaffection appears to have stemmed from a number of increasingly invasive and heavy-handed Persian policies, in particular Artaxerxes's decision to utilise Sidon as a garrison city and provincial headquarters. Things came to a head during the final preparations for Artaxerxes's planned invasion of Egypt when huge numbers of Persian troops were stationed in Sidon. Not only did this influx of troops put pressure on food supplies, it also led to the requisitioning of resources that were traditionally earmarked for trade. The resulting decline in commercial profits caused economic hardship for many of the city's inhabitants. Matters were made substantially worse by the highly insolent and disrespectful behaviour of the resident Persian officials, who arrogantly taxed and requisitioned the city's resources with little regard for the deprivation their actions might cause (Diodorus, 16.41.2).

Recognising the precariousness of Artaxerxes's position following his calamitous defeat in the winter of 351–350, the Sidonians concluded an alliance with the Egyptian pharaoh Nectanebo II (359–341) before convincing Tyre and Arwad to join a rebellion against Persian rule. In one of the first acts of defiance, the Persian royal game reserve near Sidon was ravaged before the heavy-handed officials who had caused so much misery were rounded up and executed. Although this alliance succeeded in resisting the initial advances of Artaxerxes, ultimately the rebellion was to end in abject failure. Isolated, faced with 300,000 Persian troops, and perhaps abandoned by his allies (Diodorus's account makes no mention of Tyrian or Arwadite troops in the latter years of the rebellion), Tabnit makes the strange decision to betray his own city in return for a royal pardon. His treachery resulted in a devastating catastrophe that was unparalleled in Phoenician history: 600 leading citizens were ambushed and massacred outside the city gates; 40,000 of the city's inhabitants (men, women, children and household slaves) immolated themselves in order to avoid ill-treatment at the hands of Artaxerxes's rampaging troops; those citizens who elected not to commit suicide and who survived the Persian onslaught were enslaved and deported to various cities throughout the Near East (a Babylonian text dating to 345 records the arrival of these slaves in Babylon and Susa);[16] a number of buildings and large stretches of the city walls were damaged or destroyed; and, finally, the accumulated wealth and personal possessions of the city's inhabitants (including large quantities of molten gold and silver recovered from the smouldering ruins) were pilfered and sold. Despite Artaxerxes's prior assurances, Tabnit was summarily executed once his city had been fully and violently subjugated. The brutal treatment of Sidon served as a powerful reminder of the fate awaiting any city which unsuccessfully stood against Persia. Heeding this dire warning, the panic-stricken Phoenician cities quickly capitulated and by 345 all of Phoenicia and Cyprus were once again under Persian rule.

THE ARRIVAL OF ALEXANDER THE GREAT

The short reign of Artaxerxes III's successor, Darius III (336–330), was primarily taken up with military preparations to counter the growing threat posed by Macedon and its formidable leader Alexander the Great (336–323). The classical sources record that at the time of Alexander's invasion the Phoenician contingents still held a pre-eminent position within the Persian navy (which comprised around 400 war galleys). With Alexander able to muster only 160 ships, a fleet which was a mixture of war galleys and transport vessels, it is unsurprising that one of his primary objectives was to conquer the cities of the Levantine coast. By taking control of these vital seaports, Alexander not only secured himself safe anchorages but also prevented Darius from using his navy to disrupt the Macedonian supply lines or to attack mainland Greece (both these concerns are clearly highlighted in Alexander's speech before the siege of Tyre: Arrian, 2.17.1–2). Having defeated Darius at the Battle of Issus in 333, Alexander led his forces down towards the coast of Phoenicia. The Phoenician city states were now in a very difficult position: on the one hand, if they resisted Macedonian overtures, they faced being besieged and severely punished if defeated, whilst on the other, a number of their vessels were at sea with the Persian fleet and thus any treachery on their behalf could have deadly consequences for their fellow citizens (for example, Arrian 2.20.1 records that the king of Byblos was away on a military operation at the time of the Macedonians' arrival).

According to the classical sources, stuck between a rock and a hard place, the majority of the Phoenician cities submitted to Alexander with little or no resistance (Arrian 2.13.7–8; 2.15.6; Diodorus 17.40.2). The first Phoenician city that willingly submitted to Macedonian rule was Arwad which, in an effort to demonstrate its fealty, welcomed Alexander with a royal reception and presented him with a golden crown. In the absence of their king, the council of Byblos also took the decision to open their gates voluntarily to Alexander and offer him assurances of their loyalty. Unsurprisingly, the Sidonians, still angry and resentful at their brutal treatment at the hands of the Persians less than a decade earlier, welcomed Alexander as a liberator, inviting him into their city and offering him their unconditional allegiance. Having secured the loyalty of Sidon, the Macedonians continued their march southwards towards Tyre, where they were to be met with a less enthusiastic welcome. The king of Tyre, Azemilkos (or Ozmilk, c.350–333), who was still in the service of the Persians, refused to meet Alexander and thus the ensuing negotiations were conducted via a high-ranking Tyrian princess. When Alexander demanded access to the island fortress in order to offer sacrifices at the ancient temple of Melqart (Heracles to the Greeks), the princess countered with the suggestion that he might wish to worship at the even older temple situated on the mainland. However, Alexander would not back down and so, fearing that this was a Macedonian ploy to occupy their city, the Tyrians refused to grant his request.

Despite Alexander's growing reputation as a highly talented general, the Tyrians had every reason to be confident. In addition to their powerful navy, the city was founded on an island, protected by huge walls that were an impressive 46 metres high in places, and was well provisioned with fresh water and food. Moreover, an embassy from Carthage had promised to supply Tyre with ships and soldiers if the city was besieged by the Macedonians. Azemilkos's standoffish policy towards Alexander appears to have been an attempt to maintain Tyrian independence without upsetting the army on his doorstep; however, it proved to be a dangerous miscalculation. Due to its potential to become a base of resistance against Macedonian rule, Alexander could ill afford to let Tyre retain its independence and so, with diplomacy having failed, he now gave the order to besiege the city.

The protracted siege and the subsequent destruction of the city are well documented in the classical sources and through their accounts we gain a vivid insight into the final few months of Tyre's existence. Although faced with overwhelming odds, the Tyrians mounted a dogged defence against both the Macedonian siege and the blockade of their ports by a fleet of Cyprian, Arwadian, Byblian and Sidonian vessels. In mid-July 332, after a siege lasting seven months, the city's walls were finally breached, signalling the end of Tyrian resistance. The reprisals for Tyre's opposition to Alexander were to be even more severe than those inflicted on Sidon by Artaxerxes III: 6,000 of the surviving population were summarily executed, 30,000 were sold into slavery, 2,000 young aristocratic men were crucified and their bodies displayed along the coast, and, finally, the defensive walls were torn down and much of the city destroyed. Although Tyre would eventually recover, it would never again achieve the power and prestige it had enjoyed previously. The destruction of Tyre not only marked the end of Persian rule in Phoenicia, it was also one of the first steps in the Hellenisation of the Levant.

2

GOVERNMENT AND SOCIETY

With regard to governance, the Phoenician cities were monarchies and so can best be conceptualised as sovereign states which operated under the auspices of a powerful local dynast or potentate. Royal rulers in Byblos can be identified as early as the third millennium, and in Tyre from at least the nineteenth century, indicating that monarchic rule was an early development in Phoenicia. By the mid-fourteenth century Sidon, Berytus and Arwad were also governed by well-established, powerful dynastic houses at the head of which was a male monarch. A lack of contemporaneous political documents, however, means that very little is known about the governance and administration of the Phoenician city states or about their political institutions and infrastructures. Furthermore, unlike their Canaanite, Egyptian, Assyrian and Persian counterparts, Phoenician monarchs did not, as far as is known, recount their exploits and political endeavours in monumental commemorative inscriptions or reliefs. Consequently, aside from a few royal inscriptions (which typically record the monarch's name and a superficial outline of his major achievements), the main sources of information regarding the power and prerogatives of Phoenician kings date to the Hellenistic or Roman periods and tend to be derived from non-Levantine traditions. This means that the interactions between the state and civic society, and the form, nature, duties and powers of Phoenician political and administrative institutions and officials, are difficult to reconstruct. Despite the scarcity of indigenous sources, the actions of kings such as Hiram I, Ithobaal I and Elulaios of Tyre reveal that Phoenician monarchs ruled with almost absolute power until the seventh century. Hiram I, for instance, expressed his personal authority and aspirations through the construction of a lavish new royal palace, a decision that is indicative of a ruler who wields considerable power (in democracies, oligarchies, or in states ruled by a more limited form of monarchy, political statements were more typically made through the construction of communal amenities such as markets, harbours and fortifications). Significantly, these sources also hint at the nascent power and prestige of the local city elite, or 'merchant aristocracy', which, by the seventh century, appears to have accrued considerable political and economic influence. However, any study of Phoenician governance must keep in mind that for long periods of their history the Phoenicians were subsumed within the political systems of more powerful empires (including Egypt, Assyria, Babylon, Persia and Macedonia).

Given the scarcity of documentary evidence, understanding the complex political interactions between the Phoenicians and their various overlords, interactions which must have varied significantly from period to period and from city to city, is a challenging task. Nevertheless two general conclusions can be drawn: firstly, that political oversight lay with either a resident foreign official (such as a governor or satrap) or with a compliant local ruler; and, secondly, that as long as taxes and tributes were paid in a timely manner, and services were provided when requested, most foreign rulers were content to allow local dynasts to retain much of their political autonomy.[1]

KINGS AND KINGSHIP

In many Near Eastern cultures, kingship was considered to be the very basis of civilisation. According to such beliefs, it was only the uncivilised which lived without a king to provide them with security, freedom, peace, prosperity and justice. Comparisons between the political activities of Phoenician kings and those undertaken by their Near Eastern counterparts reveal little difference in the patterns of thought and behaviour and thus there can be little doubt that Phoenician royal ideologies were inspired and influenced by Mesopotamian and Canaanite traditions. The three fundamental and intertwined tenets of Near Eastern kingship can thus be identified in Phoenician royal ideology: that the monarch belonged to heaven and thus his kingship was a god-given gift; that he had a judicial responsibility to guard and protect his subjects against the harsh realities of life; and that kingship was sacred. According to this conceptualisation of monarchy, kings ruled as mediators and intercessors of a divine agency and thus were considered to be intercessors between the earthly and divine realms. At the heart of secular royal ideology was the concept of a patron–client relationship in which the king functioned as the primary benefactor of his people. In his guise as patron the king promised to protect his citizens against war (in the forms of banditry, piracy and military invasion), want (especially poverty brought about by famine or drought) and injustice (pertaining to both the mortal and divine realms). In essence, the patron–client relationship was a practical means of safeguarding against the harsh realities of daily life in the ancient Near East.

In order to protect against physical threats and to ensure military success, the king functioned as commander-in-chief of the city's military forces (although the inscription from the tomb of Ahiram reveals that the day-to-day running of the army could be delegated to a trusted general). In the ancient Near East, kings who were remembered as great warriors were also remembered as great hunters: therefore, in order to promote their martial prowess, Phoenician monarchs often selected hunting scenes for their royal seals. Significantly, providing for their people could involve conquering or raiding other towns and cities in order to acquire spoils or additional lands – especially during times of drought or famine (e.g. the inscription of Eshmunazar II, *ANET*, p. 662). There is also evidence that the Phoenician kings functioned as supreme commanders of their cities' naval forces. For instance, a coin minted by the Sidonian king Baana (dating to *c.*409–402) bears the Phoenician word *TM'* which can be translated as 'chief commander', whilst a number of the classical texts record that during the Persian Wars each of the Phoenician kings acted as commander-in-chief of his own fleet whilst campaigning with the Persian navy.[2]

Another patronal duty of the king was to protect his citizens against want or poverty (often conceptualised in agrarian terms). The agricultural origins and connotations of this facet of the king's role can be identified from a study of wider Near Eastern royal ideology, in which kings are frequently cast in the role of shepherds of their people.[3] The use of shepherd/sheep imagery not only enabled the monarch to connect with the agrarian community, who at times could feel isolated or separate from the urban centre (see below), it also highlighted his care and compassion for all his people. Just as the shepherd would tend his flock, ensuring that it was fed and watered, so too would the king provide for his people. This highly symbolic image also provided reassurance to those pursuing non-agrarian occupations but who relied on the foodstuffs produced by the agricultural community that the king would always ensure they were provided for. The metaphor of the population as sheep also subtly reminded the people of their duty to passively follow the orders of the shepherd–king as he alone could determine what was in their best interests. This was an important point to emphasise as Phoenician kings, like their counterparts throughout the Near East, feared the divisive, and sometimes destructive, power of wilful disobedience or defiance against their rule. Finally, kings were also directly responsible for administering justice on behalf of the gods who were believed to have established law and order in the universe. Phoenician kings can therefore be found presenting themselves as righteous and just individuals (e.g. the Byblian king Yehavmilk, *ANET*, p. 656, who stresses his 'lawfulness'). The king was considered to be the final earthly judicial authority within his realm and thus once he had made a ruling, it could not be reversed or overturned. Like other Near Eastern kings, Phoenician monarchs appear to have clasped some form of symbolic implement when dispensing justice (for example, King Ahiram appears to have used a royal mace, *ANET*, p. 661). Although little is known about Phoenician judicial institutions or procedural guidelines, it is likely that the king was assisted in his jurisdictional role by a series of court officials and adjutants.

The Sacral Roles of Phoenician Kings

According to Phoenician theology, kingship was one of the basic institutions of human existence that had been designed by the gods and then bestowed on mankind as a gift. As the gods were responsible for selecting the right king, they were often credited with a role in his creation and upbringing. Kings were therefore considered to be the gods' representatives on earth and thus Phoenician kingship had an overtly religious dimension. This divine approval was particularly important as there were no unequivocal secular criteria which made a man eligible to rule. Thus, as in other Near Eastern monarchies, the power and authority of Phoenician kings was intrinsically linked to their sacred role as intermediaries between the earthly and heavenly realms. This role was often explicitly acknowledged through the incorporation of divine names (such as Ba'al, Eshmun, Melqart and 'Ashtart), into the king's dynastic or family name – the names of King Hiram's sons, Abdastratus (Servant of 'Ashtart) and Baalbazer (Servant of Ba'al), are illustrative of this practice. Similarly, rituals of monarchy and the royal ideologies from which they emerged were also designed to articulate the complex interconnection between the cosmological and earthly aspects of kingship. Consequently, one of the king's primary roles was that of chief priest and religious representative.

The priestly connotations of monarchy are attested by the religious titles and duties assumed by Phoenician kings at different points throughout the first millennium. Thus the Sidonian kings Tabnit I and Eshmunazar II referred to themselves as 'priest of 'Ashtart', whilst the Byblian king, Ozbaal, is listed as a priest of 'The Lady' (i.e. Ba'alat Gubal) in the Batno'am inscription (*ANET*, p. 662). Typically, however, Phoenician monarchs only appear to have functioned as chief priests in the temple dedicated to their dynastic patron, a situation that arose for two reasons: firstly, because it helped confirm which god was pre-eminent within the city's pantheon and, secondly, because it highlighted the close relationship that the king enjoyed with the god or goddess who had legitimised his rule and under whose auspices he now operated. If one of the main functions of a Phoenician monarch was that of chief priest, then it is logical to assume that they would have undertaken a number of religious duties, such as public sacrifices and the examination of entrails during important religious festivals. Phoenician kings also demonstrated their piety through the building or restoring of temples and altars (sometimes laying the first brick or clearing the first basket of earth). Although these projects added to the personal prestige of the monarch, they were also important as the construction of religious buildings and monuments was thought to be able to secure the prosperity of the whole state. This is clearly seen in an inscription of the Byblian king Yehavmilk in which the Lady of Byblos, in response to the king's pious prayers and offerings, is recorded as having bestowed peace and grace upon the king and by extension his people. Although there is no evidence to suggest that Phoenician kings ever had themselves formally deified, occasionally some seem to have confused divinely granted authority with divinity itself. For instance, the king of Tyre was harshly criticised by the Hebrew prophet Ezekiel (28:1–2) for being swollen with pride and claiming: 'I am god. I am sitting on the throne of God, surrounded by seas'. Ezekiel continues, 'you are a man and not a god', indicating that the prophet's ire was caused by the Tyrian king's belief in his own divinity.

Kingship as a Hereditary Position

Ideally Phoenician kingship was hereditary and passed from father to son. Consequently, in order to emphasise their legitimacy, monarchs can often be found recording that their father, and occasionally grandfather, had ruled before them (e.g. the Byblian king Yehavmilk: *ANET*, p. 502). If, at the time of his father's death, a boy was too young to ascend the throne, there could be a period of regency (as was the case with Eshmunazar II whose mother, Amo'ashtart, reigned as regent until he was old enough to rule). The king's mother seems to have been a particularly revered and respected figure in Phoenicia as attested by the inscription found on the sarcophagus of Batno'am (the mother of the Byblian king Ozbaal). Batno'am's epitaph, the existence of which immediately reveals her importance, records that she was buried in full royal regalia comprising a fine gown, headdress and gold plate covering her mouth (the latter appears to have been a uniquely Byblian tradition).

Evidence for a convention dictating that a king's successor must come from within the royal household can be identified in the curious tale told by Curtius Rufus (4.1.1–20) and Diodorus (17.47). According to these sources, following his invasion of Phoenicia, Alexander the Great asked his companion and trusted friend Hephaestion to identify a suitable successor for the recently dethroned Sidonian king. Having become close to two young Sidonian aristocrats, Hephaestion offers them the opportunity to rule. However, each in turn declines his generous offer pleading that in conformity with Sidonian custom the throne should only be allowed to pass to a member of the existing royal family. Having praised them for their lofty and noble spirit, Hephaestion then asks them to choose a suitable king from amongst the extended royal family and they select Abdalonim who, although destitute at the time, was a distant relative of the deposed king and known for his wisdom and integrity (significantly, the discovery of a votive inscription dedicated by a royal prince named Abdalonim suggests that at least part of this story is true, *SEG* 36.758).

Although it was preferred that a king's successor came from within the immediate, or at the very least extended, royal family, there were occasionally usurpers who seized the throne and were able to reign for a number of years. For instance, the grandson of Hiram I, King Abd'ashtart, was assassinated by the four sons of his wet-nurse, the eldest of whom went on to reign for 12 years. Significantly, Josephus records that at least three Tyrian kings were assassinated (one by his brother) and that a number of others were overthrown after short reigns. A similar picture is likely to hold true in most, if not all, of the other Phoenician cities, as royal dynasties throughout the ancient Near East frequently suffered from the strains of familial rivalry and personal ambition.

COUNCILS AND ASSEMBLIES

Although there was a danger that absolute power could eventually corrupt a monarch, most kings were acutely aware that their reign could be ended prematurely by a popular revolt or palace coup and thus they were mindful of their subjects. To rule effectively and to ensure the continuation of their dynastic lines monarchs were reliant upon the support of their people: hence, in order to avoid isolating themselves from their subjects, and to demonstrate that they listened to the will of the people, many Phoenician kings appear to have taken guidance from a variety of citizen councils and assemblies.[4] For example, the Amarna correspondences reveal that the kings of Tyre, Byblos, Sumur and Arwad consulted a 'council of elders' (or 'important men') when deciding matters of state. Although little is known about these councils, what is certain is that they were not symbolic as they are occasionally shown opposing the will of the king (e.g. *EA* 243) and even acting independently when they believed it advantageous to do so (e.g. *EA* 172).

That these councils retained, and at times increased, their political importance is attested in a variety of later sources. For example, the *Report of Wenamun*, which dates to the early eleventh century (i.e. around 250 years after the Amarna Letters), reveals that the Byblian council of elders still held considerable political power. This council is also referred to in Ezekiel (27:9) as: 'the ancients of Gebal (Byblos) and the wise men thereof'. Similarly, the Tyrian council, referred to by the Israelite prophets Isaiah and Ezekiel as 'Princes of the Sea', appear to have monitored and, when necessary, regulated the behaviour and decisions of their king. In the seventh-century treaty between

Esarhaddon of Assyria and Baal of Tyre, the terms of agreement, which state that the Assyrian governor will work in conjunction with Baal and with the elders of his country, suggest that Tyre's council of elders governed alongside the king. Viewed holistically, the evidence from Tyre shows that as the profits from inter-regional exchange increased, the power of the king became progressively more constrained by the city's wealthy mercantile families who were keen to influence public affairs. The power of Tyre's council of elders was to be dramatically highlighted following the invasion of the Babylonian king Nebuchadnezzar II in the early sixth century, when it governed the city for seven years in place of a king (Josephus, *Against Apion*, 21.154–60). An inscription recovered from Sarepta offers tantalising evidence for a council of 10 who were responsible for helping govern the city and its territory; however, as the text is highly fragmentary it is far from certain that this interpretation is correct.

Frustratingly, aside from periods of crisis, it is impossible to determine whether the role of Phoenician councils was purely consultative or played a direct part in decision making. All that can be said with any real confidence is that they were comprised of high-ranking nobles and officials (Phoenician = špt), who advised on matters of state and who could be trusted to assist the king in resolving judicial, fiscal and religious issues. There is also evidence for the existence of a larger, more encompassing political body referred to as the 'Peoples' Assembly' which seems to have operated alongside the more exclusive council of elders. Documented in both Tyre and Sidon, admission to this political body appears to have been open to all freeborn, adult male citizens. Although the existence of this body is confirmed in a few sources, none provides any information about its function or authority and it is unclear whether it had the power to suggest or introduce new legislation, or was simply there to affirm decisions made by the king and the Council of Elders (although, if it follows the model found in Carthage, then the latter is most likely).

SOCIAL STRUCTURES AND HIERARCHIES

Although reconstructing the social hierarchies (or structures) of the Phoenician city states is a difficult task, there are nevertheless some indications that a system of social ranking (or stratification) was in effect from the Early Bronze Age. In essence social stratification is a method for defining an individual's position within society according to their occupation, income, wealth, social status or derived power (either social or political). Consequently, a stratified society is one in which members of the same sex, and of equivalent age, do not have access to the same basic resources that sustain life. There are typically three distinguishing features of a stratified society: at least one section of society is socially and politically excluded or marginalised; high-ranking officials and courtiers group together to form an exclusive social group; and the presence of a social elite which preserves its position and status by ensuring its members gain some form of economic advantage. The clearest evidence for social stratification in the ancient world is a disparity in the size and type of people's homes (e.g. if there is a considerable difference between the dimensions of the largest and smallest houses within the city) and the clustering of houses of a similar size (which indicates some form of social or communal bond). Social ranking is also apparent in the mortuary evidence as evinced by the different types and quality of graves and grave markers found in Phoenician cemeteries. Archaeological excavations at sites throughout Lebanon have revealed that socio-economic inequality increased significantly during the Iron Age as Phoenician society became increasingly complex in terms of both political and social organisation. However, despite a considerable divide between rich and poor, with the vast majority of a city's wealth being controlled by the king, various priesthoods, and the aristocracy, there is little evidence for political tensions between the various social classes.

Despite a scarcity of evidence, it is still possible to reconstruct a schematic overview of Phoenicia's social hierarchy. In general, each of the city states appears to have informally divided its populations into five main socio-economic classes, namely: Royalty, Nobility (or Noble Class), Middle Class, Working Class and Servant Class. As has been seen, the king was at the top of the social hierarchy and thus had ultimate control over his city's land, people and assets. Aside from royalty, the uppermost class within Phoenicia's social hierarchy was the Noble Class, which comprised government officials, generals, wealthy merchants and landowners, and priests. These were the richest and most influential people who were thought to be of utmost importance to the physical and spiritual safety and prosperity of the city. In cities such as Tyre, Byblos and Arwad, members of the Council of Elders were drawn from the Noble Class. The Middle Class encompassed occupational groups such as farmers, fishermen, craftsmen, artisans, industrialists and merchants. As this class of people were responsible for fulfilling the day-to-day needs of all other sections of society (in regard to both goods and services) they were afforded certain rights and privileges that provided them with legal protection from exploitation. The Working Class included both the poorest citizens (such as shepherds, seasonal workers, day labourers and mariners) and freedmen. Aside from slaves, this group had the least amount of legal and political rights and privileges and so were easily exploited (although as citizens it is likely that they still retained a voice in the Citizen Assembly and had some legal recourse if treated particularly harshly). The final class, the Servant Class, was comprised of slaves who, although politically and legally disenfranchised, were nevertheless granted the right to earn money with which they could pay for their freedom.

Though it is possible to create a schematic overview of Phoenicia's social hierarchy, the lack of contemporary source material prevents more detailed analysis. Thus, for instance, it is impossible to detect the exact status attributed to individual occupations or to rank against each other the mass of individuals who comprised the so-called 'Middle' and 'Working' classes. When analysing the social makeup of the various Phoenician city states it is also worth noting that, due to their commercial focus, they contained a highly transient and itinerant population which comprised not only those whose profession relied on travel (such as merchants, hauliers, sailors and prospectors), but also those who by choice or by necessity worked abroad (including artisans, craftsmen, miners, scribes and envoys). Most of the major Phoenician cities would therefore have accommodated a significant number of transient foreigners who had taken up temporary residence. The overall picture which emerges is one of socially diverse and ethnically varied societies that were willing to welcome and assimilate foreigners and foreign culture.

THE WOMEN OF ANCIENT PHOENICIA

Although all the social classes identified above included female members, reconstructing the daily lives of women is still a challenging task. Like almost every aspect of Phoenician society, the existing sources (textual, representational and archaeological), as well as their interpretation, present a series of problems, the greatest of which is the unequal representation of different genders and social groups. For instance, the textual and representational sources which comprise a large part of the current dataset were predominantly produced by, and intended to serve the needs of, urban elite males and thus social and cultural bias serves to distort the picture they present. Thus, despite the majority of women coming from a non-elite background, those recorded in the textual and visual corpora are typically priestesses, queens or the wives of high-ranking officials. Even then, none of the surviving texts were written explicitly by or for women and nor do women appear to have been professional artists. Consequently, the idealised image of women presented in Phoenician literature and art is almost certainly produced by men. Accordingly, all these depictions should be used with caution as they do not represent the daily experiences or lifestyles of non-elite women, many of whom would have come from an agrarian background. Recognition of this fact means that in order to reconstruct the lives and roles of non-elite women it is first necessary to understand the social makeup and composition of agricultural communities within ancient Phoenicia.[5]

Despite archaeology starting to provide scholars with a clearer understanding of Phoenicia's agrarian communities, the picture that emerges is still distorted by male elite bias. For example, due to their better state of preservation and visibility in the archaeological record, excavators have tended to focus their attention on uncovering monumental structures such as palaces, temples and fortifications, rather than small domestic buildings. As the majority of these buildings are associated primarily with elite males, and since a major sphere of authority for women lay in the home, this lack of attention to domestic spaces means that once again the daily lives and experiences of non-elite women are missing from the evidence. This problem is compounded by the fact that the majority of locations chosen for excavation tend to be large urban complexes rather than rural or agricultural sites. Although the situation is slowly improving due to the excavation of small rural settlements such as Khalde, recovering the lives of women is still extremely challenging. Domestic spaces and artefacts require careful analysis as very few objects or spaces are gender specific (i.e. most were used by both sexes) and so we must be

Fig. 5: Basalt grinding stone recovered from Tell-Arqa

extremely careful when assigning the use of an object or location to any particular gender.

To overcome the limitations of the surviving source material, and in an effort to present a more nuanced picture of the daily lives of non-elite women, scholars are now beginning to engage with research conducted by anthropologists. The ethnographic studies conducted in Lebanon during the nineteenth and early twentieth centuries CE have proven to be particularly useful as the agrarian lifestyles and practices they document are remarkably similar to those of Iron Age Phoenicia. For instance, this research noted that the grinding of grain into flour was an exclusively female activity, an observation which also holds true for the Iron Age (as attested by a number of reliefs and texts recovered from Canaan, Israel, Egypt and Mesopotamia). Thus, by combining the finding of modern ethnographic research with the results of cross-cultural analysis, it has been possible to determine that the various grindstones discovered by archaeologists at Phoenician sites throughout Lebanon must have been utilised predominantly, if not exclusively, by women (see Figure 5). If used cautiously, the ethnographic studies of the nineteenth and early twentieth centuries have the potential to help to illuminate the daily lives of women in ancient Phoenicia and to assist in identifying the tools and objects they commonly used.

The Social and Legal Status of Phoenician Women

In the ancient Near East the family was patriarchal. The father, or husband, was head of the family and exercised supreme authority over his wife and children until his death. Women on the other hand were never truly independent and were always defined by their relationship with a male: the stages of a woman's life can therefore be summarised as daughter, bride, spouse, housekeeper, mother and finally grandmother.[6] The most important role of a woman in marriage was to bear children, preferably sons to continue the family name. Traditionally, studies of the ancient Near East have seen women as second-class citizens who were fully under the dominion of their father or husband; however, scholarship has now begun to make use of anthropological research in order to provide a more nuanced assessment of women's social status and relationships with other members of their family (particularly male members). Recent anthropological investigations into the daily experiences of Middle Eastern women during the nineteenth and twentieth centuries CE have challenged the long-held view that they were fully subservient to their male relatives. Instead, these studies emphasised the crucial role played by women in maintaining a functioning household and in ensuring family cohesion: resulting in wives generally being considered their husband's equal when it came to most aspects of household life. With the women of Phoenicia known to have undertaken similar familial roles it is reasonable to conclude that they, like their modern counterparts, were often in a position of parity and interdependence, rather than subservience, with their husbands when it came to household matters (a situation that is clearly attested in the Ugaritic texts). A common misconception of gender roles in the ancient world is that the father goes away to work whilst the mother remains in the homestead to take care of cooking, cleaning, laundry and raising the children.

However, the division of labour or important familial duties according to gender is not in fact typical in the Levant, especially in agricultural societies which could only function if important tasks were undertaken by both sexes. Examples of shared responsibilities include: the education and nurturing of children; the cultivation of fields, vineyards and orchards; the production of dairy products; and the performance of prayers and offerings in the hope of gaining divine protection or blessings for the family. The sharing of tasks by men and women, both in the public and private spheres, appears to have been accepted as it was thought to correspond to the sharing of tasks by gods and goddesses in the divine realm. Some women could also wield significant political power either as a function of their holding office as queen or queen mother (and in extraordinary circumstances even through reigning as monarch) or on account of their aristocratic status. Therefore, although women's access to official authority was limited in comparison with men's, this does not mean that women lacked authority or were completely dominated by male members of society.

The Religious Roles of Women

One aspect of public life in which women had particular influence and prestige was religion. In contrast to the rest of Canaan and the Levant, where there is limited evidence for women holding sacerdotal positions within temples and sanctuaries, priestesses appear to have played a significant role in Phoenician religious life. Undoubtedly this is a reflection of the importance of goddesses within the Phoenician pantheons. Female divinities, like their male counterparts, were not only associated with natural phenomena and forces but could also be worshipped as a city's primary patron, a fact which undeniably enhanced the roles and social status of mortal women. Consequently, those women who were seen to embody positive divine qualities appear to have played a significant role in Phoenician religious life. The fifth-century funerary inscription from the sarcophagus of King Eshmunazar II of Sidon (*KAI* 14) contains the clearest evidence for the presence of priestesses within the temples of ancient Phoenicia as it clearly states that the dead king's mother was a *khnt* (priest) of 'Ashtart. The earliest use of the term *khnt* when referring to a female subject appears on a funerary crater (a bowl used for mixing water and wine) dating to the eighth or seventh century.[7] The inscription records that the crater contained the cremated remains of Gerat-milk, a priestess (*khnt*) of the goddess 'Ashtart. Other instances of female high priests can be found in the Punic and Neo-Punic texts from the western Mediterranean. In all there are at least 14 inscriptions from across the Phoenician diaspora which make reference to a female *khnt*.[8]

Fig. 6: Detail from the Ahiram sarcophagus depicting female mourners who are dressed in sackcloth and who lament by either tearing their hair or beating their breasts

The depiction on several bronze and silver bowls of an all-female religious procession provides further evidence for the importance of priestesses.[9] The role of a priestess, if these scenes are an accurate reflection of reality, was to oversee the giving of food and music offerings by female votaries and to act as an intermediary with the gods. Women were also responsible for performing acts of ritual mourning which typically involved loud wailing whilst clasping their head or hair (as can be seen on the Ahiram sarcophagus from Byblos – see Figure 6). Numerous pottery figurines depicting women in this mourning posture have been found at sites throughout Phoenicia. In addition to performing private acts of mourning, women were also responsible for singing public lamentations following catastrophes that affected the entire community. These lamentations and public displays of grief enabled the community to vent their own feelings and to reaffirm the importance of social unity and cohesion. Significantly, it was not just at funerals that women were required to sing or perform musical recitals; in the twelfth and eleventh centuries it appears to have been customary that they greeted kings, military leaders and victorious armies with music, singing and dancing.

Another important group of female cult personnel were 'sacred' prostitutes. By the Iron Age, sacred prostitution appears to have been a long-established Phoenician institution which was particularly associated with the cult of 'Ashtart (see Chapter 3). In ancient agrarian societies, fertility of crops, flocks and humans was of central concern and thus religious rites were enacted to ensure the fertility of land and womb. Some scholars therefore hypothesise that women (and sometimes men) were employed to have sexual intercourse with worshippers in an effort to induce the gods to copulate with one another (an act which it was thought would ensure the fertilisation of the natural world). An alternative proposal is that sacred prostitution was an act performed by a worshipper in order to thank the goddess for an answered prayer or to ensure that she responds favourably to a request for her assistance or blessing. Herodotus (1.199), for instance, records that some of the prostitutes at the temple of 'Ashtart on Cyprus were ordinary women who had temporarily dedicated their bodies to the goddess in gratitude for an answered prayer or as the result of religious obligation. Whilst according to Lucian (*De Dea Syria*, 6), Byblian women who refused to shave their hair and offer it to the god Adonis at the annual festival in his honour were punished by being forced to spend a day prostituting themselves in the temple of 'Ashtart. It is also entirely possible that sacred prostitution was used as a mechanism for generating funds for the temple. Whatever its motive, the practice was clearly not regarded as an orgy of lust but as a solemn religious duty performed in the service of 'Ashtart.

The Economic Role of Women

It is likely, as is the case elsewhere in the ancient Near East, that women contributed significantly to the local economy. Many cottage industries, such as weaving and textile manufacturing, relied solely on the contributions of women and are well attested at Phoenician sites such as Sarepta, Sidon and Byblos. A funerary inscription recovered from the *tophet* at Carthage indicates that women could attain professional status and grow wealthy in their own right. The inscription records that the deceased, a Carthaginian woman by the name of Shiboulet operated as a 'city-merchant' (an occupation traditionally associated with men), indicating that women could play an active role in the Carthaginian economy. It is likely that the practice of allowing women to participate in economic activities originated in

71

Tyre prior to being transposed to Carthage by the city's Tyrian founders. Although lacking supporting evidence from Tyre itself, or indeed Phoenicia more generally, an examination of other contemporary cultures reveals a long history of successful businesswomen in the ancient Near East (for instance, commercial documents recovered from the city of Ugarit reveal that women could, with their husband's permission, operate independent businesses). Women were also often employed outside the family home as midwives, wet-nurses, bakers and cooks, and in the cosmetics industry.

THE CUISINE OF ANCIENT PHOENICIA

The act of cooking is almost as old as human culture. The choice of foods and their preparation is dependent on a society's natural resources, affluence, technological sophistication and the preferences of its members. The combination of these factors results in each society developing an original and distinct cuisine. Written documents, along with the visual and archaeological evidence, reveal an impressive list of foods in the diet of the ancient Phoenicians, including various meats, cereals, vegetables and fruits. Cereals such as barley and wheat were the main staples of the Phoenician diet and were eaten either boiled as a porridge (which could be infused with pulses such as peas, lentils, chickpeas and broad beans) or, more typically, in the form of bread or flat-cakes of various kinds. Archaeologists estimate that the average Phoenician consumed between 150 and 200 kilograms of wheat and barley per year; typically obtaining 50–70 per cent of their annual calories from these cereals.[10] Grain was generally ground into flour using a quern: this consisted of a fixed lower stone with a slightly curved surface, called a *metate*, and a moveable upper stone rider or *mano*. The quern was typically made of basalt, a coarse volcanic stone, which was preferred for the process because of its rough surface and relatively light weight. The grain seeds were ground on the coarse surface in order to break down their soft centres and produce flour which could then be baked into bread. It was a very laborious process and had the disadvantage of producing basalt grit which got into the bread and gradually wore down the teeth of those who consumed it regularly. The large numbers of ovens and handmills which have been recovered from sites throughout Phoenicia attest to the centrality of bread within the Phoenician diet. Grain was also important as it could be used to create beer, one of the ancient world's only true superfoods. By producing and consuming beer the Phoenicians were able to dramatically multiply the calories in their harvested grains; increase their consumption of a number of important vitamins; and eliminate a number of harmful bacteria that occurred in tainted water supplies. Consequently, for much of the Iron Age, beer was equally as important as bread within the Phoenician diet.

Vegetables and fruit were also staples of Phoenician cuisine, as were roots, bulbs, truffle-like fungi and mushrooms. Palaeoethnobotany (the study of plant materials at archaeological sites) has revealed that the cultivation of fruit trees was widespread throughout Phoenicia. Dates, figs, apples, pomegranates, quinces, almonds, limes and lotus have all been attested archaeologically. Until the Hellenistic age the 'Phoenician' fig was considered a delicacy in Egypt and thus the Egyptians consumed them in large quantities. Given their sweetness, fresh or dried figs could be used as an alternative to more expensive sweeteners such as honey, which tended to be consumed by the more affluent sections of society. Dates, in contrast, appear to have been popular amongst all sections of Phoenician society as they were an affordable source of vital sugars and vitamins. Grapes were consumed both fresh and dry, often being used to sweeten other foodstuffs, and were the key ingredient in another Phoenician speciality, wine. Due to their knowledge and technical expertise with regard to viticulture and wine production, the Phoenicians gained a reputation for producing wines that were unrivalled in terms of purity and taste. For instance, in a number of the poems and epics recovered from the Bronze Age city of Ugarit the quality of Lebanon's grapes and wine are highlighted (in fact, one of these texts claims that wine from Lebanon was nurtured by El, the chief god of the Ugaritic pantheon, thus making it fit for both gods and kings). Similarly, quotations from Greek and Roman writers, such as Columella, attest that the Phoenicians were skilled winemakers and viticulturists who were capable of harnessing the varied climatic and topographic conditions of Phoenicia to produce different flavours of wine. As Phoenicia's soil and climate were ideally suited for viticulture, wine, like beer, became a staple of the Phoenician diet. Even the icons of Phoenician philosophy, Zeno of Kition and Chrysippus of Soli, are recorded as being 'serious wine drinkers'; in fact, Zeno was so fond of wine that he is believed to have died as the result of over-indulgence. Phoenician wine would have been very sweet, and although the grapes were fermented, the alcohol level was quite low. When drunk the wine would have been diluted with water (possibly in a ratio of 50 per cent water to 50 per cent wine), and it was only during religious festivals, or when undertaking religious rituals, that wine would be consumed neat.[11] Scholars have argued that this may account for why intoxication was considered as akin to a spiritual state in a number of Near Eastern religions.

The Phoenicians' knowledge of and technical expertise in viti-culture also enabled them to grow significant quantities of olives, which could either be consumed straight from the tree or processed into oil. Like wine, the production of oil from olives, and from other types of seeds, has a long history in the Levant and can be traced back at least as far as the third millennium. Olive oil served several culinary roles: it was a medium for marinating meat and fish before cooking, it was used as a dressing for both cooked food and fresh salads (when used as a dressing, the oil was commonly mixed with vinegar and aromatic herbs), and, finally, it was used as a preservative.[12] Another foodstuff that had multiple uses was honey, which was used in medicine (to close and cleanse wounds or as an ingredient in medicinal remedies), religion (as a votive offering to the gods or to cleanse the body during purification rituals), and cooking (as a preservative for certain fruits or as a sweetener). The Phoenicians are also known to have produced and consumed a variety of dairy products including milk, cheese, yoghurt and ghee (a type of clarified butter). Milk had an unusual status as a food item in the ancient Near East as it could not be easily stored; consequently, the drinking of fresh milk was a luxury only afforded to farmers and those who were rich enough to afford express delivery. Milk was generally acquired from sheep, goats and cows but also occasionally from horses and asses.

Meat was typically obtained from sheep, goats, pigs, cows, game (such as rabbits and hares), and from a variety of birds, both domesticated and wild, including chickens, geese, ducks and doves. However, as most domesticated animals produced useful by-products (such as eggs from birds, milk from cows and goats, and wool from sheep), meat was generally a luxury that was only consumed on special occasions (such as during important religious festivals or at feasts to commemorate births, deaths or marriages). Although the hunting of game and fowl provided an alternative source of meat, they were typically only consumed by those living in rural regions or by the aristocracy who considered them to be delicacies. The discovery of numerous fish bones and fishing implements has revealed that seafood was also an essential element in the basic Phoenician diet. From the archaeological record it has been possible to identify that saltwater and freshwater fish, and shellfish were all consumed in large quantities. An important industry which accompanied fishing was salt extraction. Aside from pickling in oil, salting was the only means of long-term preservation known to the Phoenicians and thus a number of the larger coastal cities were sited in close proximity to naturally occurring saltpans. Although used to flavour food, salt is an important mineral that the human body needs in order to sustain a functioning nervous system; it therefore became an integral part of all ancient diets and a highly valuable trade commodity.

The Phoenicians utilised a variety of cooking methods when preparing their food, including roasting, grilling, boiling and baking. When grilling or roasting the Phoenicians did not simply expose their foodstuff to a naked flame or hot glowing embers directly, instead they utilised a number of intervening agents (such as ash or ceramic shards) in order to control cooking temperatures. The Phoenicians also appear to have regularly cooked their food in some kind of liquid, most likely either water or oil. Two types of vessel were developed to facilitate the use of a liquid medium when cooking. The first was a covered pot usually made from coarse fired clay that contained mica grit and large incisions that allowed the fabric of the pot to expand when exposed to heat. Examples of this type of cooking pot have been found at sites throughout Phoenicia: most display deposits of carbon on the outside, have a flaring grooved rim and were rounded at the bottom. The second type of vessel was the bronze cauldron that was crafted from a single sheet of beaten bronze. It is likely that the pots were designed to facilitate different cooking techniques; perhaps fast boiling in plenty of water for the ceramic pots, and a type of simmering in reduced liquid for the cauldron.[13] The baking of bread was done in circular ovens shaped like beehives with an opening at the bottom through which to stoke the fire. The walls of these ovens were constructed from clay and were sometimes covered with potsherds in order to provide additional insulation. This baking process, unique to the Near East, was economical and produced aromatic and highly flavoursome food. The form of these ovens has survived in the *tabun*, a clay oven shaped like a truncated cone, which is still used in Lebanon to this day.

With regards to crockery and serving vessels, food cooked in liquids appears to have been eaten from small, deep bowls which could easily be held in the hand, whilst for everything else there were variously sized ceramic plates. Drinks were consumed from a wide range of beakers, of different sizes, shapes and styles, and cups, with beer being imbibed from spouted jugs or jars. As only a small number of eating utensils, such as spoons or forks, have been recovered from Phoenician sites it is likely that the majority of such implements were fashioned from perishable materials.

THE PHOENICIAN LANGUAGE AND SCRIPT

Phoenician is a member of the Semitic language family, specifically the West (or Canaanite) branch of Central Semitic, and as such is closely related to Biblical Hebrew, Moabite and Ammonite, as well as Amorite, Edomite and Ugaritic.[14] The Phoenician language coalesced in the course of the second millennium and became distinct from Aramaic, which at this time was becoming popular throughout the northernmost regions of Syria and which would eventually spread all the way to Assyria and Babylon. The Phoenician language first emerges in the city states of Arwad, Byblos, Sidon, Tyre, Sarepta and Akko before merchants and settlers help spread it to regions of Sicily, Sardinia, Italy, Spain and North Africa. Through close contact with a number of indigenous languages, including the different branches of Numidian and Berber, the Phoenician dialect spoken in North Africa (especially in Carthage) was to develop a number of unique characteristics which resulted in the emergence of the Punic language in the sixth century. Linguistically, Phoenician can be divided into two primary phases: an archaic phase from the tenth to seventh centuries, and a classical phase from the sixth to first centuries (additionally, the classical phase may be further divided into Middle, sixth to fourth centuries, and Late, third to first centuries).[15] The modern decipherment of Phoenician occurred in the mid-eighteenth century when John Swinton, then Keeper of the University Archives at Oxford University, began to translate some of the Phoenician inscriptions that had been recovered from Kition. Despite the fragmentary nature of the inscriptions, Swinton identified that the extant portions of the texts bore a remarkable similarity to Biblical Hebrew and so he found he could decipher them. Were it not for the close connections with Hebrew, an ancient Semitic language which was well understood thanks to the Bible, the decipherment of Phoenician would had been a much more arduous task due to the limited amount of available material. Swinton's translations, first published in 1750 CE in a volume entitled *Inscriptiones Creticae*, were quickly supplemented by the work of the Parisian scholar Abbé Barthélemy who offered his own linguistic analysis of the Phoenician language based on a series of coin legends and on a single bilingual Greek/Punic *cippus* recovered on Malta.

As Phoenician is now an extinct or 'dead' language, information about its development, grammar, use of idiom and vocalisation must be gleaned solely from the extant written sources. Although the pronunciation of words and phrases is largely lost to us, it is widely thought that Biblical Hebrew bore a close resemblance to the language spoken in Tyre. Evidence which supports this conjecture can be found in the rendering of Phoenician geographical and personal names in Assyrian royal inscriptions and in the occasional mention of Phoenician words in the works of Greek and Latin writers (such as Philo of Byblos, Dioscurides and Eusebius of Caesarea).[16] Generally, however, the legacy of the Phoenician language has been severely undermined by the almost complete loss of literary categories such as epics and myths, prayers and hymns, poetry, chronicles and historical reports. Although the classical sources record that there were a great number of lengthy Phoenician treatises exploring a diversity of subjects (including history, philosophy, law, religion, natural history and economics), not a single fragment of these texts has survived in its original form. The reason for such a dearth of evidence may be the change in writing medium which accompanied the introduction of a cursive rather than cuneiform script. Whereas cuneiform had been written on highly robust and durable baked clay tablets, cursive scripts were written on perishable materials such as wood, ivory, papyrus and parchment, all of which were poorly suited to long-term survival in the humid environment of the coastal Levant. Consequently, although there are a few inscriptions written in ink on sherds of broken pots (*ostraca*), or very rarely on fragments of papyrus, the vast majority of the epigraphic corpus is comprised of texts incised in stone or metal. Frustratingly, the vast majority of the texts on which scholars are reliant when trying to reconstruct the Phoenician language are either commemorative, votive or funerary dedications which are typically brief, stereotyped and formulaic in nature, or are found on seal stones or various types of ceramic vessel and so simply record the owner's name or the contents of the container. In total, the entire corpus of Phoenician inscriptions from the eastern mainland and western colonies (excluding Carthage) number only several hundred (as is to be expected, the dialects of Tyre and Sidon are the dominant linguistic form attested abroad, reflecting the primary role these two city states played in the founding of overseas settlements). Inscriptions can generally only be dated by palaeographical analysis (the study of ancient or historical handwriting) or by utilising archaeological dating techniques such as carbon dating or stratigraphic analysis (although the mention of an important king or ruler can provide a clue as to when an inscription was composed).

For a brief period the Phoenician language functioned as a diplomatic *lingua franca*, as is clearly attested by its prominent use in the royal inscriptions from southern Anatolia during the ninth and eighth centuries.[17] However, the scarcity of the textual record, combined with the fact that the overwhelming majority of the evidence is formulated in a highly official style (normally in the third person), means that the grammatical features and development of the language are only partially known. What these inscriptions do reveal is that the Phoenician tongue was marked by dialectical differences from both a diachronic (i.e. changes in a linguistic system between successive points in time) and a geographic perspective. These dialectical differences are likely to have been similar in nature to the vernacular and idiomatic differences between the English spoken by Londoners and that spoken by Glaswegians. In fact, these dialects were so closely related that the Israelite prophet Jeremiah (27:3) suggests that two speakers versed in different Canaanite vernaculars could still understand one another.

The Alphabet
Phoenician inscriptions are written in a 22-consonantal alphabet (a writing system in which each symbol represents a consonant, leaving

Fig. 7: The standard Phoenician alphabet

the reader to supply the appropriate vowel sound), which was known to the Greeks as *Phoinikeia Grammata* ('the Phoenician Letters'). Despite a general agreement that the modern linear alphabet arose somewhere in the Levant during the second millennium, the precise date and point of its origin are still unclear. Although classical authors such as Herodotus and Pliny the Elder believed that it was the Phoenicians who invented the alphabet, there is now evidence of a much earlier alphabetic script known as 'proto-Canaanite'. The earliest known examples of proto-Canaanite are two graffiti found near Luxor in Egypt which date to around 1800 (a few slightly later examples have also recently been recovered from Serabit al-Khadem in the Sinai Peninsula). This writing system was entirely consonantal in origin and operated according to the acrophonic principal (that is, using a pictogram to symbolise the first consonant of the word which the picture represents). For instance, an image of a house denotes the letter 'b' the first letter in the Semitic word for house ('*bayt*') whilst an image of a hand (Semitic word '*kapp*') is used to denote the letter 'k'.[18] The Canaanite-speaking tribes who conceived of this system were clearly familiar with Egyptian writing but simplified the process so that each of the original symbols corresponded to only one distinct consonantal phoneme. Throughout the second millennium the consonantal script continued to develop, with the characters becoming gradually simplified and more abstract. Thus, by the eleventh century, virtually all of the pictographic forms had evolved into stylised 'linear' equivalents. These developments ultimately led to the emergence of the Phoenician alphabetic script at the close of the millennium (see Figure 7).

The first substantial Phoenician texts are a series of Byblian royal inscriptions dating to the tenth century. Although earlier inscriptions can be dextrograde (written and read left to right), sinistrograde (written and read right to left), or boustrophedon (a method of writing in which the lines run alternately from right to left and then from left to right) and written either vertically or horizontally, by the tenth century the direction of Phoenician writing had been standardised as horizontal and sinistrograde.[19] Significantly, despite initially using short vertical strokes to delineate individual words, this practise was quickly abandoned, meaning that in the majority of Phoenician and Punic texts the words are presented in an unbroken sequence with many straddling two lines if they could not be fitted onto one. A study of the distribution of Phoenician inscriptions reveals that the Phoenician alphabet was quickly transmitted beyond the borders of Phoenicia. Thus by the ninth century, a number of neighbouring cultures had adopted and adapted the system to meet the needs of their own languages; these included the Ammonites, Edomites, Israelites and Moabites. Furthermore, as Phoenician merchants traversed the Mediterranean, they exported their language and alphabet alongside their commodities. In around 900, the inhabitants of Cyprus were the first non-Levantine culture to adopt the Phoenician alphabet. A little over a century later, the Phoenician alphabetic tradition had also begun to be adopted by the peoples of the western Mediterranean including those of southern Spain and Sardinia. Significantly, the Phoenician language died out earlier in Phoenicia itself than it did in the western colonies as it was gradually superseded by Aramaic and Greek. Of those cultures which adopted the Phoenician alphabetic tradition, it was the Greeks who were the most proactive in embracing and developing it, with the names, shapes, values and order of the letters in their alphabet clearly attesting a Phoenician influence.

THE ECONOMY: AGRICULTURE, INDUSTRY AND COMMERCE

Recognising that attempts to categorise ancient economies according to modern, post-industrial classifications often results in a tendency towards explanatory reductionism, scholars studying the ancient Near East have now begun to move beyond simply trying to identify what kind of economy was present, or which was the dominant mode of exchange, in any given society. Instead, economic historians are now beginning to approach ancient economies from the perspective of social and commercial networks, seeking to understand how these networks were organised, operated and maintained (an approach which is starting to yield far more positive results).[20] By studying ancient economies from the perspective of networks and network theory scholars can avoid creating holistic or unified models and are instead able to present reconstructions that highlight the subtle nuances of ancient economic and commercial practices. For instance, by recognising that no ancient 'economy' was purely market driven, purely redistributive or purely reciprocal, and that no mode of exchange was so dominant that it determined the nature of every social and economic relationship within a given society, it becomes possible to illuminate the varied and complex interactions and connections which underpinned ancient economic activity. Although removing the need for a single all-encompassing theory or model, a network-based approach nevertheless helps to simplify the data (in some cases data that is particularly diverse and complicated) in such a way that it can still be understood and analysed. Finally, by recognising the importance of human choice in economic activity it becomes possible to analyse ancient economies from the perspective of constraints and possibilities rather than simply identifying and cataloguing different kinds of commercial transactions or occupations.

The application of network theory has improved significantly our understanding of economic activities within the Phoenician city states as although the ancient sources tell us much about the Phoenicians' commercial networks, they are virtually silent in regard to economic relationships and institutions. Furthermore, as the palace-dominated economies of the Phoenician city states are characteristic of those found throughout the Near East during the late second and early first millennia (i.e. they incorporated prominent agricultural, industrial and commercial sectors), cross-cultural analysis can be used to tentatively fill in some of the blanks. Therefore, by synthesising the indigenous evidence with cross-cultural analysis it has been possible to identify that throughout Phoenicia private or independent landowners, merchants and family-owned firms and businesses operated in close harmony with royal or temple enterprises. The following discussion will therefore utilise both network theory and cross-cultural analysis when reconstructing the institutions, activities and relationships within the economies of Phoenicia.

The Agricultural Sector

Although there is little direct evidence pertaining to the Phoenicians' agricultural systems, methods or equipment, it is still possible to piece together a plausible reconstruction of their agrarian operations by examining the farming practices and technologies found in contemporary societies, such as Canaan and Israel, and by studying the 40 fragments of the agricultural manual written by the Carthaginian author Mago.[21] Despite the scarcity of evidence, it has been possible to identify that the original basis of the Phoenician economies was agriculture and husbandry and that the Phoenicians exploited to the greatest possible extent the small areas of arable land under their control. By utilising both the fertile plains located in the coastal regions and the rocky lower slopes of the Lebanon Mountains, the former for cereals and the latter for viticulture and plantations, the Phoenicians were able to grow a wide variety of crops, vegetables and fruits. Due to its ability to withstand salinity and aridity better than wheat, barley became the staple of the Phoenician diet. Significantly, as barley had an accepted value like gold or silver, it was often used as a medium of exchange and so could be offered as payment for services rendered. Once harvested, crops were stored in large stone silos which not only helped preserve them but also protected them against the elements and from pests, thus allowing any surplus to be stockpiled for future use.

In order to help increase yields, protect against the frequent water shortages that often plagued the region and that could destroy a harvest, and reduce the high salinity of the soil that hindered the cultivation of all but the hardiest crops, the Phoenicians became experts in irrigation. By using artificial canals, feeder channels, weirs and dykes to channel water from the rivers and streams that criss-crossed the coastal plains, the Phoenicians were able to irrigate their fields easily and efficiently. This system of irrigation was so effective that it facilitated intensive cultivation of the land and ensured that crops could be grown during all but the harshest of droughts.[22] Evidence for the effectiveness of Phoenician irrigation techniques and technologies is alluded to by the Israelite prophet Ezekiel who compares the lush verdant plains controlled by Tyre with the Garden of Eden (Ezekiel 28:13).

However, the diminutive size of the alluvial coastal plains severely limited the potential for large-scale agricultural production and so the total volume of cereal crops which could be grown was insufficient to meet the needs of a population that had been expanding constantly since the start of the Iron Age. Therefore, in addition to barley and wheat, the Phoenicians also grew vegetables and fruits including onions, garlic, leeks, turnips, lettuces, cucumbers, apples and pomegranates. As vegetables and fruit needed more careful attention than cereal crops they were often cultivated on separate, smaller plots of land that were owned by a specific community or farmstead. Of the alternative sources of food available to the Phoenicians, the most important were grapes, olives, figs and dates. Olives and grapes were particularly important for four reasons: first, they were grown with limited rainfall and on relatively poor ground; secondly, they were harvested at different times from cereal crops, meaning that manpower could be productively exploited throughout the year; thirdly, they provided storable crops (olives as oil, and grapes as dried raisins or fermented wine) that could be used to supplement the daily diet or which provided some insurance against crop failure; fourthly, as wine and oil were both part of the staple diet, they were also a major source of income for Phoenician farmers since any surplus could be taken to market and sold.[23] As is still the case today, the region's soil and climate were ideally suited for viticulture and thus by the end of the fifth century, Phoenicia had gained a reputation for producing the finest olives and grapes. This reputation for excellence meant that Phoenician fruits were exported throughout the Mediterranean both in their raw and processed forms (i.e. as wine or olive oil).

Agricultural production appears to have been the responsibility of several sections of Phoenician society, including: the temples and palace which farmed the extensive land under their control (either directly, or through a system of leases or freeholdings); wealthy and moderately affluent farmers each of whom owned land holdings and farmsteads of various sizes; and, finally, poor nomads and shepherds who were allocated small tracts of land to cultivate. Due to the scarcity of evidence it is impossible to determine accurately either the amount of land held by each of these groups or the volume and types of crops they produced at any given point or in any given city state. In general, however, it seems likely that the most fertile territories were used to support the palace, important temples and households of high-ranking state officials. Middle or minor-ranking officials held moderate landholdings which would have been worked by others but which would nevertheless provide a comfortable standard of living. By comparison, the small-scale, independent farmers (who made up a significant percentage of the agrarian population) most likely worked the land themselves and utilised seasonal labourers only at peak moments in the agricultural calendar (such as during the ploughing or harvesting seasons).[24] The costs of farming were relatively high and included seed, plough, tools, draft animals (which were expensive to keep as they consumed large quantities of fodder when undertaking sustained labour), seasonal workers (who would also need to be paid, either in rations or by a residual share of the crops), and the expenses incurred for maintaining the farmstead. Furthermore, adverse weather, an infestation of pests, or any number of crop diseases could significantly affect the harvest and thus eliminate any potential profit. The successful management of a farm therefore required a combination of luck, timing and hard work.

The Industrial Sector

By the dawn of the first millennium, the Phoenician cities had become large industrial and commercial centres which specialised in the manufacture of luxury and prestige items. Due to the exceptionally high prices such items could command, they were either destined to be exchanged in markets outside of the Levant or, less frequently, to satisfy the needs of a very restricted number of wealthy clients within Phoenicia itself. As many of the states and empires which neighboured Phoenicia had neither the crafting traditions nor access to the raw materials required for the production of prestige goods, they were content to acquire such items from the Phoenicians. By procuring Phoenician prestige goods, whether by way of tribute and taxation, trade and exchange, or reciprocal relationships, states such as Israel and Assyria helped to consolidate and strengthen the Phoenician economies. Consequently, during the ninth century, the Phoenicians rapidly became the primary suppliers and purveyors of manufactured, luxury and prestige goods within the Near East. In particular, their workshops became renowned for the production of exquisite items of carved ivory, of gold, silver and bronze receptacles, and of ornate jewellery adorned with precious stones. As the manufacture of these items required exotic materials and precious metals not readily available within the local vicinity, Phoenician craftsmen often formed close relationships with the mercantile community. Within such relationships both parties expected to benefit: the craftsmen relied on merchants to obtain the raw materials they required for production and to find new and profitable overseas markets in which their finished products could be sold; in return merchants expected to be supplied with high-quality items at a price which allowed them to make a decent profit. These relationships not only helped to keep transaction costs low and profits high, they also enabled greater specialisation.

In addition to the luxury items produced for export, there were also a number of industries which manufactured everyday items that were intended for local consumption. These non-prestige industries included woodworking, masonry, ceramic and pottery production, and the fabrication of textiles and metal items using inexpensive materials (see Chapter 4). Significantly, cities could also benefit from selling (or exchanging as part of a reciprocal agreement) the services and expertise of their craftsmen and artisans. An illustrative example of one such arrangement is the treaty between the Tyrian king, Hiram, and his Israelite counterpart, Solomon, concerning the construction of the Jerusalem temple. In return for large annual contributions of agricultural products (primarily wheat and oil), Hiram not only agreed to provide the necessary building materials (cedar and fir) but also the services and expertise of his own men (both in terms of cutting and transporting the timber, and of preparing and conditioning it on site). Similarly, the Assyrian kings often hired the services of Phoenician ivory workers when constructing or furnishing their palaces; although these men were required to move their workshops to Assyria, they would be handsomely rewarded for their labour.

The Commercial Sector

For their contemporaries, the Phoenician cities of the Levantine coast were inseparably linked with long-distance exchange. For example: a variety of Egyptian texts stress the shrewdness of Phoenician rulers when it came to selling or redistributing the raw materials they controlled; the Hebrew Bible records that Tyre's merchants grew wealthy and behaved like princes (e.g. *Isaiah* 23:8); a number of Neo-Assyrian documents present vivid accounts of the success and wealth of Phoenician merchants (some of whom even continued to pursue their commercial interests whilst their city was besieged by Assyrian troops, Saggs, no. 2715); and the Homeric epics depict the Phoenicians as unscrupulous businessmen who turned a profit by travelling from region to region selling and buying large quantities of commodities. Thus, in the eyes of their neighbours, the Phoenicians were pre-eminent merchants who did little else other than trade and so garnered both the admiration and resentment of their contemporaries.

Though such views are highly exaggerated, they nevertheless emphasise the centrality of trade within perceptions of who the Phoenicians were and what they did. Even a cursory examination of the literary and archaeological evidence supports the idea that the economies of the Phoenician city states were heavily dependent upon the revenues and resources acquired by inter-regional exchange (both long- and short-distance). Despite the scholarly attention given to prestige goods, the Phoenicians are known to have dealt in an extensive range of commodities: for example, the *Report of Wenamun* highlights the importance of the trade in cedar wood; Homer (*Odyssey* 15.444–527) records a Phoenician crew who spent a year in Syrie trading *athyrmata* (trinkets) and *biotos* (believed to be foodstuffs); whilst the Israelite prophet Ezekiel (27:1–23) provides a lengthy list of Tyrian imports. During the period 1400 to 400 there was a steady increase in the diversity of goods being traded, indicating that the Tyrians were more than just purveyors of luxury goods (a conclusion supported by excavated material recovered from sites in Lebanon and from a number of Phoenician shipwrecks).[25] Significantly, these studies have also shown that manufactured or fully processed goods travelled east–west, whilst raw materials, foodstuffs (excluding wine) and semi-processed objects tended to travel in the opposite direction.[26] By the end of the fifth century, the trade routes along which these commodities travelled stretched from India in the east to at least as far west as Mogador (modern Essaouira) in western Morocco, creating networks which encompassed the entire Mediterranean and significant parts of the Black Sea, Red Sea, Persian Gulf and Arabian Gulf.[27]

State versus Private Commerce

In Late Bronze and Early Iron Age Phoenicia, as was the case in most other Levantine societies, merchants were economic agents who depended on the great institutions of the palace and the temple. For the Phoenicians private and 'public' commerce (i.e. commerce that was undertaken by, or on behalf of, the palace or temples) overlapped and thus independent merchants worked closely with the state. As independent and state trade were both motivated by a search for profit and a desire for gain, the two types of commerce were considered to be perfectly compatible. Even when merchants appear to have operated independently, the evidence suggests that they did so alongside, or in conjunction with, commercial agents who were charged with representing the interests of the king. Within such a system both parties needed the other if they were to profit: the palace required the services and expert market knowledge provided by private merchants, whilst traders relied on the palace to gain access to certain markets and for protection from piracy and privateering. The palace also sought to protect the commercial interests of merchants by signing financial treaties and trade agreements with other states and kingdoms so as to establish fixed terms of exchange. In return, merchants were expected to supply the palace with information about the profitability of faraway markets and the political climate in the places they visited.[28] During the twelfth to tenth centuries, the Phoenician royal households appear to have been the driving force behind long-distance trade in a manner that was reminiscent of their counterparts in large commercial cities such as Ugarit during the Late Bronze Age. Evidence for the palace's commercial prominence at this time can be found in the account of Wenamun, which documents that the Byblian king, Zakar-Baal, sat at the head of a large administrative organisation, held a monopoly over the felling and export of cedar wood and monitored and regulated commercial activities within his city's port and territorial waters. The Byblian king is also recorded as owning 20 passenger (or cargo) ships which were harboured in Byblos and a further 50 smaller coastal vessels anchored at Sidon.

Although the close co-operation between the palace and independent merchants is clearly attested in the last decades of the eleventh century, the dearth of textual evidence pertaining to the tenth century means that it has only been possible to identify instances of state commerce. The best known of these co-operative trading ventures were those undertaken by Hiram and Solomon. According to the biblical texts, Hiram oversaw the negotiation and signing of interstate commercial agreements, had the right of ownership over Tyre's timber reserves and could organise and sponsor a number of large overseas trading ventures in conjunction with an international partner (1 Kings 5:6–10; 7:13). The Tyrian royal palace therefore played an active, and indeed vital, role in the city's economy: a fact highlighted by the profitability of the overseas commercial ventures arranged under its auspices. Despite being undocumented in the extant sources, it is likely that private commercial ventures and individual enterprise continued during the tenth century.

From the ninth to eighth centuries, the operation and organisation of commercial ventures appear to have changed significantly as a result of Assyrian expansion; however, the extent of these changes is still the subject of scholarly debate.[29] For some scholars, the arrival of the Assyrians heralded the end of the palace as a significant influence within the commercial life of the Phoenician cities. According to this view, the increase in private commercial interests that accompanied the decline of royal economic power and prestige accounts for why overseas trading posts suddenly started to evolve into genuine colonies during the eighth and seventh centuries (see Chapter 5). It would also explain the prominence of independent Tyrian merchants operating large-scale businesses in Babylonia, Ur and Uruk from the ninth until the sixth centuries.[30] Evidence of independent trade can also be found in a series of correspondences informing the Assyrian king Tiglath-Pilesar III (745–727) that one of his officials had permitted the people of Sidon to work and trade cedar wood on condition that they did not sell it to the Egyptians, Palestinians or any potential enemy of Assyria. Homer's Phoenicians are also depicted as economically independent entrepreneurs rather than royal representatives carrying out state-administered trade. However, the palace should not be completely dismissed as an economic agent, as a treaty signed between Esarhaddon and King Baal of Tyre, dating to c.670, refers explicitly to the 'ships of Baal' and the 'ships of the people of Tyre', suggesting that the royal household still maintained an interest in long-distance commerce. It seems likely that, although the primary responsibility for the organisation and operation of commercial ventures had shifted from the state to private individuals and organisations, the two parties still worked in tandem with one another. When studied in conjunction, the literary and archaeological evidence show that, from the sixth century until the arrival of Alexander the Great, the palace continued to play a role in long-distance trade.

Trading Syndicates

Although the sources are virtually silent on the institutions and organisations that were responsible for the Phoenicians' commercial success, one, the ḥubŭr (*hubur*), seems to be of particular importance. The term, which has equivalents in Ugaritic and Hebrew, is understood to mean syndicate, company or trading partnership and is first attested in *The Report of Wenamun* in which it is used twice.[31] According to Wenamun's account, the king of Byblos, Zakar-Baal, boasts that he has 20 ships in Byblos that are in *hubur* with Smendes the ruler of Egypt and 50 coastal vessels in partnership with Urkatel a resident of Tanis (scholars believe that Urkatel was a powerful and influential merchant). The willingness of Zakar-Baal to enter into a *hubur* with Urkatel, a non-royal as far as can be ascertained, suggests the existence of a highly developed form of private commercial syndicate which operated in tandem with, or under the protection of, a royal house. This conclusion is supported by a variety of passages in the Old Testament which suggest that merchant consortia first emerged in order to offer protection against piracy, risk and loss (e.g. Ezekiel 27:3; 5). By forming commercial syndicates, groups of merchants could jointly provide the necessary resources to construct and equip a fleet of trading vessels and to secure protection from a king or other powerful individual (a system that is widely recorded in Ugarit).

The men who made up these guilds are likely to have been high-status individuals who were closely linked to the palace or temple but who were still independent. They have often been seen as analogous with the Assyrio-Babylonian *tamkarum* (pl. *tamkaru*) who were merchants *par excellence*.[32] If this analogy is correct, and the evidence is compelling, the members of a *hubur* were responsible for organising and financing trading ventures, and for conveying their merchandise to overseas markets (although the more prosperous are likely to have employed agents). As commercial experts they possessed the appropriate specialist knowledge, expertise and connections to make them highly useful assets to the palace and to temples. When in the employ of the state, these men pursued both their official and personal commercial interests simultaneously, meaning that public traders and private entrepreneurs were often one and the same. Moreover, due to their close relationships with the two most powerful state institutions, these men were to play an increasingly important role in the political life of the Phoenician cities.

Mechanisms of Exchange

Though the Phoenicians are known to have employed three primary forms of voluntary exchange mechanism (gift giving, barter and monetarised market exchange), the prevalence, importance and degree of overlap between these types of exchange are far from certain.[33] Some scholars advocate a linear progression from gift giving, to barter, and then finally to market exchange; however, it is likely that for much of the Iron Age all three types of exchange functioned alongside one another. By maintaining a flexible approach to exchange, Phoenician merchants were able to operate profitably in regions that had vastly different rules and expectations, and which varied considerably in regard to their level of economic sophistication and development.

The first of these mechanisms, gift exchange, involved the transfer of goods or services that, although deemed voluntary by the participants, was part of expected social behaviour. Gift giving is distinguishable from other types of voluntary exchange in several respects: firstly, the initial offering is intended to be generous and there is no haggling between giver and receiver; secondly, the exchange is an expression of an existing social relationship or the establishment of a new one which contrasts with the impersonal nature of market exchange; thirdly, the profit in gift exchange may be assessed in terms of social prestige rather than in material advantage; and, finally, the gift exchange cycle creates obligations to give, to receive and to return, thus tying the participants into a long-term relationship. Gift exchange features prominently in the relationships of the Late Bronze Age rulers who used it as a means to engender goodwill and support from their fellow monarchs. The Amarna Letters reveal that by the Late Bronze Age gift exchange was used to procure a number of goods, including precious metals, foodstuffs, manufactured products, raw materials (such as timber or bronze) and even the services of foreign troops. Gift giving could also be used to gain access to a particular market or region. For example, a group of Phoenician merchants gifted to the Greek hero Thaos an ornate silver mixing bowl in order to gain permission to trade freely at Lemnos (Homer, *Iliad*, 23:740–9).

The second mechanism, barter, is considered to be one of the oldest forms of commerce and is commonly found in pre-monetary societies that have a need for terminable, non-reciprocal forms of exchange to facilitate the redistribution of goods and services. Barter involves the direct transfer of goods or services without an intervening medium of exchange such as money. Such transfers can either be made according to a pre-agreed rate of exchange or after face-to-face negotiation. In such systems the worth of the goods or services being exchanged is determined by the value of their usefulness. Commodities or services may be exchanged internally or externally, although in societies where barter and gift exchange coexist, the barter of mundane items is distinguished from prestige exchange. Herodotus (4.16) provides an insight into the operation of Phoenician barter when he recounts a story that was supposedly told to him by some Carthaginian merchants. According to this account, when exchanging with a primitive North African tribe, the Carthaginians would deposit their wares on the beach for the natives to inspect. The indigenous traders would then set out a quantity of gold. Once both parties were satisfied, they would collect their goods and depart. Although this is likely to be a fictitious incident, it nevertheless reveals the Greek perception of how Phoenician barter functioned.

The final mechanism, market exchange, involved the transfer of goods or services via an intervening medium (most typically money). In market transactions every exchange is supposed to produce 'utility', which means that the value of the items or services traded by each party is less than the value of those they receive. For instance, in a market transaction the buyer needs to believe that it is worth the money to do so, whilst the seller must be convinced that it is more profitable to part with their goods than to hold onto them. Significantly, the 'worth' or 'value' of a particular commodity was contingent upon its availability, consumption and ideological significance in any given region. Inter-regional trade therefore provided the opportunity for both parties to feel like they had profited (i.e. one man's luxury is another man's staple). Usually, the emergence of market exchange is accompanied by monetisation – a process involving the selection of an object (or substance) which becomes a generally accepted medium of exchange (i.e. the development of money). Because of their high value and desirability, gold and silver came to be the most commonly accepted mediums by which equivalences were calculated in the ancient Near East and thus can be considered as functioning as 'money'. Although today money most commonly takes the form of coins and banknotes, in Phoenicia for much of the first millennium it was conceived in terms of the weight and purity of silver (consequently, wages and payments were specified according to measures of silver which could be weighed out in the form of ingots, disks, bars or rings). Over time, the weight and purity of silver was stabilised through the use of 'hallmarking' (placing an official mark on silver objects to indicate their purity), a process which was often carried out by temples. Because many of the prestige items exchanged in the Late Bronze and Early Iron Age were made from precious metals, it is hard to determine when monetarisation first occurred (although there is compelling evidence supporting a date in the early ninth century). By the close of the fifth century, the Phoenicians had slowly begun to move away from weighed silver as a medium of exchange and had instead begun to use coinage.

Money and Coinage

Although by the early years of the sixth century coinage had become fairly commonplace in Greece, the Phoenicians did not introduce their own coinage until the mid-fifth century. The first Phoenician cities to strike coins were Byblos and Tyre (quickly followed by Sidon and Arwad), which recognised their importance for regulating and facilitating local transactions. Despite these advantages, however, none of the other Phoenician cities began minting their own coinage prior to the Hellenistic period (although it is possible that some, like Beirut, adopted the Sidonian currency).[34] The reason for the Phoenicians' reluctance to adopt coinage is poorly understood, though it seems likely that it was a deliberate decision intended to safeguard inter-regional exchange. A study of the earliest-known coinages found in areas of Lydia (modern western Turkey) and amongst the Greek cities of Asia Minor reveals that they emerged due to local needs and socio-ideological demands rather than to facilitate inter-regional trade. As each city, kingdom or empire established its own set of equivalences for silver (for example, 1 gram of silver might equate to two loaves of bread in Babylon, but three in Phoenicia), no state could guarantee the value of its coinage beyond its own sphere of influence and so the use of coins as a medium of exchange within inter-regional commerce was problematic. Consequently, the Phoenicians, whose commercial interests lay largely outside their immediate spheres of influence, continued to trade in bulk quantities of raw goods and precious metals as it was easier and more profitable to do so. Early Byblian and Tyrian coins, therefore, would have functioned as measured bullion rather than as a local currency which could be used in day-to-day transactions.

By the beginning of the fourth century, however, the situation had changed. Excavations at Al Mina and in the port district of Byblos have unearthed large quantities of small-denomination coins struck from both silver and bronze, indicating that coinage was now being used to facilitate local commercial transactions. Significantly, although using shekels, all of the major city states adopted their own preferred weight standard and thus a shekel ranged from 6 to as many as 13 grams of silver. The coins of Tyre and Sidon were the most widely circulated and have been found in significant quantities at sites throughout the Mediterranean; in contrast, the coinage of Arwad enjoyed a fairly limited, regional distribution, whilst the currency of Byblos was almost entirely reserved for internal use.

PHOENICIAN CITIES

Cities were the physical focus for the emergence of civilisation in ancient Phoenicia. Whilst what constitutes a 'city' in the modern world is generally agreed upon, there is no such consensus when it comes to the ancient Near East. In archaeological studies, the terms 'village', 'town' and 'city' are often interchangeable and there is no agreed-upon distinction between the three. A working definition proposed in *The Oxford Encyclopaedia of Archaeology in the Near East* is that an ancient city should be thought of as a relatively permanent, compact form of human settlement, intimately connected to the settlements and communities on its periphery and populated by a diversity of family groups which were socially differentiated.[35] This definition stresses the importance of recognising that ancient cities, and other types of permanent settlements, were part of an interdependent network which included a centre (typically a walled city) and its periphery (typically a number of unwalled villages). Thus, in contrast to the modern idea of a rural-urban dichotomy, ancient cities were perceived and defined by their inhabitants as including both. Furthermore, as all of the major Phoenician cities were dependent on agrarian resources, they were required to sustain a symbiotic relationship with the rural communities on their peripheries.

Within this relationship, city dwellers relied upon the rural population to provide them with victuals and other natural products (such as leather, wool and oil), whilst the rural communities depended

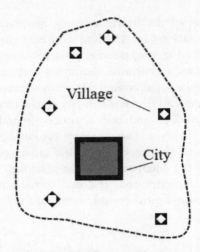

Fig. 8: The relationship between a Phoenician city (centre)
and its rural communities (periphery)

on the city for security, judicial and administrative services, temples and markets. The intensity of this interdependence also limited the size of territory which a city could control as every rural settlement had to be located in close enough proximity to the centre that continuous exchange could occur (see Figure 8). The extent of a city's rural hinterland was also limited by regional topography. For instance, a rugged and broken landscape, such as that of ancient Phoenicia, made travel and transport slower and more difficult, hence reducing the maximum distance at which a rural settlement could be located from the centre. This perhaps helps to explain why, in comparison with other urban centres in the ancient Near East, Phoenician cities were relatively small in size, ranging from an average of 2–6 hectares (5–15 acres) for smaller cities (such as Berytus and Sarepta) to 40-plus hectares (100-plus acres) for the largest cities (Arwad and Sidon).

The Urban Characteristics of a Phoenician City

As many of the major Phoenician cities have been continuously occupied since antiquity, most traces of the Iron Age settlements have either been destroyed by subsequent building projects or lie beneath modern structures and are thus inaccessible to archaeologists. Consequently, charting the unique urban development of any particular site has proven impossible and so the following sections provide a more general introduction to Phoenician architectural forms and decorations, efforts at town planning, and construction techniques. Despite the paucity of archaeological data, it has nevertheless been possible to identify a number of common features which, when combined, serve to delineate a specifically 'Phoenician' type of settlement. One of the most immediately obvious of these common characteristics was the choice of topographical location as, where possible, Phoenician cities and colonies were founded on coastal promontories or clifftops, or on islets situated just off the mainland. These locations were preferred as they not only provided easy access to the sea and its associated resources but also because cities founded on promontories, clifftops or islets were difficult to storm or blockade. Furthermore, as the majority of Phoenician foundations were established with at least one eye on trade, nearly all were located near sheltered anchorages. The cities of the Phoenician mainland were generally situated within narrow, agriculturally fertile stretches of the coastal plain, whilst overseas settlements tended to be founded within close proximity to a hinterland that was rich in raw materials (especially ores and minerals).

Strikingly, the majority of Phoenician trading posts, industrial towns and large urban centres, whether established in the homeland or abroad, demonstrate a remarkably similar layout, suggesting that some form of proto-city 'planning' was in operation. However, a distinction must be drawn between ancient 'ordered' towns and the modern concept of urban planning. Modern urban planning is a complex technical and political process that is concerned with the use of land, the protection and use of the environment, public welfare, the layout of urban space and the infrastructures that govern transportation, communication and distribution networks. In contrast, most Phoenician cities and towns should be more accurately considered as 'ordered' rather than 'planned'.[36] Although appearing planned, the order of Phoenician towns occurred almost unconsciously due to the location and arrangement of key elements such as the fortification walls, the city gates, the location of any port or harbour facilities and, finally, the main streets that connected these features to the centre of the city. These elements were the key points around which the rest of the city was arranged.

The archetypal Phoenician settlement was composed of two distinct districts: an 'upper city' which accommodated a fortified citadel, the main palace, major temples, administrative buildings and the residences of the aristocracy, and a 'lower city' which housed the commercial and industrial zones, and the residential districts occupied by the less affluent sections of the city's population. The whole city was often enclosed by a series of tall stone walls that were designed to divide the city into defensible zones (for instance, the upper city formed a defensive citadel which could be isolated from the lower district during times of siege). On the Balawat gate reliefs, for instance, Tyre is shown as being encircled by a monumental wall that has two huge arched entranceways which are sealed shut with double-leaf bronze or wooden gates. Tyre is also shown enclosed by monumental walls on a stone relief recovered from the palace of Sennacherib at Nineveh; significantly, a series of round shields is shown strung from the top of the battlements, a custom which is also alluded to by the Israelite prophet Ezekiel (27:10–12). Public cemeteries and ritual burial precincts (i.e. *tophets*) were located outside a city's walls (or boundaries if the city was unwalled) and were, when local topography permitted, sited in: clearly demarcated zones on the opposite bank of a fast flowing river; along a sandy shore; or on an adjacent ridge or hill.

Commercial and Industrial Districts

As is to be expected, the commercial life of a Phoenician city was centred on its harbour facilities, wharves, markets and warehouses. The most important of these facilities, *emporia* (large communal marketplaces), were generally situated in locations that were accessible from the city's harbour and main gate. *Emporia* were fundamental to a city's economic prosperity as they: facilitated the import of vital goods; could generate revenue through taxation and other tariffs; helped to boost exports, thereby promoting the interests of local farmers, craftsmen and traders; enhanced the influence and prestige of a city; and, finally, if well provisioned and maintained, could undermine the commercial attractiveness of rival states. Harbours were another central feature of most towns and settlements due to the Phoenicians' dependence on the sea for trade, communication and various marine resources. In terms of configuration, Phoenician harbours were either 'open' (unsheltered and exposed to the sea) or 'closed' (sheltered from the sea with a narrow entrance that was easily defensible), depending on the local topography. Recent studies have revealed that, prior to the fourth century, most harbours were formed by modifying the local topography, either by carving out the natural rock or by adapting reefs or rocky islands so as to create moles or breakwaters. From the end of the fourth century, the Phoenicians began to reinforce natural reefs by placing large, finely cut ashlar stones on top of them (ashlar = hewn rectangular stone blocks with finely worked edges). By laying these stones as 'headers' (i.e. they were positioned so that only their short end was presented to the incoming waves), Phoenician engineers ensured that these underwater walls provided the maximum resistance to the destructive motion of the sea.

A number of cities (including Tyre, Arwad, Sidon, Tell-Sukas and Carthage) had twin harbour complexes which allowed them to separate commercial and military shipping. In order to facilitate the transport of commodities intended for export, the industrial quarter of most Phoenician cities was located adjacent to the harbour, or, if not adjacent then close by and linked to it via a major road or thoroughfare. Due to the inherent risks (i.e. fires or disease) and the awful smells that were associated with heavy industrial activity, metal-working, dye production and tanning facilities were, as far as was practical, located away from the residential areas of the 'lower district'. Smaller cottage industries, such as weaving and pottery production, were typically spread throughout the city rather than being centred in or around one particular location.

Residential Districts

Aside from the royal family and a select number of wealthy aristocrats and high-ranking officials who dwelt in the upper city, the general population of a Phoenician city lived in residential districts that were located in the lower city. Organised around an irregular network of narrow streets and winding paths, these residential districts tended to be overcrowded and densely packed. With little or no room to expand outwards, many homeowners solved the problem by expanding upwards, meaning that the typical Phoenician house had two or more storeys (when present, the upper floors replicated the layout of the lower storeys). The use of multi-levelled dwellings enabled a larger number of inhabitants to be accommodated within the limited available space, which in turn resulted in many of the Phoenician cities (in particular Arwad, Sarepta and Tyre) having a much higher urban density than towns and settlements in neighbouring regions.

With only a handful of private dwellings having been fully excavated in Lebanon, none of which have retained their upper floors, archaeological findings from Tunisia and northern Israel can be used to shed light on Phoenician house design and construction. Further information can also be obtained from the classical texts and from the depiction of Phoenician towns and cities in a variety of reliefs and frescos. The foremost visual evidence for Phoenician domestic architecture is contained in a number of Assyrian reliefs which document both the style and form of private dwellings. For instance, a relief recovered from the palace of the Assyrian king Sennacherib (which takes as its subject the sacking of a Phoenician city) depicts a number of individual houses that are tightly grouped together. These houses are all multi-levelled and are adorned with elegant features including columns on either side of the front doors, ornate upper-floor windows framed by balustrades embellished with scroll-like decorations, and crenellated roofs. These dwellings are remarkably similar to those portrayed both on the Balawat Gates and in the cruder tomb paintings discovered at Djebel (the most striking of which depicts a compact town comprised of 17 two-storey houses of varying sizes). Significantly, these images cohere closely with the descriptions provided by classical authors such as Strabo (*Geography*, 16.2.13; 16.2.23), who records that the houses of Tyre and Arwad typically had two or more storeys with some Tyrian high-rises being taller than those found in Rome.

The archaeological record reveals that two types of dwellings predominated during the Middle and Late Bronze Age: the courtyard house (which has been found in both rural and urban settings), and the row house (which was characteristically found in an urban setting). Courtyard structures, which are usually much grander, are thought to have been typical of large, rich households, whilst the more modest-sized row houses are likely to have been occupied by poorer families. Variations within each category of house can be accounted for by the number of inhabitants, their affluence and the location of the house within the residential district. Although both types of house continued to be built during the Iron Age, their popularity declined and they were slowly replaced by a new type of dwelling consisting of three or four modestly sized rooms that could be arranged in various configurations. One of the most prevalent configurations consisted of three parallel rooms (sometimes separated by pillars) which were backed by a fourth larger room. The middle of the three parallel longitudinal spaces is widely thought to have been an open-air courtyard as it contained the entrance to the building. Courtyards were a common architectural feature of dwellings throughout the Levant as they helped illuminate, aerate and cool a building. Recent research has shown that in regions with scorching hot summers, the presence of an internal courtyard can considerably reduce the air temperature within a building. The cooling effect of courtyards results from convection as the warm air of the courtyard, which is open to direct radiation from the sun in the evening, slowly rises to be replaced by the cool air of the night. This cold air gradually seeps throughout the house leading to a significant drop in air temperature. The courtyard itself retains its coolness for most of the day and so was the location of most household activities as well as recreation. The cooling effect of a courtyard could be further enhanced by the presence of pools of water or simple fountains.

Construction Methods and Materials

Phoenician architectural styles and construction techniques were heavily influenced by Phoenicia's climate, geography and abundance of natural resources. Significantly, these factors not only influenced the appearance of buildings and how they were decorated but also their survival in the archaeological record (i.e. mud structures are far less likely to survive than those constructed from stone). Sometimes the level of preservation is quite spectacular but typically archaeologists find only a building's ground plan (i.e. the foundations, floor and lower parts of any walls). Even the most complete Phoenician buildings are still lacking their upper storeys and roofs – the presence of which are typically indicated by the thickness of the lower walls, the remains of staircases, or any fallen roof material that might lie on top of collapsed walls. Consequently, even though the corpus of Phoenician architecture is quite extensive, all the building and structures are incomplete to some degree. Nevertheless, from the surviving ground plan, construction materials and contents of a structure, archaeologists can gain important insights into a building's size, shape, method of fabrication and original appearance.[37]

The primary building materials employed in ancient Phoenicia were clay, mud, stone and wood, and it was common for two or three of these to be used in a single structure.[38] The ways in which these materials were employed, and in what quantities, varied significantly in different periods and in different regions according to availability, climate, geography and socio-cultural factors. Due to the large number of rivers and streams that criss-crossed the coastal plains, the Phoenician cities could easily acquire large quantities of clay and mud suitable for construction. The earliest mud walls were constructed using a mixture of soil, water and straw and were formed either by hand or by using a vertical frame with wooden sides. The result was crude, uneven walls of varying thicknesses which were prone to crumble and collapse. The development of mud bricks helped to overcome many of these problems as they allowed for the construction of straight, uniform walls. These bricks were created from the same mixture as mud walls and were either shaped by hand or by using a four-sided wooden frame; once formed the bricks were left in the sun to dry. A mud-based mortar was used to bond the bricks together once they were in place, whilst bitumen was used as a sealant against damp and water. Aside from mud, Phoenician builders also made extensive use of timber. Good-quality timber was plentiful in Phoenicia and so the Phoenicians utilised wood from a range of different trees in their constructions: for general purposes, such as fittings and frames, they used sycamore, fig, Aleppo pine, and oak (*terebinth*), whilst for roofing planks and structural timbers they utilised cypress, poplar, pine and oak. The most prized wood came from the region's famous cedar trees which were immensely strong and supple and so ideally suited for monumental building projects. The wooden sections of Phoenician buildings are rarely preserved, although their former presence is sometimes detectable due to the discovery of post holes, stone bases for wooden columns and gaps in stone walls where wooden beams had been placed, or if a building had been destroyed by fire resulting in its wooden fittings and frames being preserved as charcoal.

The stone used in construction was obtained either by gathering loose surface rocks (known as 'fieldstones') or by quarrying blocks of various shapes and sizes directly from bedrock. Stone was a versatile material that could be used in the construction of various architectural features including: freestanding and retaining walls, platforms, columns (including bases and capitals), door sills and sockets, and stairs. Typically, stone was used only in the construction of a building's foundation and lower walls (the upper sections would be built using timber frames and mud bricks). When fieldstones were used to construct a freestanding wall they would be left in their natural shape and simply piled on top of one another (normally with the largest stones at the bottom), any spaces between the stones would be filled with smaller pebbles or chippings in order to create a tight-fitting bond. Once finished, the wall would then be covered with mud before being sealed with a coat of bitumen. In order to use as few small stones as possible, the larger fieldstones were commonly arranged so that their edges formed the closest possible bond. This style of construction is known as rubble (or fieldstone) masonry and was widely used in both the Bronze and Iron ages.[39]

The first monumental stone architecture appears in Phoenicia during the Middle Bronze Age with the emergence of ashlar masonry. Ashlar were hewn, rectangular (or, occasionally, cuboid) stone blocks with finely worked edges that were laid in horizontal courses when constructing walls, podiums or foundations. The Phoenicians gained renown for being extremely skilled masons who created some of the largest and most uniform ashlar.[40] Ashlar were typically carved from limestone of varying hardness and colour, but could also be formed from basalt or sandstone. Due to the expense of quarrying and transporting ashlar their use was originally confined to isolated blocks around which fieldstones were arranged; however, during the late Bronze Age they began to be used to construct more extensive walls (or sections of a wall). Freestanding ashlar walls were constructed from regular sized and shaped blocks which would be laid horizontally so as to create two parallel lines with a small gap between them, this gap would be filled with smaller irregular stones and then packed with mud (significantly, only the outward-facing side of the ashlar blocks would be finely worked). Thus, although presenting the appearance of finely jointed ashlar (a squared block of uniform ashlars), this type of monumental masonry belonged to a very distinctive style of stone dressing known as 'ashlar-faced coarse rubble'.

At the same time as the emergence of ashlar masonry, it is also possible to see an expansion in the use of columns. Although pillars and columns had previously only been used for doubling or reinforcing walls, they were now utilised to construct large porticos and halls. Despite this, however, the Phoenicians never developed their own columnar style but instead adopted different column types from neighbouring cultures (principally Greece and Egypt). Since there is no evidence in Phoenicia for lifting devices such as hoists, winches and pulley blocks, lifting lugs, or lewis holes, it is still unclear how the Phoenicians manoeuvred heavy stones and columns into position. The traditional view is that they used some sort of ramp to raise the blocks; however, this solution was both unpractical and labour intensive. Consequently, some archaeologists are now of the opinion that the Phoenicians used a simple machine that employed levers and counterweights. Such a machine, called a shadoof, was widely used in Egypt and could raise blocks of stone weighing in excess of two tons. Although there is currently no archaeological evidence for the use of shadoofs in Phoenicia, the close contact that the Phoenicians enjoyed with Egypt means that it is possible that they could have encountered this type of technology and adopted it.

3

RELIGION

Any study of the religions of ancient Phoenicia is hindered by the pronounced lack of documentary and material evidence from which to construct a diachronic overview of religious beliefs and practices. The almost complete loss of indigenous literature means that scholars seeking to reconstruct Phoenician religion are lacking the hymns, prayers and incantations which often provide valuable insights into the nature of the gods, religious ideology and sentiment, and different forms of worship. Despite Phoenician and Punic epigraphic sources numbering in excess of 6,000, these inscriptions offer few insights into contemporary religious beliefs or rituals. In fact, except for a few rare documents, such as the sacrificial tariffs recovered from Carthage or the expense ledgers of the temple of 'Ashtart/Aphrodite at Kition, the majority of these inscriptions do little more than list the names of particular gods, worshippers or sacraments. Furthermore, by their very nature, written remains are likely to record the religion of royalty and of the wealthy rather than that of the poor who leave no monuments or texts: consequently, the religion of the masses has probably perished forever.

Although archaeology has helped fill in some of the blanks, the monuments, palaces, temples and tombs uncovered by archaeologists are generally mute on the specific meaning or importance of religious rituals, symbols and beliefs and on the character, life-stories or functions of different deities. As comparison with written texts remains a fundamental step for correctly interpreting material culture, the dearth of literary sources means that any interpretation of Phoenician religious iconography or architecture remains speculative at best. With the indigenous literary and material sources providing an unsatisfactory picture, scholars are in the unfortunate position of having to rely on indirect sources when trying to reconstruct Phoenician religious beliefs and systems. One such indirect source of evidence is the Ugaritic texts, which contain ample information pertaining to the religion and mythology of a Bronze Age city located on the Syrian coast just north of Phoenicia. In fact, the recovery and subsequent publication of the Ugaritic texts have provided scholars with the most extensive corpus of West Semitic religious writings outside of the Bible. With many scholars considering Ugarit as the most northerly Canaanite city, these texts are frequently used when reconstructing the religions of other Levantine coastal settlements during the Late Bronze and Early Iron Ages. As the Ugaritic texts are far more extensive than the cursory inscriptions found in Phoenicia, it is tempting to place undue importance on this material: however, the substantial differences between the two corpora mean that it is impossible to assume simple continuity between the religions of Ugarit and those of Phoenicia. As the Ugaritic texts were created prior to the city's destruction in c.1200, and as their place of composition was outside of Phoenicia, the evidence they contain is both chronologically and geographically removed from the Phoenicians. Despite this, we should not be too pessimistic as they do record elements of religious worship and beliefs that were common to many, if not most, of the major religions of the ancient Near East.

Other indirect evidence is contained in a variety of Greek and Latin texts and in the Old Testament. This evidence, although scant and often condemnatory, nevertheless provides narrative and historical information lacking in other sources. In the Old Testament, for instance, snippets of information about the worship of Tyrian and Sidonian deities can often be gleaned from the diatribes delivered by the prophets and priests of Yahweh. The most sustained discussion of Phoenician religion is contained in Philo of Byblos's *Phoenician History* which was written in the late first or early second century CE. Though the work is now lost, extensive excerpts have been preserved in later Christian literature (e.g. Eusebius of Caesarea's *Praeparatio Evangelista*, an apologetic text written in the fourth century CE). The sections of Philo's work preserved in these excerpts include a cosmology, a history of Phoenician culture, a history of the god

Kronos and brief discussions of human sacrifice and the religious significance of serpents. Although all of the indirect sources require particularly careful treatment, if their agenda, bias and perspective are always kept in mind they can provide useful insights into Phoenician religious beliefs and practices.

CONTINUITY OR CHANGE?

As is to be expected when studying Phoenician religion from a *longue durée* perspective, it is possible to identify a marked evolution in religious practices, beliefs and styles of worship during the first millennium. In fact, much has been written about the revolutionary changes that were thought to have transformed Phoenician religion at this time. Recognising that the final years of the Bronze Age were marked by political and economic instability, scholars were keen to prove there had been a coinciding spiritual revolution which radically altered religious belief and observance within the coastal cities of northern Canaan. Ultimately, this new line of thought led scholars to question whether or not it is possible to discern a significant development in the religious system depicted in the Ugaritic texts and those described in later sources. The religious reforms instituted in Tyre under the auspices of Hiram I were used to support the hypothesis that there was a fundamental change in religious beliefs and practices during the Early Iron Age. The rise to prominence of previously minor deities (such as Ba'al and 'Ashtart) led many scholars to conclude that there had been a sudden and dramatic change in the conception and composition of the Canaanite-Phoenician pantheon during the eleventh and tenth centuries. This conclusion resulted in Phoenician religion being conceptualised as an ever-evolving series of cults that were constantly being changed and modified according to the beliefs and needs of each subsequent generation of worshippers.

By the middle of the 1970s, however, this view was being called into question as scholars began to stress the longevity of the Ugaritic and Canaanite influence on Phoenician religion. Scholars now suggested that any change should be understood as a modification of existing practices rather than as outright innovation. For instance, the reforms of Hiram did not in fact introduce the cult of Melqart to Tyre, as was previously believed, but rather promoted and institutionalised it. According to Herodotus (2.43–4), who claims to have spoken directly with a group of Tyrian priests, the cult of Melqart could trace its origins back to the founding of the city in the third millennium. Similarly, Josephus claims that all three of Tyre's main sanctuaries were well established by the time of Hiram (*Against Apion*, 1:13; 18; and *Antiquities of the Jews*, 8.146). Hence Hiram's so-called 'revolution' of the Tyrian religious system seems to have consisted of enlarging or renovating the temples of Melqart and 'Ashtart (providing each temple with a newly cut cedar roof) and the declaration of Melqart as Hiram's personal and dynastic patron. Although Melqart is not attested prior to the first millennium, the incorporation of the divine term *mlk* within royal titulature of the fourteenth century indicates that he was venerated from a much earlier date.

A continued reverence of Bronze Age deities is also documented at other Phoenician cities during the first millennium. At Byblos, Ba'alat Gubal (Lady Byblos), who is first attested in the third millennium, retained her prominence within the Byblian pantheon and continued to be venerated throughout the first millennium, as was Ba'al Shamaim (Lord of the Heavens). Prior to his invocation in the tenth-century royal inscription of Yehimilk, Ba'al Shamaim is recorded in the Egyptian texts of the New Kingdom (*c.*1550–1070), and in a number of Amarna correspondences sent by both Byblos and Tyre (*EA* 108; 147; 149), thus indicating the longevity of his cult. Ba'al Shamaim may in fact be equated with the Bronze Age Semitic storm deity Haddu who is worshipped at Ugarit during the second millennium.[1] The primary deities of Sidon, 'Ashtart and Eshmun were also worshipped for well over a thousand years prior to the dawning of the Iron Age. Both are recorded separately in a number of ritual texts from Ugarit before appearing together in a north-west Semitic incantation from an Egyptian medical papyrus dating to the fourteenth century.[2]

During the Iron Age it is also possible to identify the continued worship of a number of the other deities recorded in Ugaritic texts: for instance, El, the primary deity and father of the gods in Ugaritic mythology, and Reshef, who enjoyed widespread popularity at Sidon and on Cyprus, are both mentioned in an eighth-century inscription from Karatepe (located in modern Turkey); Ba'al Saphon, who is known to have been highly venerated at both Tyre and Carthage, appears in the seventh-century treaty between the Assyrian king

Esarhaddon and Baal I of Tyre; whilst the Semitic god Shed is mentioned on a number of votive offerings. Furthermore, it was at Byblos in the Late Bronze Age that the Egyptian cults of Osiris, Isis and Amon, all of which are well documented within the pantheons of Iron Age Phoenicia, were apparently first introduced. Finally, evidence for the longevity of the Ugaritic-Canaanite pantheon can tentatively be identified in *De Dea Syria (The Syrian Goddess)*, a text dating to the second century CE which is attributed to Lucian.[3] *The Syrian Goddess* (1–10) contains a discussion of several Phoenician religious sites followed by a lengthy description of the myths, sacred area and cults of the north Syrian city of Hierapolis (which is situated north-east of Aleppo near the Euphrates River). Significantly, the text indicates that a number of the deities worshipped in Ugarit were still being venerated throughout Phoenicia in the second century CE (sometimes in a manner that closely resembled the rites and practices of the Late Bronze Age). From the surviving evidence, it is possible to identify that many of the religious innovations of the Iron Age were clearly rooted in the beliefs, traditions and practices of the Bronze Age.

However, the recording of divine names, such as El, Ba'al, 'Ashtart or Reshef, in documents that are chronologically and geographically diffuse, does not mean that the characteristics and functional features of these deities remained unchanged. Although some aspects of Phoenician religion clearly retained a sense of continuity with the past and with wider Canaanite traditions, the individual city pantheons and cults that emerge in the Iron Age are largely the product of an autonomous development process. The turbulent period marking the end of the Bronze Age enabled the Phoenician city states to free themselves (or, perhaps more accurately, be freed from) Egyptian suzerainty. Keen to assert their newfound independence, the Phoenician city states sought ways of distinguishing themselves from one another, and from the cities and states of the wider Levant. In the religious sphere this resulted in the reorganisation of each city's pantheon and the introduction of modified forms of public worship. Consequently, from the Early Iron Age, each of the Phoenician cities had its own religious calendar, festivals, feasts and celebrations, traditions and deities. Although some deities were worshipped in a multitude of towns and cities, they were not necessarily afforded the same prominence or importance in each (this tendency towards religious autonomy and regional distinctiveness can also be identified in Phoenician overseas settlements).

This restructuring also resulted in the emergence of a two-tier hierarchy within each city's pantheon. The top tier comprised a supreme male and female deity – a Ba'al (master/lord) and Ba'alat (mistress/lady) – whilst the lower tier included all other deities recognised and worshipped in the city. The deities of the upper tier symbolised local religious identities and distinctiveness, whereas those of the second tier were worshipped because of their particular competences or functions (such as the sea, mountains, war, birth, adolescence and even death). The deities of the upper tier were also intrinsically linked to the ruling dynasty and thus embodied all of the powers and functions that had previously been assigned to deified sovereigns during the Bronze Age. Although these pairs of deities (Melqart and 'Ashtart at Tyre, Eshmun and 'Ashtart at Sidon, and Ba'al and Ba'alat at Byblos) are often seen as the chief gods of the city, this may not necessarily be the case. In the seventh-century treaty between Esarhaddon and Baal I, it is the elder god El and his consort who are recorded as the chief gods of Tyre, not Melqart and 'Ashtart.[4] Although the older generation of gods are less visible in popular religion since they played no major role in the spiritual life of the city, they were, nevertheless, powerful individuals who could be invoked when necessary. Melqart and 'Ashtart should therefore be considered as the patron gods of the royal household rather than as the chief gods of the city. The emergence of dynastic patrons and the differing compositions of each city's pantheon are reflections of a general move towards cultural distinctiveness and independence. Consequently, a tendency towards religious autonomy came to dominate Phoenician religious life throughout the first millennium and was even sustained during periods of submission to more powerful empires such as Assyria, Egypt and Persia. Significantly, as evinced in *De Dea Syria*, the Phoenician cities still showed signs of religious autonomy in the second century CE despite all of the inducements towards syncretism which had been offered firstly by Hellenisation and then by Romanisation.

THE PHOENICIAN PANTHEONS

Byblos

From at least the middle of the second millennium the city of Byblos housed two large and important temple complexes. The oldest of the two, dating to the first quarter of the second millennium, was consecrated to a female deity known as Lady Byblos (Ba'alat Gubal) whilst the second, an L-shaped building which remained in use until the Roman period, was dedicated to a male, menacing god who has tentatively been identified as Reshef. Although Ba'alat Gubal has traditionally been seen as a manifestation of the polymorphic 'Ashtart (especially as she was recognised by the Egyptians as Hathor or Isis, and by the Greeks and Romans as Aphrodite and Venus respectively), recent scholarship has challenged this belief. Consequently, it is now widely accepted that Ba'alat Gubal was a deity in her own right who shared some of the primary features, characteristics and functions of 'Ashtart (discussed below).[5]

Ba'alat Gubal is recorded in a variety of royal inscriptions including funerary texts, dedications on altars and votive offerings, demonstrating her importance to the city and her role as dynastic patron. Although Ba'alat Gubal's connection with the Byblian monarchy is attested in the Middle Bronze Age, it was not until the Late Bronze Age that she assumed the role of dynastic patron. In the Amarna Letters King Rib-Addi usually began his messages by invoking the goddess of Byblos to bless or protect the Egyptian pharaoh. From other extant sources it is also possible to ascertain that Ba'alat Gubal's role as dynastic patron included selecting the king, securing his status as monarch and judge, protecting him during his lifetime, and ensuring his progeny and succession. Her importance as royal patron is evinced in a number of Byblian royal prayers in which the king either thanks her for her assistance (*KAI* 10.2–3, 7–8) or petitions her to prolong his days and give him favour with the gods (*KAI* 5).[6] In addition to being a dynastic patron, Ba'alat Gubal also appears to have been venerated due to her association with fertility, birth and seafaring.

Much less is known about Ba'alat Gubal's consort, the unidentified male, menacing god, as there are no specific references to him in either the literary or epigraphic corpora. Although this deity, who is thought to be Reshef, was traditionally known as a 'smiting god', scholars now prefer the term 'menacing god', as he is never actually depicted striking an enemy.[7] The tentative suggestion that this god should be identified as Reshef results from the discovery of a large number of votive offerings that had been buried under the floor of the L-shaped temple. The majority of these offerings are small, male figurines which are posed in a menacing stance. The marked similarities between these figurines and those dedicated in the temple of Reshef at Ugarit have led scholars to conclude that they must have been intended for the same deity. Whether or not this identification is correct, the fact that the god is depicted in a menacing pose (the epitome of male power) suggests that he was the natural counterpart for the charismatic authority of Ba'alat. Thus, as is also true in Tyre and Sidon, the basis of the Byblian pantheon was a divine pair who watched over and protected the king, his dynasty and the city. In addition to Ba'alat and Reshef, a number of Byblian texts also refer to the 'Assembly of the Holy Gods of Byblos' (*KAI* no. 4; no. 10) members of which included Adonis, Ba'al Shamaim, Ba'al Addir ('The Powerful Lord') and El; however, very little is known about the worship of these deities.

Sidon

Information pertaining to the composition of the Sidonian pantheon can be obtained from a variety of epigraphic sources including royal building inscriptions, dedications, funerary texts, votive inscriptions and temple records, which range in date from the ninth to the third centuries. The most informative of these inscriptions are those found on the royal sarcophagi belonging to Tabnit and Eshmunazar II, the Eshmun temple dedications of king Bod'ashtart and the votive offering of crown prince Baalshillem, all of which date to the fifth century (*KAI* 13; 14; 15; 16; 17). An analysis of the epigraphic corpus indicates that the principal dynastic deities of Sidon were the god Eshmun and his female consort 'Ashtart; a divine couple who were intrinsically linked to the ruling dynasty and who embodied all of the powers and functions of earthly monarchs.

Eshmun was a local variant of Ba'al who seems to have been worshipped both as a dynastic patron and as a healing god. These two facets of Eshmun's divinity are perhaps reflected in the etymology of his name, the root of which, *šmn*, means 'oil'. Oil played an important role in rituals of royal investiture and in cleansing rites at healing sanctuaries and so its association with Eshmun is unsurprising. Eshmun's healing role is also clearly attested in his sanctuary at Bostan esh-Sheikh which was founded in close proximity to the supposedly therapeutic waters of the Yidlal Spring. Moreover, votive offerings recovered from the temple were typically dedicated either in thanks or as a prayer for healing. During the Hellenistic period, Eshmun's assimilation with Asklepios, the Greek god of medicine, increased the popularity of his cult and led to its diffusion to Tyre and Arwad. As Eshmun's therapeutic skills were more universally applicable than his dynastic functions, this aspect of his character was increasingly emphasised: however, within Sidon itself his two roles are likely to have been equally revered and thus his importance as dynastic patron should not be underestimated. For instance, Eshmun's assimilation with Melqart, the dynastic god *par excellence*, highlights the significance of his patronal duties. Eshmun's royal patronage is also highlighted though his skill at hunting and his dispensing of justice, both of which are typically royal activities. Finally, a number of inscriptions recording requests by the kings of Sidon for Eshmun's assistance in fulfilling their roles as father to their people, protectorate of their city, dispenser of justice and bringer of peace, further demonstrates Eshmun's intimate link with the Sidonian monarchy.

Eshmun's consort, 'Ashtart (or Ashtoreth), was also a multi-faceted deity whose functions included that of dynastic patron, celestial and maritime goddess, and fertility deity. The close association between 'Ashtart and Eshmun is evinced by King Eshmunazar II's decision to erect their temples adjacent to one another and by 'Ashtart's divine epithet *šm bʿl* (Name of Baʿal). 'Ashtart's importance as dynastic patron is clearly established in Sidonian royal titulature: for instance, in the inscriptions on the sarcophagi of Tabnit and Eshmunazar II, the title 'chief priest of 'Ashtart' precedes all others including 'King of the Sidonians', whilst Eshmunazar's mother identified herself as a priestess of 'Ashtart. It was also common for the kings of Sidon to have theophoric names which referred to their relationship with the goddess (e.g. Bodʿashtart = servant of 'Ashtart). As with Baʿalat Gubal in Byblos, 'Ashtart was considered to be one of the primary sources of royal power (see Figure 9). In her guise as a maritime deity, 'Ashtart is often depicted on Sidonian coins standing on the prow of a galley, with her right hand stretched forward holding a crown as though pointing the vessel on its way. Although there were undoubtedly a number of other lesser deities being worshipped, aside from a letter sent by the king of Sidon to his counterpart in Ugarit complaining that blasphemy had been committed in the temple of Baʿal, there is no evidence for the wider Sidonian pantheon.

Fig. 9: The throne of 'Ashtart at Bostan esh-Sheikh. The empty throne functioned as a cult statue and was thus an object of veneration

Tyre

The general composition of the Tyrian pantheon can be recovered thanks to the survival of a seventh-century treaty between Baal I, king of Tyre, and Esarhaddon, king of Assyria (*ANET*, p. 534). The treaty, signed in *c*.675, invokes a number of deities to act as guarantors and who would punish any transgression; amongst this list are a number of Tyrian gods and goddesses including 'Anath, 'Ashtart, Ba'al Shamaim, Ba'al Malage ('Lord of Plenty'), Baitylos (the deified personification of a baetyl), Ba'al Saphon, Eshmun and Melqart. Although this document does not portray a normative image of the Tyrian pantheon, as the gods invoked are chosen because of the potential harm they can inflict if the treaty is broken (e.g. Eshmun and Melqart are invoked because they could deprive Tyre of food, oil and clothing, whilst Ba'al Shamaim, Ba'al Malage and Ba'al Saphon are called upon to destroy the fleets of Tyre), it nevertheless emphasises the diverse range of deities that were venerated in Tyre. The prominence given to the three manifestations of Ba'al within the treaty emphasises his role as the supreme storm

112

deity and his importance within the Tyrian pantheon (there are many manifestations of Ba'al both as a regional god, e.g. Ba'al of Sidon, and as a weather god, e.g. Ba'al Saphon and Ba'al Shamaim).

Despite the importance of Ba'al Saphon and Ba'al Shamaim to nautical travel and commerce, the pre-eminent male deity of Tyre was Melqart ('King of the City') who was worshipped as a dynastic patron, fertility god and maritime deity. Known to the Tyrians as Ba'al of Tyre (i.e. 'Lord of Tyre'), Melqart represented the all-pervasive power of the monarchy and was considered to be the divine personification of the ideal Phoenician king. Due to his early synchronism with the Greek god Heracles, much of what we know about Melqart and his worship is recorded by Greek and Latin authors. Herodotus (2.44) and Lucian (*De Dea Syria*, 3), for instance, record that Melqart's temple in Tyre was very ancient and was believed to have been founded at the same time as the city. Although originally worshipped as the founder and patron of Tyre, Melqart was increasingly revered as the protector of Tyrian social and economic interests. In particular, he was considered to play an active role in the founding and protection of Tyrian colonies: a role attested by the numerous dedications made in his honour at temples in Cyprus, Carthage, Sardinia, Malta and Spain.

Melqart's consort was 'Ashtart ('Queen of Heaven'), who was recognised and worshipped as Tyre's chief goddess. 'Tyrian' 'Ashtart, like her Sidonian counterpart, was a multi-faceted deity who functioned as a dynastic patron, celestial and maritime goddess, divine warrior and fertility deity. Her warrior characteristics are evinced in the treaty between Baal and Esarhaddon, wherein she is called upon to smash the bows of potential violators whilst her dynastic connections are emphasised by the royal title 'chief priest of 'Ashtart' held by Tyrian kings. 'Ashtart's temple, like that of Melqart, was believed to be very old. According to Josephus (*Antiquities of the Jews*, 8.145–6), the temple was already long established by the time Hiram I decided to renovate it in the tenth century. Evidence for the private worship of 'Ashtart has been provided by a small limestone throne recovered from a family temple close to Tyre. An inscription on the throne's plinth records that Abdoubast, son of Bodbaal, had dedicated the statue in his personal sanctuary to 'Ashtart. Cult statues of 'Ashtart were also dedicated as votive offerings in temples and sanctuaries as a way of encouraging the goddess to provide good harvests, fertility of land and womb, and protection and tranquillity in the home.

Berytus

The only detailed accounts of Berytian religious beliefs and practices are found in a number of Greek and Roman texts written in or after the first century CE. These texts must be used cautiously, however, as they describe a belief system that had already been transformed by Western traditions and customs. One of the most detailed accounts of Berytian religion is provided by Philo of Byblos, who, although reflecting contemporaneous religious beliefs and practices, nevertheless does provide some insights into early traditions. According to Philo, Berytus was founded by the supreme god El following his marriage to a mortal woman named Berout. In order to prove his devotion to his new wife, El decided to build a great city which would be named in her honour (although a later tradition suggests that the city was named after the nymph Beroë – Nonnus, *The Dionysiaca*, 43.118–1.32).

Despite founding Berytus, El bestowed the patronage of the city to Poseidon and the seven *Cabiri* (the 'Great Ones'), which, for Philo at least, explained the importance of these deities throughout the city's history. Although it is unclear which Semitic god Philo equates with Poseidon, what is certain is that both deities must have had similar characteristics and duties in order to justify the syncretism.[8] It is therefore customary to refer to the Semitic god who was widely worshipped in Berytus as either 'Semitic Poseidon' or 'Berytian Poseidon'. As god of the sea, every maritime occupation was under Berytian Poseidon's protection and thus the seafaring inhabitants of Berytus looked upon him with great reverence. In fact, he was held in such high esteem that when a group of Berytian merchants established a commercial enclave on the Greek island of Delos during the second century, they referred to themselves as the *Poseidoniastes of Berytus* and erected a temple in his honour. On Berytus's early coinage Berytian Poseidon is depicted riding in a chariot that is drawn by four hippocampi or seahorses, whilst on later issues he is portrayed standing proudly, clutching a trident in his hand. The trident was an important symbol of Poseidon's power as he could use it to lash the seas into frenzy or calm them following a storm. Berytian coins also commonly depict Poseidon alongside or atop a dolphin, further emphasising his role as protector of maritime industries.

Like Poseidon, the *Cabiri* were also venerated due to their maritime associations, in particular their connection to navigation and ship construction. Philo credits the *Cabiri* as being the first to construct seaworthy vessels and to navigate the open seas, which perhaps accounts for why their image was a popular choice of figurehead on Phoenician vessels. Representations of 'Ashtart (or her temple) also appear on a number of Berytian coins, suggesting that she may have been venerated as the city's chief goddess. Nevertheless, although her role as patroness of seafarers makes this conclusion plausible, it has yet to be supported by either the literary or archaeological evidence. Finally, Pausanias (7.23.6) records that Berytus housed a large temple dedicated to the healer god Eshmun; however, like Berytian 'Ashtart, little is known about his specific characteristics or duties.

Sarepta

The main shrine at Sarepta, which was constructed with considerable care and attention, was built on the edge of a large mound overlooking the harbour. The identity of the deity to which the temple was consecrated was revealed by the chance discovery of an ivory dedicatory plaque which reads: 'The statue which Shillem, son of Mapa'al, son of 'Izai made for Tanit-'Ashtart'.[9] The inscription is highly significant as it contains the first unequivocal occurrence of Tanit in the Phoenician homeland. Prior to the excavations at Sarepta scholars considered Tanit to be a Libyan goddess who had been assimilated into the Punic pantheon; however, this inscription suggests that the origins of her cult lay in the east rather than in Africa. There are two ways of interpreting the inscription's conjoining of Tanit and 'Ashtart: firstly, that by the seventh century the cult of Tanit had been fused to that of 'Ashtart, or, secondly, that the dedication was made to both goddesses as they were worshipped in the same shrine.

Another deity known to have been worshipped in Sarepta was the chthonic god Shadrapa whose name appears incised on a fifth-century potsherd. As the inscription had been scored into the wet clay prior to firing, and as the pot appears to have been of particularly high quality, it is likely that the object was deliberately manufactured as a votive offering. The imagery and symbolism that are associated with Shadrapa suggest that he was a deity who embodied supreme strength, power and vitality.[10] Due to the fragmentary nature of the surviving dataset it is impossible to ascertain Shadrapa's importance within Sarepta's pantheon; however, references to the worship of Melqart, Ba'al and Eshmun suggest that he was probably not the city's patron deity.

Dying and Rising Gods

A common feature of the Phoenician pantheons was the veneration of a male deity who died and was resurrected. In fact, many of the religions of the ancient Near East incorporated deities which scholars have identified as dying and rising gods.[11] Three such gods are recognised to have been worshipped in Phoenicia: Eshmun at Sidon, Adonis at Byblos and Melqart at Tyre. Although united by their common fate, and despite tendencies towards association and syncretism, each of these gods was very different. For instance, Adonis was primarily a demi-god associated with beauty and desire, Melqart was the tutelary god of Tyre, whilst Eshmun was a god of healing, regeneration and rejuvenation. Traditionally, the dying and rising gods of the ancient Near East have been closely related to the seasonal cycle and to the agricultural calendar. Since the late nineteenth century, scholars have accepted that the death and return of these deities was a metaphorical analogy for the life cycle of plants: the summer drought, a period when no vegetation could flourish, symbolically represented the deity's death and absence, whilst the winter rains and spring floods, which brought about the renewed fertility of the earth, represented the god's resurrection and return. This model seemed to be supported by the timing of the annual festivals held in honour of Adonis and Melqart (Adonis had a single festival held in mid-summer which commemorated both his death and resurrection, whilst Melqart was honoured with two separate festivals – one in summer to commemorate his death and one in spring to rejoice at his reawakening). However, advances in archaeoastronomical research have led some scholars to question the assumption that these festivals were intended to coincide with the agricultural calendar. The discovery that many of the altars and temples of the Phoenician colonial diaspora have a helioscopic orientation (i.e. are aligned with the sun) has given rise to the hypothesis that Phoenician worship, in particular that relating to a dying and rising deity, was connected to the annual solstices and equinoxes rather than the agricultural cycle.[12] However, this innovative research is still in its infancy and thus further work is required before the newly proposed model can be considered as a convincing alternative to traditional interpretations.

PHOENICIAN PRIESTS AND ADJUTANTS

Priests

Public worship was overseen and administered by a body of professional clergy. At the head of this body was the chief priest or, occasionally, priestess, who presided over the city's most important cultic affairs. Due to the power and prestige that temples could accrue, the office of chief priest/priestess was always closely linked to the royal household, meaning that many who held the position were immediate relatives of the king. Although by the Persian Period it had become common for kings to hold the position of chief priest in cults dedicated to their dynastic patron, it is likely that a member of the royal family or a highly trusted religious adviser was assigned the task of overseeing the daily running of cultic life. In general the priesthood appears to have been a hereditary position drawn from the ranks of the aristocracy. The importance and high social standing of the priestly class is perhaps most clearly evinced in a number of grave markers recovered from the cemetery at Tyre Al-Bass. An analysis of these funerary stelae revealed that those dedicated to priests (and very occasionally, priestesses) tended to be of much higher quality than those commemorating recipients from other occupational backgrounds.[13]

Male members of the Phoenician priesthood are traditionally represented barefooted and clean-shaven, dressed in a long, pleated, linen tunic which had wide, open sleeves and a conical hat that is reminiscent of the modern Lebanese tarboush (see Figure 10). The few surviving visual representations closely match the description of Phoenician priests provided by the Latin author Silius Italicus. According to Silius (3.21–8, the priests of the temple of Melqart in Gadir (modern Cádiz) wore white pleated robes, shaved their heads and abstained from sexual acts. Shaving was apparently part of the cultic preparations that priests were required to perform, thus explaining the need for temple barbers (see below). The discovery of large numbers of hatchet razors in both funerary and temple contexts in Phoenician colonies (in particular those of North Africa, Sardinia and Spain) highlights the ritual importance of shaving.

Fig. 10: Stone stele depicting a Phoenician priest dressed in long flowing robes and
conical hat. Ny Carlsberg Glyptotek Museum, Copenhagen

Aside from overseeing the day-to-day running of the temple,
the main duties of a Phoenician priest were to supervise religious
ceremonies and festivals, offer regular sacrifices to the gods and
divine the future. In addition to performing sacerdotal functions,
contemporary sources also testify that Phoenician priests were

responsible for maintaining and updating the temple's library. Although operating in tandem with royal archives, it is likely that temple libraries preserved documents detailing the most outstanding and praiseworthy achievements of the local king, achievements which needed not only to be brought to the attention of the gods but also recorded for posterity.

Adjutants

Phoenician priests were supported in their duties by a number of minor functionaries and adjutants who were employed to undertake the more mundane tasks associated with temple life (such as cleaning, maintenance and administration). An inscription recovered from the sanctuary of 'Ashtart at Kition offers a unique insight into the various adjutants and personnel employed in the service of a Phoenician temple (*KAI* no. 37). The inscription, which is in essence an administrative document recording the various types of cultic personnel and their monthly salaries, provides a vivid picture of life in the temple which can be supplemented by what Herodotus (1.119) tells us about the temple of 'Ashtart at Paphos. According to these two sources, Phoenician temples (at least those consecrated to 'Ashtart) employed guards, servants, barbers, scribes, musicians, butchers, bakers, a 'water master', a 'sacrificer' and sacred prostitutes.

Like their contemporaries in Ugarit and Canaan, Phoenician cultic personnel are believed to have received a share of the temple's income in the form of food, drink, textiles, wool and occasionally silver. The most important cultic personnel were charged with taking care of the god. Their duties included making sure that the cult statue was always clothed and sheltered, overseeing ritual offerings and libations to ensure that they were conducted in the correct manner and, finally, ascertaining the will of the god through the use of divination. However, the majority of staff were employed to perform more mundane tasks such as guarding temple property, upkeep of temple grounds, cleaning, maintenance and administration. Orphans and children from poor families could be dedicated as an offering to the goddess and would become temple slaves charged with performing menial work or hard labour. Although these children were strictly supervised and required to undertake unpleasant tasks, they were normally well fed and well treated. Temple slaves could also be captives of war dedicated by a victorious king, second- or third-generation slaves born into captivity, or privately owned slaves lent to the temple by a pious master. In order to deter slaves from absconding, those belonging to the temple were prominently branded in order to prove ownership.

CULTIC RITUALS AND PRACTICES

The cultic life of a Phoenician city revolved around a calendar of feasts, festivals and celebrations, occasions that brought people together and helped reinforce the idea of a collective religious identity. As it was believed that the gods were present and receptive to the requests of their worshippers during these events, it was important to ensure that they corresponded with important dates within the city's sacred and secular schedules. For instance, as survival depended on farming and agriculture, many of the most important cultic events coincided with significant points within the agrarian cycle (such as the start of the new ploughing season and the beginning and end of the harvest).

The Phoenicians, like the Canaanites, considered sacred time to be cyclical and so divided their liturgical calendar into 12 lunar rather than solar months. The New Moon (*Neomenia*) appears to have regulated the rhythm of Phoenician religious life and so a number of cultic ceremonies were performed to mark its rising and setting (*KAI* 43). The importance of the new moon is prominently attested in the Kition inscription, which shows that the monthly billing of temple expenses began with the rising of the new moon, and in the popularity of the Phoenician name *Bnḥdš* ('son-of-the-new-moon').[14] Religions that adhere to a lunar calendar traditionally considered days of a full moon to be auspicious and it is likely that the same was true in Phoenicia.

Another significant date in the Phoenician calendar was New Year. In contrast to modern conventions, Phoenician New Year celebrations were held in the month of *Peritia* (February–March) so as to coincide with the first spring equinox. The most famous New Year celebrations were those initiated by Hiram I at Tyre which comprised a lavish annual festival commemorating the resurrection or reawakening of the god Melqart. The festival was of immense importance to the Tyrians as they believed that the death and resurrection of Melqart had instigated the annual lifecycle of the earth's vegetation. As part of the festival, an effigy of Melqart would be placed on a giant raft, ceremonially set ablaze and then cast adrift. The intention of this ritual appears to have been twofold: firstly, to revive the god and make him immortal by virtue of fire and, secondly, to ritually purify him by virtue of water. After the body of Melqart had been consumed by fire and sea, the king and his chief consort symbolically assumed the roles of Melqart and ʿAshtart in a ritual marriage intended to guarantee the fertility of the monarch and to enshrine and legitimise his authority. The role played by the average citizen in these events is unclear but at the very least they could observe proceedings. In addition to these larger festivals, smaller ceremonies were used to mark a variety of occasions in the public and private life of a citizen including their birthday, naming day, marriage, induction to public office, and death.

Dance, Music and Song

Music and dancing were two common yet important features of Phoenician cult worship. The centrality of movement in worship has a long history in the ancient Near East and is attested in both the literary and material records.[15] The earliest textual evidence for cultic dance is provided by the Old Testament which records that the 200 prophets of Baʿal who confronted Elijah on Mount Carmel performed ritual dances as part of their efforts to evoke their god's support (1 Kings 18:25–6).[16] The importance of ritual dance within Phoenician cult practices is also attested by its depiction in a variety of contemporary artworks. For instance, a number of Phoenician silver and bronze bowls (ranging in date from the ninth to the seventh centuries) are decorated with images of female cultic dancers. In general, the ritual processions depicted on these bowls are somewhat stately and sedate affairs with the dancers showing minimal signs of animation. However, a much freer form of dancing has been identified on a Phoenician silver bowl in the collection of the Cleveland Museum of Art.[17] The central medallion of this bowl depicts two highly animated male dancers who are holding leaves in each hand and who appear to be located in a field. The scene has been interpreted as a ritualistic dance that was intended to ensure the fertility of the fields.

The continued importance of cultic dance throughout the Phoenician period is attested by a third-century inscription etched into an altar at Deir el Qal'a (near Beirut). The altar is dedicated to the god Ba'al Margod (from the root *rqd* meaning to 'dance' or 'skip'), whose cult was widespread in the ancient world. Ba'al Margod is believed to have been given his name either because he was the inventor of dance or because his adherents utilised ritualistic movement when worshipping him. The Greek author Heliodorus of Emesa (*Aithiopika*, 4.17.1), writing in the third century CE, provides further evidence for the importance of cultic dancing when he describes a group of Tyrian sailors performing an Assyrian-style ritual dance in honour of the god Melqart. Significantly, this dance was not part of a fertility rite but rather was intended to curry favour with the god in order to gain his protection for the forthcoming crossing to Sicily. Cultic dances could therefore be performed in a variety of contexts and settings and for a multitude of reasons.

The inclusion of cultic singers (*šrm*) in the Kition temple accounts and the various depictions of cultic musicians found at sites throughout Phoenicia attest that music and song were also prominent features of Phoenician worship. These were particularly important forms of worship as both were thought to enable communication between the mortal and divine realms. Instruments which made a loud or explosive sound, such as drums and tambourines, were also considered to have an apotropaic function (i.e. they could ward off evil). People in a liminal state (such as brides, new-born babies and the recently deceased) were particularly vulnerable to demonic attack and thus drums and tambourines were commonly played at births, weddings and funerals. Finally, music and singing were also believed to have the power to restore and rejuvenate and so became particularly vital forms of worship within the healing cults and sanctuaries consecrated to Eshmun and other 'healer' gods.[18]

Divination

As in many other ancient Near Eastern religions, divination appears to have played an important role in the cultic life of ancient Phoenicia. Divination involved observing omens and signs from the gods in order to gain knowledge of the future. Omens were either solicited or unsolicited: in the case of the former, a priest or specialist observed or examined a situation which he had induced, whilst in the case of the latter, signs could be seen or observed by anyone (e.g. an earthquake or lightning strike). Both private individuals and state officials consulted omens when making important decisions or when trying to determine the will of the gods. One of the most popular methods of divination was extispicy which involved searching for divine omens or messages in the entrails and organs of a sacrificial animal. The discovery of any unusual blemish or deformity would be taken as a message from the gods and interpreted according to its form and position. The discovery of a small but significant number of inscribed arrowheads from religious sites throughout Lebanon indicates that belomancy (the study of the flight of arrows) was also utilised by the Phoenicians.[19] There is also evidence for ecstatic prophecy, a form of divination in which the prophet is believed to be completely possessed by the spirit of a god and thus can reveal 'divine truths'. The most explicit example of this type of prophecy is recorded in the *Report of Wenamun* (*ANET*, p. 26). Although undocumented, it is believed that the Phoenicians also used necromancy (the consultation of the dead), uranomancy (divination through the study of the heavens), libomancy (observing the smoke from a fire or oil lamp), and lecanomancy (observing the pattern of oil poured onto water). Another important way of divining the future was the consultation of oracles. Oracles were individuals who were thought to have been specifically chosen by the gods to serve as portals through which divine messages could be conveyed to the mortal realm. As the gods were believed to speak directly to the oracle, they differed from priests and seers who merely interpreted the divine signs they observed around them. Oracles are particularly prominent in the foundation myths of various Phoenician cities and colonies: for instance, according to Strabo (*Geography*, 3.5.5) the founding of Gadir (modern-day Cádiz) occurred because of a command that had been issued by a Tyrian oracle.

Prayers, Libations and the Burning of Incense

Perhaps the central feature of any religious event or ceremony was the offering up of prayers. Illustrated seals and dedicatory stelae depict worshippers in varying gestures of prayer (most commonly with the right hand raised in front of the mouth; with both hands lifted heavenwards; or with their hands clasped at waist level). Prayer was in essence an invitation for the gods to manifest themselves in the mortal realm as a precursor to ritual communication. The worshipper calls upon the deity by emphasising their supreme qualities (size, strength, justness etc.), an act which not only proves the worshipper's supplication but also demonstrates their complete confidence in the god's ability to assist them. In essence, then, prayer should be seen as public acclamation of the deity's awesome majesty and an invitation to dialogue and exchange rather than a moment of personal reflection or contemplation. Unfortunately, aside from a few cursory blessing formulas, we are lacking any substantial Phoenician prayers or liturgies. Nevertheless, these standardised blessing formulas do reveal that one of the prominent aims of Phoenician prayer was to highlight the worshipper's faithfulness and piety in order to solicit divine blessings and favours.

The burning of incense was another important feature of Phoenician religion and is one of the most widely attested forms of worship in the ancient Near East. Incense had first been used in a secular setting to mask the odours from sweat and putrefaction that commonly occur in warm and temperate climates. There is little doubt that the original domestic use of aromatic materials was intended to alleviate the unpleasant odours of everyday life. It is likely that the practice was subsequently introduced into cultic life in order to combat the foul odours that were generated by the sacrificial slaughter of large numbers of animals. From its more practical uses, incense gained abstract significance once it entered into Phoenician cultic life. For example, incense was believed to have a purifying power which cleansed the air both literally and spiritually. In line with Egyptian beliefs, it also appears that the Phoenicians considered smoke to be a conduit connecting the mortal and divine realms which could be used to carry messages to the gods. The prevalence of incense burning is also attested by its depiction on a number of Phoenician seal stones and grave markers, and by the discovery of incense burners (and related paraphernalia) at numerous Phoenician sites from across the Mediterranean. Significantly, the ritualistic burning of aromatic material also appears to have been a common feature of private worship as indicated by the discovery of small incense burners in domestic settings and on several Phoenician shipwrecks.

Another popular form of offering which frequently accompanied the burning of incense and the offering of prayers was the pouring of libations, that is the ritual pouring of a liquid as a form of offering or sacrifice to a god, spirit or ancestor. The most common type of libation consisted of a mixture of wine and water, but unmixed wine, oil, water, milk, honey and even blood could be used. Libations would be poured onto something of religious significance (such as an altar), or directly into the earth. The vessels used when pouring libations, the most prevalent of which was a shallow bowl known as a *phialē*, often had distinctive forms in order to differentiate them from similar items employed in a secular setting. Although the Canaanite and Ugaritic ritual and mythic texts show that libations were normally made alongside other food offerings (in particular, at ritual feasts and sacrifices), evidence from Phoenicia suggests that the pouring of libations was considered to be a significant cultic act in and of itself. For instance, a Phoenician silver bowl recovered from Etrurian Caere depicts a scene of ritual libations in which a procession of female water-bearers is in the process of pouring an offering.

SANCTUARIES, TEMPLES AND SHRINES

Although the Phoenicians left many traces of their cultic activities, scholars are generally much better informed about the religious architecture of the latter half of the first millennium than they are for that of the Late Bronze or Early Iron Age. This is largely due to the fact that many of the early first-millennium cultic sites lie either beneath the foundations of modern towns and cities or are yet to be fully excavated. In contrast, many of the most important Classical and Hellenistic temples (such as those at Ain el-Hayat in Amrit, Bostan esh-Sheikh near Sidon, and Umm el-Amed near Tyre) have largely been left untouched and so are accessible to archaeologists. A quick survey of the archaeological, literary and visual evidence immediately reveals that Phoenician cult places generally adhere to the concept of 'sacred space' which is found throughout the ancient world. In essence, Phoenician 'sacred space' can be understood as an area that was owned or inhabited by a god (or gods) and was thus considered as untouchable, holy territory. The holiness of sacrosanct land was often protected by sacred laws or by a codified set of rules which were designed to regulate conduct in order to protect the purity and sanctity of the space. Moreover, the extent of a temple's landholdings was of major importance for the perception of the deity's prominence and power. Many temples are known to have owned large swathes of agricultural land which, although still sacred, was leased out in order to generate revenues that could be used to cover the costs of running the temple. Although temples and sanctuaries are the most archaeologically visible form of sacred space, Phoenician holy places also included the location of lightning strikes, and sacred vineyards, groves, grottos, caves, springs and wells.

The most important places of worship were large, monumental buildings that had been commissioned by kings or by members of the royal household. As was the case in contemporary societies, the construction of temples was considered to be the pious duty of the royal family and thus kings, queens and princes were keen to advertise their involvement in founding, or substantially restoring, large cultic centres. For instance, the funerary inscription of the fifth-century Sidonian king, Eshmunazar II, proudly records that he and his mother had built a number of urban and extra-urban sanctuaries consecrated to the most important gods of Sidon. In general, the Phoenicians constructed two types of temple: the open-air precinct and the built, enclosed temple. Open-air precincts consisted of a paved, elevated, open courtyard (*temenos*), which housed some form of cultic installation such as an altar, shrine or baetyl (sacred stone). Where possible this type of sanctuary was constructed on high ground (ideally on top of a mountain or high hill) or in close proximity to other natural features such as springs, rivers or ridges. When not constructed on top of a hill or mountain, open-air complexes tended to be elevated by means of a built platform or raised terrace.

The most monumental open-air precinct is that of Bostan esh-Sheikh, which is situated at Nahr el-Awali, two kilometres to the north-east of Sidon. The sanctuary encompassed a large open area which contained sacred trees and streams, and which housed a variety of cultic buildings and chapels dedicated to both Eshmun and 'Ashtart. The undulating, rugged topography of the site meant that the original temple of Eshmun, which is believed to have been constructed in the early sixth century, took the form of a huge truncated pyramid reminiscent of the ziggurats (step pyramids) found in contemporary cultures. During the Early Persian Period the original temple was supplanted by a monumental ashlar podium that was 70 metres long, 50 metres wide and 20 metres high. In order to overcome the uneven terrain, and as a way of alleviating the threat of subsidence, the new podium was terraced against a large slope and protected by thick retaining walls (see Figure 11). The upper terrace of the podium housed an elevated open-air precinct, at the centre

Fig. 11: The open-air precinct and temple of Eshmun at Bostan esh-Sheikh

of which was a prismatic altar made from dressed stones. During the fourth century, a new chapel was constructed at the base of the podium. Consecrated to 'Ashtart, the chapel contained a monumental throne (which was flanked on either side by a griffin or sphinx), and a large, ornately decorated ceremonial basin (which is often referred to as 'the pool of 'Ashtart'). Water was obviously an important part of the cultic life of the sanctuary as, in addition to the ceremonial basin, it also possessed an elaborate network of water channels and basins which were fed by the 'Yidlal Spring'. With many Phoenician cultic sites containing some form of sacred well or spring, it is likely that ritual ablutions were an essential feature of religious observance.

Although contemporary literature records that the Phoenicians were famed for their construction of magnificent roofed temples, there are very few traces of enclosed temple complexes in the archaeological record. This holds particularly true for urban complexes. Currently Temple One of the Kathari precinct at Kition is the only excavated example of a large Phoenician enclosed sanctuary in the eastern Mediterranean. With so few archaeological remains, and with contemporary sources providing limited information regarding the size and layout of urban sanctuaries, estimates for the average dimensions of a Phoenician temple are tentative at best. However, if the few surviving examples at Amrit, Tell-Sukas, Sarepta and Tell-Arqa are a representative sample, then Phoenician urban sanctuaries were generally much more modest in size than their equivalents in Syria-Palestine. Even more monumental temples (such as those at Tyre, Sidon and Arwad) are still considerably smaller than sanctuary complexes found in the rest of the Levant.

The key features of the typical Phoenician urban or enclosed temple complex were: a central temple or chapel; a large open courtyard; imposing perimeter walls; and an ornate portico through which the site was entered. The central temple, a tripartite structure consisting of an entrance hall, cella (outer chamber), and holy of holies (inner chamber), housed a large effigy in which the god or goddess was believed to dwell. Surrounding the temple was a large, open-air courtyard at the periphery of which was a variety of service buildings and storehouses. As the courtyard housed the sanctuary's primary altar (which was normally positioned opposite the temple's main entrance), it was considered to be sacred space and so was commonly delineated by some sort of decorated fence or balustrade. Most complexes were encircled by an imposing perimeter wall and so could only be accessed via a single portico (a roofed and columned entrance way or porch). Although none of these porticos has survived, it is possible to gain a general sense of their size and form from their depiction in contemporary artworks. A terracotta plaque depicting the ornate portico constructed by the Byblian king Yehaumilk at the temple of Ba'alat Gubal shows it as having a tall façade that included two Ionic columns, an entablature decorated with a winged sun disk (entablature = the horizontal upper section of a classical building which rested on top of the columns), and pedimental ornaments (*acroteria*), which take the form of lions. If the proportions are represented accurately then the portico would have been six metres wide and approximately ten metres high, dimensions which closely align with the size of the plinth and column bases found at the entrance to Ba'alat Gubal's sacred precinct in Byblos.

In addition to open-air precincts and enclosed temple complexes, the Phoenicians also considered a number of other locations or natural features to be sacred space. For instance, both Philo of Byblos and a second-century CE inscription from Arwad (*IGLS* VII, 4002) attest to the importance of sacred groves within Phoenician cultic traditions, thus providing some credence to Silius Italicus's largely fictional description of the sacred grove of Elissa in Carthage (*Punica*, 1.71–7). It was also common for the Phoenicians to consider grottos and caves to be sacred spaces. One particularly well-known example is the cave at Afqa (or Afka), which is located at the source of the Adonis River, known today as Nahr Ibrahim. The force of the water gushing from the mountain produced a large cave at the mouth of which the Phoenicians constructed a temple consecrated to both Adonis and 'Ashtart. In Greek mythology, Adonis was believed to have been born and to have died at the foot of the waterfall, thus explaining the cave's importance to his worshippers. Caves and caverns, such as the one at Magdhdouché (located between Sidon and Tyre), were also commonly linked to the worship of fertility deities such as 'Ashtart as they were seen to symbolically represent the womb. Although the cave at Magdhdouché has now been converted into a Christian chapel dedicated to the worship of the Virgin Mary, early visitors to the site recorded that its walls had been covered in sexual images, leading the famed French archaeologist Ernest Renan to describe it as a Phoenician 'grotto of prostitution'. As is the case at Afqa, the remains of a temple of 'Ashtart lie close to the sacred cave. Recent research has also shown that grottos were a popular place of worship amongst mariners and acolytes of underworld divinities (with the latter believing that they were gateways to the netherworld).

Other natural features which helped to define and shape both the secular and sacred landscapes were rivers and streams. The importance of water within Phoenician religious beliefs (in particular the veneration of streams and rivers) is attested by the large number of temples and cult structures located close to some form of watercourse. Water, which is essential for life, was manifestly symbolic within Phoenician religion and was thus often a central feature of cultic rituals and practices.[20] For instance, free-flowing water was considered to be 'alive' as it had both motion and voice and, like the gods, could bestow life on dry and barren regions. According to the Levantine and Mesopotamian worldview, a 'sweet ocean' was located both beneath the earth and above the heavens. It was through streams, wells, rivers and rain that these life-giving 'sweet waters' (i.e. fresh water) reached humanity. As water helped sustain life, ensured the fertility of the land and was a pre-eminent purification agent, it was considered to have restorative properties. Consequently, the majority of Phoenician spring sanctuaries, including those at Afqa, Amrit and Bostan esh-Shiekh, were consecrated to the fertility goddess 'Ashtart, the healing god Eshmun, or to both. Certain springs or streams were also believed to have prophetic qualities. At Afqa, for example, votive offerings would be thrown into the sacred waters in order to please the deities and secure their favour: if the supplicant's offering remained floating on the water's surface it was predicted that the year ahead would be prosperous; however, if the offering sank then hard times were to follow.

DEATH AND AFTERLIFE

The precariousness of human existence means that every society develops mechanisms or belief systems which are intended to soften the brutal reality of death. Although these differ depending upon the social and cultural contexts in which they emerge, one that was common to many of the civilisations of the ancient Near East was a belief in a continued existence after death. The nature of the evidence means that the task of reconstructing Phoenician beliefs concerning death and the afterlife is a challenging one. While the inscriptions and artefacts recovered from Phoenician necropoleis have provided insights into the types of funerary rites and rituals that were commonly performed, the dearth of literary texts means it is impossible to identify the ideological beliefs that inspired them. Therefore, in order to gain a more complete understanding of Phoenician eschatological beliefs, scholars have cautiously used comparative evidence in order to try and fill in some of the lacunae. From this comparative material it is possible to infer that both the Canaanites and the Phoenicians conceived the afterlife as a subterranean world which was shrouded in darkness.[21] Located somewhere beneath the earth's surface, it was a place of rest to which the spirits of the deceased travelled to spend eternity with their ancestors.

Inscriptions from several Sidonian royal sarcophagi indicate that the Phoenicians called their dead *rephaim*, a term that had previously been used in Ugarit to denote divine ancestors or individuals that had been posthumously deified.[22] Although there is no explicit evidence for the practice of ancestor worship in ancient Phoenicia, the root meaning of the term *rephaim* ('to heal') strongly indicates that the Phoenicians believed in a continued existence after death.[23] This hypothesis gains support from a first-century CE Latin-Punic inscription from Libya which renders the Semitic *rephaim* as *di manes* (the *di manes* were chthonic deities thought to represent the souls of deceased loved ones). Philo of Byblos also suggests that the Phoenicians believed in some form of afterlife. According to Philo, the Phoenicians associated the notion of death with the god Muth, a primordial deity that presided over the muddy, putrid netherworld to which spirits were believed to descend. Philo's account appears to reflect a wider religious tradition which held that after death the soul of the deceased transitioned to an unknown, bleak and desolate place where it joined the spirits of its ancestors.[24] If Philo accurately portrays Byblian eschatological beliefs during the Late Iron Age, then the worship of Muth provides further evidence that the Phoenicians believed in some form of life after death. The closing lines of the burial epitaph of King Tabnit of Sidon, which contain a curse preventing anyone who violates the sanctity of the sarcophagus from finding rest in the afterlife, provide further evidence of the belief in a continued existence after death (*ANET*, p. 62).

The iconography and symbolism used in the decoration of tombs and sarcophagi (such as the Egyptian *ankh* and lotus flower) also indicate that the Phoenicians believed in the notion of spiritual rebirth and continuation. In Egyptian funerary reliefs a lotus flower, which is commonly used to represent the concept of regeneration, is often shown being sniffed by the deceased and their family in a symbolic act intended to ensure the rebirth of the soul in the afterlife. A similar gesture is also depicted on the Ahiram sarcophagus where the king's son, Ithobaal, is depicted raising the flower to his nose. In contrast, the lotus flower held by the king is shown as wilted and drooping, signifying that Ahiram is deceased (see Figure 12). The lotus flower became a common feature in Phoenician and Punic religious art and was often used to represent the protection and renewal of the spirit. Similarly, in funerary art, images of birds and fish became popular eschatological symbols that were used to represent the journey of the soul into the afterlife. The funerary assemblages and grave goods recovered from Phoenician necropoleis are also strongly indicative of a culture that believed in a continued existence post-death. As the burials at Tyre-Al-Bas attest, the deceased was provided with

Fig. 12: Detail from the Ahiram sarcophagus depicting the deceased king clutching a
wilted lotus flower in his left hand

everything that would be required for, or wanted in, the afterlife
including both luxury objects (i.e. personal adornments such as
jewellery) and more utilitarian items (such as cooking utensils).[25]
Significantly, many of the grave goods recovered from Phoenician
tombs, such as painted ostrich eggs (magical items that helped ensure
a smooth transition to the afterlife) and apotropaic amulets, plaques
and figurines, were intended to ward off evil and to provide physical
or spiritual protection to the deceased.

Mortuary Rites and Rituals

A study of funerary rites and rituals also provides a compelling case for
accepting that the Phoenicians conceived some form of life after death.
Although unable to shed light on the ideological beliefs that underpinned
them, archaeology has been extremely helpful in reconstructing
Phoenician burial rituals which are otherwise poorly documented in the
literary texts. Archaeology has shown that the Phoenicians practised
both inhumation (burial) and cremation (burning) when disposing of
the deceased. Inhumation was the predominant form of burial practice

during the Late Bronze Age but was replaced in the first millennium by a new method of disposal, cremation. The excavation of the necropolis at Tyre-Al-Bas has revealed that cremation was used as early as the tenth century and may have been a practice that originated in Phoenicia before spreading to the rest of the Levant. Although cremation was generally more common than interment during the Late Bronze to Early Iron Age, there appears to have been no eschatological difference between the two practices and thus members of the same family were free to choose whichever they preferred. The excavations also revealed that Tyrian funerary ceremonies were protracted and must have lasted several days, or perhaps even weeks. Phoenician cremation rituals are generally believed to have been divided into four phases: firstly, the preparation and cremation of the body; secondly, the performance of ritual lamentations and a funerary procession; thirdly, the interment of the deceased's ashes; and, finally, the rituals and ceremonies that accompanied the closing of the tomb. Although omitting the cremation stage of phase one, Phoenician interment ceremonies are likely to have followed a similar process – albeit with the body rather than the ashes being interred.

The ritual preparation of the deceased for interment appears to have varied according to their social class. Typically, the body was washed and cleansed, doused with perfumed oils, and then carefully swathed in linen or cloth bandages. The discovery of clothing pins and jewellery in the tombs of high-status individuals suggests that it was common for the deceased to be dressed in their finest clothes. It is likely that those being cremated were also dressed or wrapped in a piece of cloth as this was a common practice throughout the ancient Near East. An inscription from Byblos attests that before being interred the wealthier members of society had their bodies swathed in myrrh and bdellium (a resin that could be extracted from certain plants) and it is likely that their purification rites would have involved the use of expensive imported aromatics and fragrances. The practice of embalming was rare and seems to have been reserved for royalty or highly important members of the royal court. Members of royalty were also occasionally buried with gold death masks or with a gold band across their mouths (e.g. Batnoam, the mother of the Byblian king Ozbaal, *TSSI* no. 26) and their eyes and fingernails would be covered with gold or silver foil. Following the preparation and cremation of the body was a funeral procession that incorporated ritual acts of lamentation such as loud wailing, the wearing of sackcloth, the tearing of hair and the beating of breasts.

The central, and perhaps most meaningful, phase of the whole ceremony was the ritual interment of the body (or ashes) and the subsequent depositing of two jugs and a drinking vessel. In essence, the act of placing the remains into the grave, a liminal place of transition between the world of the living and the world of the dead, symbolised the beginning of the deceased's journey to the afterlife. As the grave was to be the occupant's final resting place, great care had to be taken when depositing the remains. Before the tomb was finally closed, new objects were deposited for the deceased's personal use post-mortem and, on occasion, small aromatic fires were lit in order to purify both the grave and the spirit of the departing. Once the final items had been deposited and the aromatic fires had burnt out, the grave was covered with a layer of stone or sand. The ceremonial closing of the grave was then followed by a sacrifice, the pouring of libations and the consumption of food and drink – the accoutrements of these activities (plates, bowls and jugs) were ritualistically smashed before being deposited on top of the tomb. Feasts in honour of the deceased were a common feature of funerary rituals throughout the Levant and are well documented at Ebla, Ugarit, Qatna, Byblos, Tyre and Israel. Though these feats were primarily symbolic expressions of continuity with the past, as the living and the dead shared the same food and drink, they were also intended to reinforce the bonds of social cohesion and to create an ongoing relationship between the deceased, their family and the wider community.

Graves, Tombs and Necropoleis
Due to a concern with spiritual and physical pollution, Phoenician cemeteries were normally located at some distance from the settlement to which they were associated and, where feasible, were separated from it by some form of natural barrier such as a river or valley (for instance, island cities like Arwad and Tyre located their cemeteries on the mainland). Most of the urban centres appear to have had multiple burial grounds which catered for different societal groupings. The graves of children, for example, appear to have been kept separate from those of adults and thus infants were either interred in separate precincts (known as *tophets*) or under the floor of the family home. The Phoenicians constructed their tombs

in a variety of different shapes, sizes and styles according to fashion and utilitarian requirements: despite this, however, it is possible to identify four primary types of grave or tomb during the Iron Age.

The most simplistic form of burial was the *fossa* grave which was a single-occupancy grave consisting of a shallow oblong pit that had been excavated directly into soft soil or rock. The second type of tomb, the shaft grave, consisted of a narrow vertical well which was enlarged at the base in order to accommodate the body. The third tomb type, known as a pit grave, was constructed by digging a simple rectangular trench of roughly human dimensions into which the body would be deposited. In order to prevent the body from being disturbed, the pit was sometimes lined and covered with large stones. From the sixth century, it is possible to identify a great diversity in the type and quality of pit graves, ranging from a simple stone-lined pit to elaborate stone edifices (the latter being known as cist graves). The final category of grave was the built or rock-cut chamber tomb (*hypogeum*). These tombs could be designed for multiple or single occupancy and were either subterranean stone-lined caverns or single-roomed chambers constructed using well-cut ashlar blocks and covered by a flat ceiling with a pitched roof. Access to these tombs was via a shaft or a stepped open-air ramp called a *dromos*. The use of monumental, above-ground tomb structures (such as the pyramid and cube-shaped funerary towers at Amrit) was a relatively late development and did not appear until the fourth century. The bodies of royalty or high-ranking individuals were often placed in coffins before being interred. These coffins ranged from simple wooden caskets with flat or ridged covers to decorated anthropoid sarcophagi crafted from terracotta or imported marble, with the latter becoming the preferred choice for the aristocracy from the mid-first millennium.

The funerary pyres used in cremations were generally situated at the periphery of the cemetery as close as possible to the intended final resting place of the deceased (occasionally the pyre could be constructed in the tomb itself, although examples of this are rare). Once the pyre had burnt itself out, the charred remains of the deceased would be collected together and carefully wrapped in cloth before being deposited in an urn or amphora and then finally buried (see Figure 13). There were three types of pit grave into which urns were interred: those that accommodated one urn, those that accommodated two urns, and those that accommodated multiple urns.

Fig. 13: A terracotta burial urn with rounded body, small circular base, wide rim and two looped handles

In 'single-urn' graves, all of the ashes and remains collected from the funerary pyre were gathered together and deposited in a solitary urn which was then buried. Once placed in the grave, the urn was covered with a plate or flat stone before two jugs were positioned at its base and a drinking bowl leant against its shoulder. As its name suggests, a 'double-urn grave' contained two urns: in one were the ashes of the deceased whilst in the other were any bones or personal items which had not been fully incinerated. Just prior to the grave being shut, both urns were carefully covered with a plate and two jugs and a drinking vessel were deposited. The third type of grave contained groups of single and double-urn burials that were positioned adjacent to one another and which had been deliberately deposited in the same space over several generations. In some cases the older urns had been relocated so that they were either beside or above more recent additions. Although it is unclear why these urns had been grouped together, the most probable explanation is that they contained the ashes of successive generations of one family.

The discovery of rectangular imprints in close proximity to a large number of Phoenician graves provides evidence for the use of grave markers. For the majority of citizens these markers would have been crafted from perishable materials, such as a wooden plaque; however, the more affluent, or those individuals who held an important position within the community, could commission a marker made from stone. These markers are likely to have had a dual purpose: firstly, to demark the burial space and to record who had been previously buried at a particular location, and, secondly, to commemorate the deceased and ensure the survival of their name for eternity. By ensuring that the deceased's memory was kept alive, these markers perhaps represented a metaphor for the continuity of life. The markers that were positioned above communal graves appear to have recorded the original occupant and a few select members of the family who were subsequently interred at the same site. A burial site could also be marked by a gravestone that had been crudely carved from local sandstone and which typically included some type of religious symbol or motif and an inscribed epitaph. The epitaphs generally record the deceased's personal name and patronymic (although this is not always present) and, on very rare occasions, their occupation. Significantly, nearly all of the personal names found on Phoenician gravestones incorporate the name of an important deity (e.g. Ba'al, 'Ashtart, Melqart, El).

4

ART AND MATERIAL CULTURE

Tracing the origins and emergence of a distinctly Phoenician artistic tradition has proven to be no easy task. Although the literary accounts from the Old Testament and Assyrian annals point to a vibrant and well-developed craft tradition at the end of the second millennium, these testimonies are not currently supported by the material record. With the notable exception of the Ahiram sarcophagus, whose date is still contested, few Phoenician artworks can be definitively assigned to the Early Iron Age. This lacuna in the material record is largely due to the fact that the Early Iron Age strata at many of the major urban centres have yet to be subjected to controlled archaeological investigation. Furthermore, the surviving material record provides only a partial or incomplete picture as the products of two of Phoenicia's most renowned artistic traditions, carved woodwork and textiles, are highly biodegradable and thus rarely survive in the prevailing environmental conditions and soil types found in Lebanon. To further compound matters, many artworks were produced specifically for export and thus modern typological and stylistic analyses of Phoenician arts and crafts are, for the most part, based on finds recovered from sites outside of Phoenicia itself. Relying on such finds is problematic as there is a growing body of evidence to indicate that some of these objects may have been manufactured *in situ* by resident or itinerant craftsmen.[1]

Despite such restrictions, it is still possible to create a general overview of Phoenician artistic developments from the Late Bronze

Age through to the end of the first millennium.[2] The use of comparative evidence has been particularly helpful in this regard. For instance, a number of metal and ivory objects recovered from the Bronze Age city of Ugrarit show remarkable parallels with similar items produced in Phoenicia during the Iron Age. Such similarities suggest that there was a direct continuity between the Syrian traditions of the Late Bronze Age and those identified in Phoenicia at the start of the Iron Age. Moreover, dispersed finds from sites throughout the Levant indicate that Phoenician artisans, in particular those working with metal or ivory, were heavily influenced by the surrounding Canaanite and Syrian cultural and artistic traditions.[3] However, generalisations regarding the early inspirations for Phoenician art are best avoided as there is clear evidence that craftsmen working with materials other than metal took inspiration from the Cypriot (terracotta) and Egyptian (pottery and glass) artistic milieus.[4] In fact, recent studies have shown that the choice of artistic tradition from which to draw inspiration was often the result of political or economic considerations and thus varied from city to city. Consequently, a fundamental question that needs to be addressed before examining the various categories of art and material culture is: what exactly is it that makes Phoenician art 'Phoenician'?

The answer to this question has generally been that Phoenician art can be defined by its eclecticism, which is most clearly evident in its unique and unprecedented blending of contrasting styles and motifs. Although liberally borrowing elements from other artistic traditions, Phoenician craftsmen did not simply replicate existing artworks but rather drew upon a range of styles and influences in order to produce unique composite designs. This is particularly true with religious motifs and symbols which are often removed from their original context or imbued with new meaning or significance by Phoenician artists. However, now and then Phoenician artists elected to imitate specific foreign styles or designs without modification or without the introduction of new elements and thus Phoenician art can be difficult to recognise if it copies an original too closely. To make matters worse, Phoenician artists were not the only ones to copy or borrow foreign iconography. Phoenician art is therefore seen as an amalgam of many different cultural elements, leading scholars to categorise artworks according to the borrowed style or cultural influence which is considered to dominate. It is thus common for Phoenician art to be classified as 'Egyptianising' (i.e. includes common elements of Egyptian art – such as the regular spacing of figures; figures that are depicted in profile; large expanses of undecorated flesh or clothing; symmetry in regard to motifs, symbols and patterns; decoration with colours that were common to the Egyptian palette; or incorporation of specific motifs that were common to Egypt), 'Assyrianising' (i.e. includes elements of Assyrian or Hittite art – such as Assyrian-style lions, clothing, hairstyles, deities, demons, emblems of royal office, or winged sphinxes; giving predominance to animals and nature scenes; or depicting human figures as relatively rigid and static), 'Syrianising' (i.e. draws inspiration from Syrian manufacturing and artistic traditions – utilising symbols and motifs that were common to Anatolia; presenting figures from a frontal perspective; and depicting distinctive facial features such as large eyes and noses, receding chins and pinched lips), or 'Cypro-Phoenician' (i.e. is typically found on Cyprus – having characteristics that are common to both Phoenician and Cypriot artistic traditions; displaying a largely Phoenician sense of organisation and layout; utilising certain common decorative motifs; drawing heavily upon Assyrian traditions).

Unfortunately, however, not all scholars are in agreement as to how these terms should be applied to the various sub-categories of Phoenician art and so objects can be classified differently by individual scholars. Moreover, despite being lauded in antiquity as exceptional craftsmen and artisans, the Phoenicians' willingness to borrow motifs and designs liberally from other cultures has led to their artworks being labelled as derivative by modern scholars. For instance, in his seminal study of the art and architecture of the ancient Near East, the highly esteemed historian Henri Frankfort accused the Phoenicians of producing 'bungled' and 'crude' imitations of Egyptian masterpieces before condemning their metalwork as 'garish' (an assessment which is at odds with the high praise given to the Phoenician silver work in Homer's *Iliad*).[5] Other accusations which have been levelled at Phoenician art include: that it is simplistic and poorly expressed; that it was primarily produced for profit rather than aesthetic appeal; and that, despite mimicking other traditions and liberally adopting foreign motifs and symbols, it never achieved a sense of unity or coherence. However, since the publication and exhibiting of a much wider array of Phoenician artefacts throughout the 1980s and 1990s, scholars have begun to view Phoenician art more favourably. It is now accepted that although taking inspiration from other cultures and artistic traditions, Phoenician craftsmen managed to achieve an innovative synthesis which expressed a refined and characteristically 'Phoenician' taste. Moreover, with more careful analysis, it is possible to identify that Phoenician artworks often contain a structural balance and cohesion which are not immediately obvious.[6] It is necessary, therefore, to recognise and accept that Phoenician artisans relied on their customers' appreciation and understanding of a particular aesthetic style and iconographic language that modern scholars often struggle to decipher.

IVORY WORK

Prior to the emergence of the Phoenician ivory working industry in the ninth century, there was already a long and rich history of ivory carving in the ancient Near East. Although the earliest examples date to the third millennium, the popularity of, and demand for, ivory objects increased significantly during the Late Bronze Age. Thus the period *c*.1600–1200 witnessed an explosion of competing ivory carving traditions stretching from Greece in the west to Iran in the east. With so many competing traditions, scholars have thus far struggled to determine which, if any, influenced the Phoenician craftsmen who began producing large quantities of finely carved ivory during the ninth century (although there is clearly an Egyptian influence on the artistic style and choice of subject). The rarity of ivory made it a highly prized commodity and thus it became synonymous with luxury, decadence and power: eventually, its reputation and desirability led to it being seen as having a corrupting and immoral influence and so it was often condemned in the Hebrew Bible (e.g. Amos 3:15; 6:4 and Ezekiel 27:6). There has been much debate about where the Phoenicians acquired their ivory. During the second millennium the most coveted ivory was that which was extracted from the teeth of hippopotamuses and it is likely that this was sourced from Egypt; however, during the Late Bronze Age, fashions changed and ivory procured from elephant tusks became the most desirable. With no local supplies it is likely that the Phoenicians sought to acquire elephant tusks from North Africa and perhaps even India.

Phoenician craftsmen were particularly known for their skill in producing decorated ivory work, numerous examples of which have been found in Assyria, northern Syria and northern Palestine (other isolated examples have also been recovered from sacrificial and funerary contexts in Rhodes, Samos, Crete, mainland Greece and Italy). As the biblical texts make clear, these ornate ivory carvings were crafted for an elite clientele consisting primarily of foreign rulers and aristocrats. The high quality of the craftsmanship indicates that some workshops were part of a palace-controlled industry and thus it is likely that, as with bronze casters who operated under royal patronage, ivory workers were members of a professional guild. It is also likely that the skills and techniques were passed down from father to son so as to ensure that the industry was always well supplied with professional craftsmen.

Phoenician ivory workers employed a wide range of effects and techniques in order to produce an aesthetically pleasing final product. These included: ajouré (perforated openwork), champlevé (a type of deep carving in which the background is whittled down in order to make the foreground decoration stand out), cloisonné work (a style of enamel decoration), and the use of tinted paste, glass and goldleaf to augment the ivory's natural appeal (paradoxically, considering the value of ivory, some items were completely gilded, meaning that none of the raw ivory was left showing – see Figure 14). The various types of ivory objects manufactured by the Phoenicians include: rectangular panels for furniture (such as chairs, thrones, footstools, couches and beds), boxes, chests, handles for fans or fly whisks, cosmetic implements and even horse blinkers, harnesses and bridals. The size of furniture panels was restricted by the carver's ability to obtain flat pieces of ivory from a curved or bowed tusk or tooth (thus, the more skilled the artisan the larger the panel that he could produce). When assembled on a wooden frame these individual furniture panels formed abstract and representational motifs rather than narrative scenes. As the individual panels often formed part of a larger piece, the carver would inscribe them with different letters in order to identify their correct placement. Significantly, these letters were not always written in Phoenician, perhaps indicating that the carver was not present for the final assembly process (a system which is very similar to modern flat-pack furniture).

Fig. 14: Ivory inlay of a lioness mauling an African man in a thicket comprised of lotus flowers and papyrus plants. Fragments of gold leaf remain on the man's kilt and hair indicating that the item would originally have been gilded

The largest cache of carved ivories ever discovered was found at the Assyrian capital city of Nimrud in Northern Iraq.[7] As Assyrian kings collected these ivories as gifts, tribute or plunder, they represent an unparalleled record of the artistic traditions in the regions conquered or controlled by Assyria (although it is also possible that some of these ivories were carved *in situ* by resident artists). Because of the diverse provenance of the Nimrud ivories, combined with a dearth of comparative examples recovered from Levantine or Mediterranean sites, it has proven difficult to establish conclusively when and where each object was produced. Consequently, recent scholarship has instead focused on trying to define the differences between the Phoenician and northern Syrian traditions. In general, three separate artistic styles have been identified: the 'Phoenician', the 'Syrian-Intermediate' and the 'North Syrian'. Ivories which demonstrate a strong Egyptian influence are assigned to the 'Phoenician' artistic tradition as they display motifs and symbols which are remarkably similar to those found on Phoenician metal bowls (Egyptianising motifs include those that are wholly Egyptian in origin – such as sphinxes and the various depictions of the god Horus – as well as modified Egyptian themes such as youths dressed in Pharonic crowns who are grasping fantastic plants). A few motifs seem more distinctly 'Phoenician', such as the 'woman at the window' who is wearing an Egyptian wig and may represent a queen, priestess or sacred prostitute.

A statistical analysis of the Nimrud ivories has revealed that the vast majority belong to the Phoenician tradition. This large corpus of Phoenician ivories can be divided into two approximately equal groups, those that are closest to the art of Egypt (known as 'Classical Phoenician') and those which are still clearly Phoenician in style but which tend to be of slightly lower quality (known simply as 'Phoenician'). Despite the strong links to Egypt and Egyptian art, there is a severely limited range of subjects illustrated on the Phoenician ivories – the main motifs include the birth of Horus, a cow suckling a calf, youths binding a papyrus, a lioness in a papyrus thicket, a griffin trampling a fallen human and a variety of deities, humans, snakes, sphinxes and winged animals. Significantly, although popular in Egypt, there are no examples of narrative art; instead the pieces tend to focus on rituals and religious scenes. Furthermore, although Phoenician craftsmen liberally appropriated Egyptian motifs and designs, they did not slavishly copy them but instead adapted them to serve their own purpose and meaning.

METALWORK

The appropriation of designs without concern for their original meaning is also characteristic of Phoenician metalwork. In general it has been the eclectic style and inseparable blend of elements from the diverse stylistic traditions of the Near Eastern and Mediterranean worlds which have gained the attention of specialists.[8] The best-attested objects of the Phoenician metalworking tradition were ornate bowls. Popular during the tenth to seventh centuries, examples have been found in Iran, Syria, Greece, Italy and Spain.[9] The reputation of the Phoenicians as highly skilled metalworkers is well established in both the Old Testament and the Homeric poems. Homer, for instance, displays a deep-rooted respect for Phoenician craftsmen, describing the large silver crater offered by Achilles as a prize in the funeral games devoted to Patroclus as a 'masterpiece of Sidonian craftsmanship' and 'the loveliest thing in the world' (*Iliad*, 12.74–749). The corpus of metal bowls can be subdivided in one of two ways: either according to their shape, method of manufacture, and the metal from which they are fashioned, or, according to their iconographic themes, motifs and stylistic influences. Although by the end of the ninth century ornate metal bowls were being manufactured in numerous workshops around the Mediterranean, the origins of this artistic tradition clearly lay in Phoenicia.[10]

The vast majority of Phoenician bowls were created by hammering a thin sheet of metal over a curved anvil. Once formed, the interior of the bowl would be decorated using a variety of techniques including chasing (working the metal from the front by hammering with various tools that either raise, depress or push aside the metal without removing any of the surface), engraving (the process by which the outlines of decorative patterns and reliefs are etched into the metal), embossing (the raising of smaller, often rounded areas, such as the tip of a tail or the petal of a flower), and repoussé (working the metal from the back to give a higher relief on the front). How these bowls were used appears to have been determined by the individual preference of the owner. Those that were recovered from a votive or funerary setting may have been used to pour libations as part of a religious ritual, or, alternatively, may simply have been items particularly treasured by the deceased. Many of the shallower bowls, which have generally been recovered from a private setting, were pierced, suggesting that they were suspended when being displayed.

For the most part, the iconography and motifs found on Phoenician bowls were drawn from two artistic traditions, either Egyptian or Neo-Assyrian. Typical Egyptianising motifs include: groups of Egyptian women, pharaoh smiting his enemies, winged sun-disks, various Egyptian deities, ankhs, sun-beetles, wingless sphinxes, Egyptian-style temple pylons, papyrus boats, hieroglyphs

Fig. 15: Shallow, silver-gilded bowl decorated in repoussé. The central medallion depicts a male figure in combat with a rearing lion. The surrounding scenes, which most likely represent a hunting expedition, are encircled by a serpent with patterned skin

and Egyptian-style marsh scenes with fish, fowl, wild oxen, and swimmers amongst the reeds. The Neo-Assyrian elements, which, as in other Phoenician art forms, appear at the time when Assyria was strengthening its political hegemony over the Levant, include: four-winged genies, winged sphinxes, sieges, animal hunts from the back of a chariot and a lion killing a bull or deer. Other scenes also draw upon wider Mesopotamian traditions such as the capture of the monstrous giant Humbaba or an unarmed hero in combat with a lion (see Figure 15).

Despite the disparate origins of the motifs and iconography, there is nevertheless an underlying uniformity to the bowls: for instance, all include a central medallion and have one or more concentric bands of decoration. It also appears that the craftsmen of these bowls were consciously drawing upon a fixed and precise system of typological criteria as, although at first the decorative repertoire of the bowls appears to be quite varied, in reality the number of iconographic themes is limited. The disparity between the abundance of cultural influences on which the Phoenicians could have drawn and the small number of motifs and themes actually presented suggests that there was some sort of selection process. If correct, this perhaps indicates that the bowls were specifically designed with the export market in mind, a hypothesis supported by the fact that many of the motifs had no underlying meaning (e.g. the hieroglyphic writing on these bowls is nonsensical). It thus appears that many of the elements were selected for their aesthetic appeal rather than their original meanings or connotations.

The other two main categories of metalwork for which the Phoenicians are well known are bronze statues and so-called votive razors. The production of small cast bronze figurines is first attested in the third millennium and continues through to the Early Iron Age, whereas the razors were more closely associated with Carthage and thus are principally attested in the seventh to second centuries. The statues appear to have been primarily produced as votive offerings for temples and domestic shrines. The subjects mainly consist of seated or standing male and female deities in Egyptianising dress that are often positioned with one of their hands outstretched, palm out, in a traditional pose of blessing. Another popular type is that of a 'smiting' or 'menacing' deity which is believed to represent the god Reshef. Although surprisingly few of these figures have been recovered from the Phoenician mainland, numerous examples have been found outside the Levant.[11] Recent typological analysis suggests that many of the figurines found outside of Phoenicia had actually been manufactured in Phoenician workshops and then exported. The finer-quality statues, which have inlaid eyes and faces that are covered with gold or silver foil, bear some resemblance to the forms of Egyptian statuary of the New Kingdom.

Similarly, the votive razors which are most prevalent in the colonies of North Africa, Sardinia and Iberia also seem to take inspiration from implements found in New Kingdom Egypt. The razors are generally 20 centimetres long with a flat, roughly rectangular body and a crescent-shaped blade on one of the short ends. The handle protrudes from either the middle of the blade or, more frequently, is attached to the short end of the implement opposite to the one that had been sharpened. In later examples, the razor's handle takes a zoomorphic form and is often shaped like a swan or an ibis. Birds and animals are also commonly depicted on the blade itself, as are gods, goddesses, heroes and a variety of plants (such as palm trees and lotuses). The presence of small holes in the upper portion of the blade, or the inclusion of suspension rings near the handle, indicate that the razors were designed to be suspended (whether this was for display purposes or more practical reasons is unknown).

STONEWORK – STELAE, SCULPTURE AND SARCOPHAGI

In contrast to many other art forms, stone funerary monuments, sculpture and sarcophagi are more reliably identified as the products of Phoenician craftsmen since they are found in Phoenicia and are not easily portable. The Phoenician cities were located in a region devoid of stone or marble which was suitable for the production of high-quality sculptures. The local stone was far inferior to that used by Egyptian and Assyrian artists, and thus for important projects or artworks better-quality materials were imported. In the sixth century, importation of marble from Greece commenced and it became the primary material for prestige or luxury items crafted from stone. However, stone sculptures and reliefs, such as anthropoid (human-form) sarcophagi, statues of gods, votive or commemorative stelae and architectural decorations, constitute a very incomplete series which does not fully represent the history of Phoenician sculpture.

The most widespread products of Phoenician masons were stelae and *cippi* (small, squat pillars), which have been recovered in significant quantities from the cemeteries at Khalde, Sidon, Tell-el-Burak and Tyre.[12] The vast majority of the funerary monuments were cut in local calcareous sandstone (or occasionally limestone); were rather crudely made (with only the front, and to a lesser degree the lateral sides, being smoothed); were small in size (with a maximum length of 76 centimetres, width of 40 centimetres and thickness of 34 centimetres); usually bore a symbol and/or inscription; were found in so-called 'common' cemeteries (i.e. cemeteries used by citizens who occupied the lower echelons of society); and were dateable to between the tenth and sixth centuries (although a small number are believed to date to the fifth century). The stelae and *cippi* present in a variety of shapes and styles and so can be trapezoidal, rectangular, rectangular with a rounded top, L-shaped or pyramidal. As these monuments represent the tombstones of the average citizen, their crude workmanship reflects the modest income and social background of those who commissioned them.

Although illustrating a wealth of Phoenician religious symbols and motifs (some entirely local and others which were clearly borrowed from Egypt), the stelae present a fairly simplistic and coarse iconography (which is perhaps unsurprising given the poor quality and texture of the stone from which they were formed). Some of the motifs, such as the ankh, are clear and easy to identify whilst others remain more difficult to define and interpret. The motifs and symbols can be roughly divided into the following categories: anthropomorphic motifs (including human heads, schematic faces and busts); Egyptian hieroglyphs (primarily the ankh and nefer symbols); the Tanit symbol (which consists of an isosceles triangle below a circle with a horizontal line at the apex of the triangle); baetyls (sacred standing stones) and sacred pillars; single letters (which were considerably larger than those of the inscription and which were occasionally from the Greek alphabet); astral motifs (including solar disks, winged disks and crescent moons); geometric motifs (such as circles with six spokes on the inside, sloping crosses and ovals); shrines (these only appear on Persian Period stelae); and, finally, plant motifs (palmettes, lotus flowers and ivy). The diverse and varied iconography of the stelae provides scholars with an important glimpse of Phoenician popular art which is otherwise very poorly documented.[13] The poor quality of these stelae and *cippi* stands in stark contrast to the high level of craftsmanship displayed in royal monuments and in luxury items that were produced for export. They therefore bear witness to the ways in which moderately affluent Tyrians and Sidonians could use art to express their religious views and beliefs. The tradition of using stone grave markers was to be carried with the Phoenicians as they expanded throughout the Mediterranean and thus numerous examples have been recovered from cemeteries in North Africa, Sicily, Sardinia, Cyprus and Iberia.

As well as the production of stelae and *cippi*, Phoenician stonemasons also produced ornate stone sarcophagi (see Figure 16). These were prestige items which only the most affluent citizens would have been able to afford. Unfortunately, the extant record is only a partial one as, aside from the Ahiram sarcophagus which dates to the Early Iron Age, all other examples date to the Persian Period. In addition to the 130 anthropoid sarcophagi recovered from tombs in Phoenicia, there are an increasing number being recovered from sites in the coastal regions of western Syria (significantly this is an area that was never under Phoenician control).[14] As with the stone stelae, the quality of the finished product varied according to the skill of the craftsman and the quality of the material being used (generally Phoenician stone sarcophagi were crafted from either imported marble or from local basalt).

Anthropoid sarcophagi consist of two elements, the lid and the box, and could assume both male and female form with the latter predominating (the gender can be determined by the hairstyle which was always carefully rendered). The body is normally depicted in a crude mummiform shape, which tapers to a flattened ledge that denotes the feet. Although it is possible that the person portrayed on the lid was a stylised representation of the deceased which emulated their social status, gender and age, it is more likely that the image was a generic, idealised character design that was popular at the time the objects were manufactured. Irrespective of which interpretation is correct, the use of human features as a visual icon would have been meaningful to the society in which they were created. Over time the sarcophagi became increasingly less humanoid, with the final examples consisting of a box-shaped receptacle that had a neckless head-mask appended to it. Although the roots of this artistic style can be traced to Egypt, Phoenician stonemasons clearly drew on several traditions, including Persian, Syrian and Greek. Beginning in the late fifth century, Phoenician sarcophagi become increasingly Hellenised in style and form (something that is particularly noticeable in the distinctly Greek hairstyles).

Remarkably, despite the obvious talents of their stonemasons, the Phoenicians never developed a coherent or widespread tradition in large-scale stone statuary. The few pieces which have survived are removed from each other both temporally and geographically and so do not permit the reconstruction of changing styles or traditions. As with the stone sarcophagi, it is possible to identify an Egyptian influence

Fig. 16: Greek-style, fifth-century white marble sarcophagus lid recovered from Sidon. The lid has an anthropoid form consisting of a male head, crude mummiform body and a flattened ledge to denote feet

in the early pieces and a Greek influence in the latter. Aside from the unfinished male colossus at Byblos, very little remains of the earliest monumental stone statuary. Sculpted from local limestone, the Byblian colossus displays a number of Egyptian influences including its stance (i.e. one leg is positioned slightly in front of the other as if the figure is taking a step), an Egyptian-style wig, and the presence of a supporting back pillar. During the ninth century, Phoenician stone masons clearly took inspiration from the popular art and fashions found in Egypt. This new hybrid form of statuary which freely merged Egyptian and Phoenician cultural influences was to spread from the mainland to Cyprus, where it would influence fashion in cities such as Kition.

The majority of early statues portray a common subject consisting of a male youth dressed in Egyptian-style clothing (sleeved tunic, pleated kilt and elaborate collar) positioned in a forward-moving posture with one arm held at his side and the other bent across his chest. In contrast, later variants, such as an eighth-century example recovered from Tyre, depict the youth in an upright position with both arms by his side (in one hand he clenches a scroll or 'handkerchief') and with his legs clasped together (although only the tops of the youth's legs remain, it is enough to determine that he was not shown in motion). The youth wears Egyptian dress, including a broad breastplate on his naked chest, a pleated kilt that is edged at the top and bottom by bands and is divided by a central pendant flap decorated with a pair of serpents and solar disks, and a plain dual-ring bracelet on his left arm. Other examples of this type have also been recovered from Sarepta and Sidon and reveal a remarkable consistency in form and style (see Figure 17).

The temple of Eshmun at Sidon has also yielded a number of statues that are noteworthy for their Hellenised physical characteristics such as almond-shaped eyes, straight nose, and lips which display just a hint of a smile. The statues, which are believed to date to the sixth century, provide the earliest evidence for the gradual incorporation of Greek influences (probably via Cyprus) into Phoenician artistic tradition. Over the next 300 years, Hellenic artistic traditions became increasingly popular, resulting in artworks that displayed far more Greek attributes and influences than they did Egyptian. In addition to monumental statuary, a number of smaller stone figurines have also been discovered at the temple of Eshmun. The statues, which date to the fifth century, all depict young or adolescent boys who are arranged in a variety of poses. What is particularly striking about

Fig. 17: Eighth-century stone statue portraying a young male dressed in Egyptian-style clothing. The youth is positioned in a forward-moving posture with both arms held at his side

these figures is that their style is fully Greek and is thus completely devoid of any Egyptianising features.

GLASS AND FAIENCE

Phoenician glassware was another commodity which was both highly lauded and highly prized in antiquity. For instance, Strabo

(*Geography*, 16.2.25) records that the southern coastal dunes between Tyre and Akko contained particularly high-quality sand which was ideally suited to glassmaking. Similarly, the famous Roman naturalist, Pliny the Elder (*Natural Histories*, 36.190–9), who was writing in the first century CE, praises the Sidonians for their unrivalled skill at glassmaking, a proficiency which he attributes to the fact that the Phoenicians were the first to discover glass. Although archaeology has shown that Pliny was wrong to attribute the invention of glass to the Phoenicians, as it first appears in the Hurrian kingdom of Mitanni in the sixteenth century, the material and literary records pertaining to the Late Bronze and Early Iron Age indicate that he was right to allude to the long history of glassmaking in Phoenicia.[15] For instance: the Amarna correspondences record that large quantities of raw glass were sent from Tyre and its neighbours to Egypt (e.g. *EA* 148); the *Report of Wenamun* (45–50) notes that the Byblian king had a large glass window; and a large quantity of raw glass ingots and beads were recovered from the Ulu Burun wreck.

Experimental research has shown that glass results from the complex fusion of various readily available basic ingredients such as silica in the form of sand, calcium carbonate and sodium and potassium alkalis (such as that obtained from plant ash). Once assembled, these components would be mixed together to form a paste which would then be heated to a temperature of around 1,050 degrees centigrade to ensure that the various elements fused together. The molten paste could then be poured into a mould and left to slowly set, or, alternatively, it could be carefully shaped whilst it was gradually cooling (if following the latter process, patterns could be incised into the semi-hardened glass whilst it was setting). During the Late Bronze and Early Iron Ages, glass vessels and objects were typically 'core-formed', a technique which involved the creation of a wax or clay 'core' which would be modelled into the desired shape, wrapped in a piece of cloth, fixed to a cane, and then submerged into the molten paste. Once the core was sufficiently coated in molten glass it would be rolled over a flat piece of stone or metal in order to achieve a smoother and more consistent finish. Once the glass was sufficiently hardened, the original core would be extracted and the glass would be repeatedly polished. The rims, handles and bases of jugs and flasks would be moulded separately and then, whilst still hot, would be carefully applied to the final object using pincers. The

Fig. 18: Decorative fourth-century glass amphoriskos (left) and alabastron (right) created using the 'core-formed' technique

natural colour of glass produced in this way was blue or blueish-green, but other colours could be produced by mixing different metals or mineral oxides into the original paste.[16]

Despite producing a wide variety of glass vessels, the Phoenicians were most closely associated with the manufacture of alabastra (small vessels used to hold oil or perfume) and hemispherical cups and bowels (see Figure 18). Most of the excavated examples have been found in temples, palaces and elite residencies or tombs indicating that they were luxury items which would command a high price. Phoenician craftsmen also appear to have been adept at producing intricate glass inlays which were used to adorn items crafted from ivory or wood.

In the late seventh century, the Phoenician workshops in the eastern Mediterranean began producing glass apotropaic pendants in the shape of demon masks, animals and anthropoid heads (both male and female). Examples of these pendants have been found at sites throughout the Mediterranean basin, Western Europe and the Near East and so provide evidence for primary and secondary trade during the seventh to fifth centuries. The Phoenicians also made extensive use of faience, a self-glazing silica-based frit which was widely used in Egypt (frit is the fused or partially fused materials used in glass making). The versatility of Phoenician faience meant that it was easily worked and thus could be moulded into any shape imagined by the craftsman. The most popular faience objects were protective charms in the form of scarabs, Egyptian religious symbols, apotropaic eyes, or the heads of demons, deities and heroes. As these amulets were typically made by unskilled or trainee craftsmen, they tended to be cheap, low-quality items that were easy to mass produce. Thus, although some faience ware was created for the luxury market, such as the famous Bocchoris vase discovered in Tarquinia, the majority were poorly crafted trinkets produced to meet the demands of a mass market.

POTTERY AND CERAMICS

In comparison with glass, ivory and metal objects, ceramic vessels were cheap and easy to produce. The prevalence of the basic raw materials from which they were formed, and the relative ease and speed at which they could be manufactured, means that pottery vessels are often the most ubiquitous type of artefact recovered from Phoenician sites: nevertheless, their importance should not be underestimated. As fired pottery vessels were durable, waterproof and resistant to impact and thermal shock, they were ideally suited to the collection, transport and storage of liquids, and in the preparation and storing of foodstuffs. Furthermore, as the majority of pottery items (aside from amphorae) were intended for domestic use, they provide insights into many aspects of the Phoenicians' daily lives which are otherwise undocumented. Despite its importance in antiquity, it has only been in the last 20 years that Phoenician pottery has received the same level of academic scrutiny as that of ancient Greece. This is largely due to the limited repertoire of

Phoenician pottery which, although including aesthetically pleasing fine ware bowls, mushroom-lipped jugs, and finely burnished red-slipped pitchers, was generally limited to more mundane and less interesting shapes and forms.

Phoenician pottery is most often categorised either according to common stylistic features (e.g. decorative style – bichrome, black-on-red and red slip) or shape (e.g. bowls, flasks, spherical jugs, mushroom-lipped jugs, trefoil-mouth pitchers). Although these categorisations are useful, it is nevertheless important also to consider the method of manufacture and design characteristic of ceramic vessels, as this type of analysis can reveal unexpected correlations with other pottery traditions or provide clues about the origins and uses of a particular kind of vessel. Consequently, current research attempts to combine typological analysis (form and decoration) with a study of technology (method of manufacture) and function (domestic, commercial or funerary). In contrast to the artistic innovation and creativity displayed in other mediums, the Phoenicians were extremely conservative when it came to their ceramic traditions. Throughout the first millennium, Phoenician pottery retained its plain and simple decoration whilst the quality of manufacture was generally average. Unlike items produced for export, therefore, the value of Phoenician pottery was derived primarily, if not exclusively, from its utilitarian function as tableware or as containers for other more valuable commodities.

Nevertheless, Phoenician pottery has proven to be important for establishing relative chronologies and has helped scholars to determine absolute time periods within Phoenician history. It has also been highly important for research examining the geographic, historical, economic and cultural interconnections of the ancient world in the first millennium. As Phoenician pottery has a characteristic style which makes it easily recognised, its presence at disparate sites throughout the ancient world has helped scholars to determine the extent of Phoenician trade networks and commercial interactions. The discovery of 22 kilns and associated workshops during the excavations at Sarepta has also provided scholars with a great deal of information regarding the manufacturing and processing techniques utilised by Phoenician potters.[17] Aside from slight variances in size and shape, the kilns display a remarkable consistency in terms of construction and layout throughout the first millennium. For instance, all of the kilns included an oval oven chamber that was divided into two levels: a lower tier (sub-divided into two kidney-shaped lobes) that was used for stoking the fires and for the initial firing of the wet clay, and an upper tier that was used for stacking pottery which had been fired but still needed to be left to bake. Although the kilns were built using traditional fieldstone masonry (see Chapter 2), the need to insulate the central space meant that the walls were coated in multiple layers of clay rather than mud.

The distinctive bichrome (two-colour) pottery first appears in the Early Iron Age, c.1050. It has often been assumed that the bichrome style of decoration was derived from Late Bronze Age antecedents; however, it is now generally held that it arose due to a natural desire to enhance or enliven earlier monochrome (single-colour) designs and thus might not necessarily have a direct antecedent.[18] During the Early Iron Age, the most common type of bichrome decoration consists of broad red, or more accurately reddish-purple, bands that were carefully outlined or highlighted by narrower grey or black lines. These bands normally encircled the vase horizontally, but, on occasion, they could be presented vertically on opposing sides of a vessel in order to create a pattern consisting of filled circles of alternating colours (see Figure 19). This pattern, which scholars have labelled the 'bull's eye pattern', is most commonly found decorating the sides of flasks, in particular spherical and early ring-based jugs, and on the interior of shallow bowls. The decoration on early ceramic vessels generally consists of simple patterns such as monochrome concentric circles or spirals. The popularity of circular decoration perhaps reflects the fact that many of the vessels had been manufactured horizontally on a turntable or wheel.

Other simple geometric designs that were popular during this period included combinations of undulating or straight lines, six- or eight-point stars, criss-crossed banding, pendant triangles and vertical lozenges (diamond shapes).[19] Although the majority of Phoenician bichrome ware was decorated with geometric designs and patterns, there are rare examples of floral designs and religious motifs. At some point in the mid-ninth century, bichrome began to fall out of fashion and was gradually superseded by polished 'slip ware'. This new style resulted from an innovation in decorative techniques which now saw objects completely covered in a burnished red, or, less frequently,

Fig. 19: Ceramic, mushroom-lipped oil jug with rounded body, small circular base,
curved D-shaped handle, tall cylindrical neck and flared rim

black slip (coating). This style of decoration remained fashionable
until the sixth century when Greek ceramics, especially Athenian
black and red slip ware, came into vogue due to their prestige value.

Phoenician potters were able to manufacture a wide range of
objects which can be broadly divided into two categories according
to their forms, either open or closed. 'Closed-form' vessels are those

that have parts of their body that are of greater diameter than their rim; in contrast, 'open-form' denotes vessels whose rim is its widest point. The most prevalent types of open-form objects were: cups, which had a flat base, incurved rim and hemispherical or ridged sides; plates, which adhered to a fairly simplistic design consisting of a deep concavity and a thickened or furrowed rim; and goblets, which had a high foot, large bowl, semi-circular rolled rim and a varying number of handles. There was a much broader repertoire of closed-form objects, including amphorae, kraters (vessels used to mix wine and water), cooking pots, strainer-spouted jugs, trefoil pitchers and neck-ridged jugs. Among the numerous varieties of closed-form cooking pots two types dominate: the first has two handles, a rounded body and a rim moulded in high relief which was capable of supporting a lid, whilst the second has a single handle, bulbous body and bulging rim. Significantly, an analysis of these pots reveals that they were usually made from coarse fired clay that contained mica grit and featured large incisions that allowed the fabric of the pot to expand when exposed to heat.

One of the most interesting early pottery types is the strainer-spouted jar, which has an upward-tilting side spout that contained a strainer at its base to filter sediments from heavy liquids (such as beer, wine or herbal tea – see Figure 20).[20] The position of the spout, which is on one side of the vessel and offset approximately 90 degrees from the handle, would make pouring very difficult and so the vessel appears to have been designed for personal use. Another common pottery type was the neck-rimmed jug which underwent a long developmental process: starting as a pilgrim flask with an asymmetric body, long neck and two stirrup-type handles, it gradually transformed into a more spherical jug with only one handle, before ultimately evolving into a ring-shaped vessel with a mushroom-lip. The trefoil pitcher (which has a three-lobed spout) is often seen as the most elegant item in the repertoire of Phoenician potters as its long, tapering form and ridged shoulders are reminiscent of the more developed artistic styles found in the metal working industry.

Perhaps the most important closed-form pottery objects were amphorae. Designed to be portable and easily stacked within the hull of a merchant vessel, amphorae made maritime shipping cheaper and easier and thus changed the shape of long-distance exchange. For instance, recent studies have shown that Phoenician amphorae were

Fig. 20: 'Beer' jug with striped decoration

produced in standardised capacities so as to facilitate the export of oil and wine. Consequently, their impact on inter-regional trade and commerce should be considered as similar to that of the metal shipping-container in the twentieth century CE. There were generally three types of amphorae utilised by the Phoenicians, those with a biconical shape and horizontal handles, those with an oval body and streamlined neck, and those with an ellipsoidal body, extended neck and vertical handles attached at the widest point (commercial amphorae). The style and shape of the commercial amphorae can be traced back to the pottery traditions of the Late Bronze Age and remained in use throughout the Early Iron Age. At the end of the eighth century a new form emerges which, although initially being used alongside other types of amphorae, eventually replaced them.[21] This form consisted of a sub-cylindrical body tapering to a point at the base, with either a short neck or none at all, a rolled rim and handles attached near the ridged shoulder. In order to preserve the contents and prevent spillage whilst in transit, Phoenician amphorae were sealed using a pinewood disk plug and a sealant made from a mixture of resin and clay. As amphorae were highly durable, they could be reused and recycled and so, in addition to functioning as transport containers, they were also used as toilets, for burial urns and even as weapons in naval warfare.

TERRACOTTA – FIGURINES, MASKS, PROTOMES

As clay was easily worked, malleable and readily available, Phoenician potters, in addition to manufacturing large quantities of ceramic vessels, also produced an assortment of terracotta items (ceramic/pottery wares are formed from clay that is fired to a temperature of 550 degrees centigrade, whilst terracotta results from heating the clay to 650–900 degrees centigrade). During the past 20 years excavations in Lebanon and northern Israel have produced a large corpus of anthropomorphic male and female figurines and statues. As these figurines were manufactured for the domestic market, they provide important information regarding Phoenician artistic fashions and tastes. The regional character of these items is most clearly attested by their absence from the overseas settlements and colonies, and the association of particular forms and types with specific cities or locales (e.g. equestrian figurines appear to have been particularly popular in the region of Amrit). The profitability of the terracotta industry has been highlighted by the discovery of large production centres in Berytus, Sidon, Sarepta and Achziv.

Phoenician terracotta items can be broadly divided into three categories according to their method of manufacture: those made by hand; those thrown on a potter's wheel; and those produced in a mould. All three techniques are well attested throughout Phoenicia and were in concurrent use throughout the Iron Age. The purely hand-formed figurines are the crudest and most simplistic in terms of conception and manufacturing and are an idiosyncratic group. The wheel-made figurines present a more uniform tradition with the majority having tapering conical torsos, moulded heads and limbs made from rolled clay. Neither the handmade nor wheel-thrown figurines appear to have been influenced by foreign artistic traditions or conventions. In contrast, the craftsmen responsible for producing moulded figurines appear to have taken inspiration from a much wider range of artistic styles.

Ceramic figurines created using a mould were formed either in the round (bivalve mould) or, more frequently, they were moulded on the front (univalve) and then trimmed on the reverse, either with the craftsman's finger or a smooth tool. The different methods for smoothing the back of a univalve figurine resulted in vastly different finishes: those smoothed by a finger tend to have more gently rounded backs and retain additional clay behind the body, whilst tool-trimmed figurines have a flattened back which often caused the limbs to become slightly truncated. After the figurine was removed from the mould, additional details were added such as incised lines representing strands of hair or the addition of pellets to represent curls. Facial features such as eyes, nose and mouth were partially designed in the mould then later augmented by hand (e.g. eyes were enlarged and the pupils were either painted or punctured into the clay). Paint could also be used to highlight specific features such as hair and eyebrows. Although the figurines had a vertical stance, they were not free standing due to the size and position of the head and torso which meant that they were top-heavy. Small moulded figurines of this type have been discovered in temples, graves and tombs, and in domestic cultic contexts indicating that they were primarily votive in character. One of the most common types of figurine is the nude female who stands cupping her breasts. Another ubiquitous variety is the veiled, pregnant goddess seated with her right hand placed just above her swollen belly. Both types of figurine were potent symbols of fecundity and thus unsurprisingly they are most commonly found in temples consecrated to fertility deities such as 'Ashtart.

Masks and protomes (busts), although much rarer than figurines, are nevertheless just as important as they too were manufactured for the domestic market and thus provide invaluable insights into Phoenician artistic fashions and tastes. Although the origins of the terracotta masks can be traced to the Late Bronze Age they remained popular throughout the first millennium and, significantly, examples have been recovered from sites in both the east (e.g. Akko, Byblos, Sidon and Tyre) and west (e.g. Motya, Ibiza and Carthage). Protomes have most commonly been found in the west and, although being produced in the Early Iron Age, appear to have become particularly popular during the mid-first millennium. Both the masks and the protomes could either be wheel-made or moulded, were slightly smaller than life-size, and were decorated with incised or engraved designs prior to being painted. As with the figurines, the quality of masks and protomes varies considerably according to the skill of the craftsman and the intended consumer of the finished product: moreover, the discovery of items with identical defects provides evidence for mass production.

The masks, which were predominantly male, typically had apertures for the eyes and mouth, whilst protomes were principally female consisting of a bust (or a head and neck) which was hollowed out from the back and contained no orifices for the eyes or mouth. The majority of the masks, and a few of the protomes, had suspension holes at the top or along the sides, suggesting that they would be suspended when being displayed. There is a range of interpretations regarding the exact purpose and function of masks and protomes. Since they often represent deities, the protomes have been interpreted as votive offerings for temples and sanctuaries, or as an apotropaic image designed to protect the occupant of a tomb. The apertures in the masks indicate that they were to be used or worn and so, as the majority have been recovered from sanctuaries or necropoli, it is generally held that they had some sort of religious function. However, the precise cultic purpose of the masks is still debated and thus they have been variously interpreted as death masks, apotropaic amulets, replicas of masks worn in religious ceremonies or masks used by children or young adolescents when performing sacred dances.

JEWELLERY AND SEAL STONES

The discovery of intricate gold and silver jewellery at sites throughout Lebanon offers further evidence of the Phoenicians' technical sophistication and artistic ability. Although jewellery makers primarily used precious metals when creating their masterpieces, for their less discerning or less affluent clients they also produced a wide range of costume jewellery (these were items that had been fashioned from bronze and then adorned with a thin layer of silver or gold foil). A number of techniques were used in the manufacture of Phoenician jewellery, the most common of which were: granulation (a decorative style whereby small grains of metal, or granules, are arranged in an ornamental or figurative pattern on a metal surface), filigree work (an intricate pattern made using thin gold or silver wire), and embossing (see above). Despite having to be rendered in minute scale, the decoration on Phoenician jewellery was equal in quality and aesthetic appeal to that found on other metal items (including the ornate silver and copper bowls for which the Phoenicians were famed). Phoenician jewellery makers often embellished their work with coloured glass, semi-precious and precious stones (such as lapis lazuli, carnelian, amethyst, hematite and even marble), or pendants made from hammered gold. These pendants, which were typically attached to necklaces, bracelets and earrings, could be fashioned in a variety of shapes, including: oblongs, circles, cartouches, lotus flowers, lions, sphinxes, griffins, falcons, scarabs, the eye of Horus, female figures and a solid square box surmounted by a small granulated pyramid known as the 'ball-and-cage' motif. Although the majority of earrings were commonly in the shape of a leech or elongated rod, a more elaborate and highly popular design consisted of a pendant cross and oval-shaped 'ring', which, when viewed together, created the appearance of an Egyptian ankh. The overtly religious designs and symbols of Phoenician jewellery and the fact that the vast majority of it has been recovered from a funerary context, suggests that many items had a magical or apotropaic function.

Two other items which were commonly included amongst the grave goods in Phoenician tombs are cylinder seals and seal stones (or 'scarabs'). Cylinder seals, which first came into use during the early decades of the Middle Bronze Age, consist of a small, round cylinder (typically about 3 centimetres long), which has a hole drilled through its length so that it could be worn on a string or pin, and which was engraved with figurative scenes (or occasionally alphabetic characters). Cylinder seals were used as a form of signature as they could be rolled over wet clay in order to leave a back-to-front impression of the design in relief. However, the emergence of an alphabetic script which could be written on papyri at the end of the second millennium resulted in cylinder seals gradually being replaced by seal stones. Although these seal stones originally had a conical profile, were made from soft stone types and had stylised scenes and motifs etched into their surface, at the start of the first millennium Phoenician seal engravers began to imitate the Egyptian scarab (a type of seal stone that was carved into the anatomical form of a coleopteryx beetle). The preferred choice of stone from which to carve these scarabs was steatite with a blue or green glaze, although examples of carved semi-precious stones such as jasper, cornelian, agate, rock crystal and onyx have also been discovered. The coleopteryx beetle was a sacred Egyptian symbol that was intrinsically linked to regeneration (both in the mortal realm and in the afterlife) and thus the seal stone was often pierced so it could be worn as an amulet. The inscriptions and images carved into the oval base of the stone (including ankhs, falcons, uraeus serpents, eyes of Horus and the names of various Egyptian gods such as Ra, Amun, Ptah and Horus) are presented within a series of horizontal registers and display a constant attention to the protective function of the seal.

By the end of the ninth century, this multi-registered style of composition was eventually reduced to a simplified format with a primary scene framed above by a winged sun disk and below by the Egyptian hieroglyphic sign *nub* (which was used to symbolise heaven). The less ornate seals, typically crafted from soft stone or glass paste, often feature either an individual animal (real or mythical) or floral motif, and were intended for the mass market. During the eighth and seventh centuries, Phoenician seal engravers appear to have taken inspiration form the same cultures and traditions as their counterparts in the metalworking and ivory carving industries.

TEXTILES

Textile production was the most labour-intensive of all crafts and its cultural, social and economic significance can hardly be overstated.

Textiles offer protection from the elements, function as social signals (i.e. by denoting social status), were used as a mnemonic device to record events or stories (i.e. in the form of tapestries), or could be of such economic value that they were used as a medium of exchange. Throughout their history the Phoenicians were known for their production of high-quality and brightly coloured fabrics. Homer (*Iliad*, 6.288–95), for instance, praises the colourful textiles for which Sidonian women were famed, whilst brightly coloured garments feature prominently among the Phoenician tribute recorded in the Assyrian annals and in Ezekiel's list of high-value commodities produced and traded by Tyre (27:16). Tragically, however, it is impossible to offer precise comment about the appearance or production of these highly coveted fabrics as only a handful of fragments have survived. From the representations of Phoenician men and women found in contemporary artworks it has been possible to ascertain that the Phoenicians typically wore ankle-length, loose-fitting, woollen robes that were brightly coloured, adorned with embroidered designs, and had fringed hems (sleeves could be long, short or elbow length). Sometimes the robes for men stopped at the knee and appear to have been tunics that were tied at the waist with a sash (e.g. the male figures in the Luli reliefs) or could be close fitting rather than flowing (as is the case on the Balawat gates – see Figure 21). Interestingly, at Carthage this Eastern style of dress continued to be popular and appears to have survived relatively unchanged into the Hellenistic era (Plautus, *Poenulus*, 975–6). In contrast to the rest of society, Phoenician priests are always depicted dressed in long, simple robes that were loosely fitting and plainly coloured.

Although we know very little about the appearance or production of Phoenician textiles, we are far better informed about the manufacture and use of purple dye. In antiquity the production of purple dye from murex (a type of sea snail) became synonymous with the Phoenicians leading many scholars to posit that the Greek word *Phoinikes* (from which the modern term 'Phoenician' is derived) refers to the dyeing industry for which the region was famed. According to this tradition, the term 'Phoenician' was derived from the Greek word *phoinós* which can be translated as either 'red', 'blood', 'to stain with blood' or 'death'. If this is accepted, then the name Phoenicia should be understood as either 'the country of purple dyers' or 'the

land of purple cloth'. Archaeological excavations have revealed substantial facilities for murex harvesting, processing and dyeing in Arwad, Berytus, Sidon, Sarepta, Tyre, Tell-Keisan, Shiqmona, Dor and Akko, highlighting just how important this industry was to the Phoenicians.[22]

The discovery of vast heaps of broken and discarded murex at sites such as Sidon and Sarepta revealed that both major types of Mediterranean mollusc species (*Murex trunculus* and *Murex brandaris*) were used in the manufacture of dyes.[23] *Murex trunculus* (also known as *Hexaplex trunculus*) was used to make a blue-purple dye known as 'royal blue', whilst *Murex brandaris* (also known as *Bolinus brandaris*) was used to make the purple-red dye known as 'Tyrian purple' or 'imperial purple' (both types of dye were indelible, a rare property for ancient colourants, and were thus highly prized).[24] Although the southern Levantine coast, between Tyre and Haifa, had an ecosystem which could sustain a high concentration of murex, when demand outstripped supply these molluscs could also be imported from other areas of the Mediterranean and from the Aqaba Gulf (Ezekiel 27:7.16).

Fig. 21: A decorative bronze band from the gates of Shalmaneser III's palace at Khorsaba. The scene depicts the transport of tribute from Sidon and Tyre to Assyria

It has been calculated that 12,000 *Murex brandaris* were required to produce 1.4 grams of dye, enough to colour the trim of an averaged-sized garment, and so dyeing even a small piece of cloth required large quantities of murex. The price of purple-dyed textiles could therefore be extraordinarily high; in fact, the product was so valuable and so desirable that a multitude of imitation purples of inferior quality were created to meet demand. Because of this phenomenon, purple-coloured textiles and potsherds must be subject to chemical analysis before they can be designated as genuine examples of 'royal blue' or 'imperial purple'.[25] Pliny the Elder provides the most detailed account of the extraction and dyeing processes (*Natural History*, 9.60–5). Although Pliny's account sounds convincing, scientists were unable to produce either 'Tyrian purple' or 'royal blue' by following his instructions. However, by synthesising Pliny's description with those provided in other historic accounts (and with information obtained through the use of experimental archaeology), scholars have finally been able to reconstruct the ancient process for extracting and imparting purple dye.[26]

5

OVERSEAS EXPANSION

The classical sources assert that it was during the twelfth century, at around the same time as the fall of Troy (which in antiquity was generally dated to 1190 or 1184), that the Phoenicians first began to establish overseas settlements (see Map 2). For instance, Velleius Paterculus (1:2.3; 1.8.4) claims that Gadir (modern Cádiz) was founded eight years after the fall of Troy whilst Strabo (*Geography*, 1.3.2), Pliny (*Natural Histories*, 19.216) and Pomponius Mela (3.6.46) offer the slightly less precise observation that the city was founded 'shortly after' Troy's destruction. Other urban centres which were thought to have been founded in the twelfth century include Utica on the coast of Tunisia (Silius Italicus, 3.241–2) and Lixus in Morocco (Pliny, *Natural History*, 19:63). However, these dates are not supported by the archaeological record, which suggests that the earliest overseas settlements were founded during the late ninth or early eighth century. Consequently, there is an awkward gap of some 300 years between the dates provided by the classical authors and the ones which can be securely attested by archaeology.

In order to try and rationalise this discrepancy, scholars now propose that there must have been a 'pre-colonial' phase which preceded the founding of the first permanent settlement.[1] This 'pre-colonial' phase constitutes an extended period of time during which merchants and entrepreneurs visited a region in order to ascertain: the types of resources it possessed and in what quantities; its potential profitability in terms of trade, manufacturing and industry; the receptiveness of the indigenous population to foreign influences;

and the viability of colonisation at a later date. According to this model, the initial Phoenician prospectors – who travelled in small groups, limited themselves to the creation of landing stages, trading posts or small temporary markets, and conducted trade via the institutions of guest-friendship and reciprocity (or via a simple form of barter as envisaged by Diodorus 5.35.4–5) – would have left little trace in the archaeological record.[2] In contrast, the 'colonial' phase is marked by: the founding of larger, more permanent settlements (or, alternatively, the expansion and urbanisation of pre-existing settlements); the embracing of barter and market transactions as the primary types of exchange mechanisms; and the appearance of widespread and sustained cross-cultural contact, interactions and appropriation.[3] Recognition that Phoenician overseas expansion occurred in two phases not only helps to validate the twelfth-century foundation dates recorded by the classical authors, but also explains why archaeologists have been unable to substantiate them.

Though scholars are in general agreement that the Phoenicians' Mediterranean migration occurred in two broad phases, the terminology used to describe these phases and the designations ascribed to the various settlements continue to be controversial issues. A particularly contentious subject is the appropriateness of using terms such as 'colony' and 'colonisation'. In the English language the term 'colony', derived from the Latin noun *colonia*, was originally used to denote an overseas settlement that had been founded on the directive of a state or empire and so remained subject to its rule. However, the term has become historically associated with European expansions into overseas territories during the sixteenth to the twentieth centuries CE (e.g. the British colonisation of Africa and India during the nineteenth and twentieth centuries) and so has acquired imperial connotations. Recognising that many settlements were established without official state intervention, scholars have started to reject the terms 'colony' and 'colonisation' when discussing Phoenician overseas migration during the second and first millennia.[4]

Similarly, the applicability of the term 'pre-colonial' has also been called into question as many scholars now consider the second phase of the Phoenician migration to be a period of expansion rather than 'colonisation'. An additional issue with the term 'pre-colonial' is that it also intrinsically implies a subsequent 'colonial' phase, an assumption which does not hold true for many of the regions visited by the Phoenicians during the twelfth to ninth centuries. Despite calls for 'pre-colonial' to be abandoned, it is now generally accepted that the term is useful so long as a number of caveats are kept in mind: firstly, and perhaps counter-intuitively, that the term does not necessarily indicate the initial stage of a process that will automatically end in colonisation or permanent settlement (i.e. the term 'pre-colonial' can, if clearly identified as such, be used as a chronological marker to denote a period of time during which sporadic but sustained commercial contact was established, even if there was no subsequent 'colonial' phase. In a modern setting, this is perhaps analogous to a rugby player who undertakes a series of 'pre-match' exercises only for the game to be cancelled. In spite of the match not going ahead, the player is still considered as having completed a 'pre-match' routine); secondly, that the areas in which 'pre-colonial' contacts occurred are often located at some distance from those in which subsequent colonies or settlements are established; thirdly, when not being used as a chronological marker, the term should be reserved for those instances when a direct relationship between a temporary ('pre-colonial') and permanent ('colonial') presence can be substantiated (for instance, although a region may have been visited once or twice prior to colonisation or settlement, this is not enough to justify labelling those early contacts as 'pre-colonial'); fourthly, it should not be assumed that any settlement or colony established in a region visited during a pre-colonial phase was founded by the same groups that had made the initial contact; fifthly, that the 'pre-colonial' phase began and ended at different times in different places; and, finally, that any colony or settlement which did result from 'pre-colonial' contact would not necessarily exercise political or economic control over the indigenous population. Likewise, the term 'colony' can still be useful for identifying a community that had been established away from home, so long as the emphasis is placed on the distinctive cultural elements rather than the political (for instance, the term is useful for juxtaposing the 'self' and 'other' within a colonial milieu).[5]

In the overview of Phoenician overseas migration presented below, the term 'settlement' will be used to denote an urban centre, *emporium* or staging post that was founded, or significantly expanded, without evidence of direct state intervention or directive, whilst the term 'colony' will be reserved for those instances when there is clear evidence of state involvement (e.g. Carthage). According to this model, an *emporium* which had originally been founded as a 'settlement' could become a 'colony' if any subsequent expansion was officially encouraged, and vice versa. In the same vein, the terms 'settler', 'immigrant' and 'emigrant' will be used to identify people who had moved overseas of their own free volition without official pressure, whilst the term 'colonist' is reserved to denote those who had been actively encouraged to relocate by a polity, state or empire (when there is uncertainty, the term settler will be used as it has fewer unwanted connotations). Although utilising the term 'pre-colonial phase' to denote the period of temporary interactions prior to the founding of either a colony or large settlement, it will be used sparingly and always keeping in mind the caveats listed above. Furthermore, in contrast to previous scholarship, this study will also stress the multivariate origins of the people involved in both 'settlement' and 'colonisation'. Traditionally the entire network of Phoenician settlements and colonies established in the central and western Mediterranean has been attributed to Tyre; however, recent archaeological excavations have revealed that some were likely to have been Sidonian foundations. Furthermore, the array of different Eastern funerary rites and practices which have been identified amongst the earliest burials at Phoenician settlements and colonies throughout the western Mediterranean are indicative of an ethnically diverse group which included emigrants from a number of different city states.

THE STIMULI FOR PHOENICIAN EXPANSION

By acknowledging that Phoenician overseas migration was a gradual process, it has been possible to offer a more nuanced explanation of the social, economic and political circumstances which motivated it. Rather than being an *ad hoc*, haphazard undertaking, Phoenician commercial and colonial expansion is now thought of as being perfectly programmed and highly organised. That is not to say that all of these ventures were state sponsored or endorsed (although some obviously were), but rather that groups, either public or private, invested time, energy and resources in ensuring that the right locations were chosen for eventual colonisation or settlement. This is a model that is far removed from that proposed in early scholarship, which saw Phoenician expansion to be the result of Assyrian political and military pressure. According to this view, Phoenician colonies and settlements were founded by a surge of refugees fleeing from Assyrian oppression who were forced to improvise as they went along. The result was that many of these refugees headed to places that they already knew (e.g. the small commercial staging posts that had been founded in the eleventh century).[6] As early scholarship attributed the foundation of all overseas settlements and colonies to the city of Tyre, this view of Phoenician expansion not only pre-supposes that Tyre was simply reacting to the political and fiscal demands of Assyrian imperialism, it also reduces all Tyrian emigrants to the status of refugees. As the contemporaneous sources indicate that the political and commercial power of Tyre remained virtually unaltered until its conquest by Babylon in the sixth century, this theory is easily dismissed. Although there were occasional periods during which there was significant disruption to Tyre's maritime trade, these tended to last for a few years at most and so had no real long-term effect on the Tyrian economy. Another theory, which became popular during the 1980s, ascribed Phoenician overseas expansion to the internal dynamics of Tyrian society and Tyre's inexhaustible demand for resources during the tenth century. This was a time when the city was ruled by Hiram I and the literary sources suggest that the city reached its commercial zenith. Once again, however, recent archaeological excavations have indicated that there was no significant westward expansion during this period.

The primary problem with both of these models is that they sought one overriding causal factor to explain Phoenician overseas migration: either Assyrian oppression or a resource-hungry economy. In contrast, the two-phase model recognises that the Phoenician diaspora resulted from a number of interrelated casual factors which occurred over a longer period of time. Moreover, it also acknowledges that the two phases of expansion could have been stimulated by different factors and that the importance of these factors invariably fluctuated over time. Therefore, in order to understand fully the process of Phoenician overseas expansion it is necessary to determine the various internal and external factors which motivated it. Internal factors (such as a substantial agricultural deficit, overpopulation, civil unrest and an economy that is reliant on the revenues generated by trade and industry), were particularly significant as long-distance commerce and the founding of overseas settlements normally only occur during times of shortage or political crisis, or, conversely, during periods of stability and prosperity when significant profits could be made from exporting excess production. On the other hand, external factors such as political or economic pressure exerted by a more powerful empire often generated, or exacerbated, internal socio-economic conditions which made overseas expansion desirable (i.e. excessive demands for tribute often caused an economic shortage within a tributary city thus leading it to seek new revenue streams). External factors should therefore be considered as outside influences which caused or aggravated internal tensions within a city.

External Factors

It has long been held that Assyrian suzerainty during the eighth–seventh centuries was the primary motivation for Phoenician overseas expansion. According to this school of thought, the Phoenician colonisation drive was stimulated by Assyrian economic and military pressure which caused large numbers of artisans, farmers and merchants to flee westwards in order to escape persecution, and which forced cities such as Tyre and Sidon to seek out new sources of precious and semi-precious metals in order to satisfy Assyria's demands for tribute. However, with Phoenician westward migration now being recognised as a far more gradual and protracted process, and with newly acquired radio-carbon dates indicating that some settlements in the far west had been founded during the ninth rather than eighth century, such a simplistic explanation is no longer tenable.[7] Although the revised chronology still places the foundation of Tyre's earliest western settlements after Assyria's first demand for tribute (issued by Ashurnasirpal II in *c*.870), the late ninth century was a time when Tyre was profiting greatly from inter-regional exchange and so could easily afford the sums being levied. That these payments had a negligible effect on the Tyrian economy can be inferred from the emphasis that the ninth-century Assyrian annals and royal inscriptions place on Tyre's economic prestige and wealth, and from the fact that by the middle of the eighth century Tyre was in a position to pay Tiglath-Pilesar III 150 gold talents in tribute (i.e. almost 4,300 kilograms). Crucially, the late ninth to early eighth centuries was also a period during which Assyrian power and influence were rapidly declining. Thus, as the Assyrians benefited greatly from the revenues and resources they obtained from Tyre, it was in their own best interests to ensure that the city's economic prosperity was not undermined by demands for excessive amounts of tribute. Moreover, the Assyrians are known to have considered a tributary's specific economic circumstance when calculating the amount they owed, and so the large sums demanded from Tyre should be seen as a reflection of the city's wealth and affluence rather than as an attempt to impoverish it. The value Assyria placed on Tyre is perhaps most clearly evinced by the fact that it retained its territorial independence despite repeated rebellions (including those of Hiram II, Metenna and Luli). Even during the seventh century, when Assyrian rule was far more direct and heavy handed, Tyre continued to profit greatly from inter-regional exchange. In fact, the seventh century coincides with the zenith of the Phoenicians' commercial and colonial activity in the west. Consequently, although Assyrian hegemony may have occasionally caused or exacerbated internal tensions within the Phoenician city states, it is no longer tenable to identify it as the sole, or even primary, motivation for Phoenician overseas expansion.

Internal Factors

One of the first internal factors thought to have encouraged the Phoenicians to venture overseas was the reduction of their territory following the various catastrophes that accompanied the end of the Bronze Age. Following this tumultuous period, the territory controlled by the Phoenician city states shrank from a distance of 500 kilometres from north to south, to just over 200 kilometres. The loss of large tracts of arable land in the south was particularly disruptive as it reduced significantly the agricultural productivity of cities such as Tyre and Sidon. Agrarian output was also affected by the climatic changes which occurred in the eastern Mediterranean in around 1200. Data provided by palaeoclimatic studies and analyses of the pollen records have shown that these changes caused: a substantial reduction in annual rainfall which resulted in the region's Mediterranean-type vegetation being replaced with desert-like Saharan varieties; a serious degradation of the forests throughout Phoenicia; and a significant decline in the types and volume of crops which could be grown. As a consequence, cities such as Tyre were now forced to import huge quantities of wheat and oil in order to feed their citizens; a fact evinced by the agreement between Hiram I and the Israelite king Solomon in the early tenth century (1 Kings 5:23). According to the terms of this agreement, Hiram would receive large quantities of wheat and oil in exchange for providing Solomon with the building materials, craftsmen and architects needed to construct a grand temple for Yahweh. A decline in agricultural productivity might also account for Tyre's preoccupation with expanding its territory and influence southwards into the fertile plains of northern Israel.

While there is no indication of severe droughts during this period, the significantly lower annual rainfall meant that some regions became uninhabitable, resulting in a number of towns and villages being abandoned (particularly those located in the interior of the Bekaa Valley). As the impact of these climatic changes was less pronounced in the coastal plains, many of the displaced populations relocated to this region. Research into Early Iron Age settlement patterns has shown that between the tenth and eighth centuries there was a considerable increase in the number of villages and towns along the Phoenician coast. This dense clustering of settlements exerted considerable pressure on resources and thus for the first time overpopulation became a significant problem. It is likely that the extensive construction programme initiated by Hiram I, including extending the city and improving its systems for collecting water, resulted from a need to adapt the urban space for an increasing population. Furthermore, archaeological and palaeodemographic studies have revealed that there was a significant growth in population throughout Phoenicia during the tenth and ninth centuries.[8] Overseas expansion therefore offered the opportunity to reduce overpopulation whilst simultaneously expanding the Phoenicians' sphere of economic influence. Significantly, a number of the classical authors explicitly state that Phoenician overseas expansion was due to agricultural shortages and overpopulation (e.g. Justinus, *Epitome*, 18.3.50; Curtius Rufus, 6.4.20; Tertullian, *De anima*, 30; Sallust, *Jugurtha*, 19.1–2): however, it must be kept in mind that these issues may have been highlighted as they were known to be the primary impetuses for Greek colonisation.

Another important internal factor which served as an impetus for overseas expansion was the emergence of specialised industries during the last quarter of the tenth century. Although the various crises at the end of the thirteenth century had severely reduced the number of markets for luxury goods, by the tenth century the economic fortunes of Mesopotamia and the Levant were beginning to recover and thus demand for luxury products slowly began to increase. Keen not only to take advantage of this situation, but also to fill the commercial void left by the destruction of Ugarit, the Phoenicians began to create specialised industries focused on the production of high-quality prestige items. These items, prized for their intrinsic value and as symbols of power, status and prestige, were highly desired by the elites of neighbouring states who procured them by means of tribute, taxation, trade or reciprocal agreements. Although these specialised industries were profitable and helped to strengthen the Phoenician economies, they also relied on exotic materials and large quantities of precious metals that were not readily available in Phoenicia (in particular gold and silver). It is thus likely that many of the initial overseas ventures that occurred during the pre-colonial phase were at least partially intended to identify regions where these materials could be acquired and to establish new markets and trade routes. In addition to silver and gold, Phoenician overseas ventures were also motivated by a desire to find deposits of non-precious metals such as tin, iron and copper which were used in the manufacture of farming equipment, weapons and armour, tools and household utensils. Iron, for instance, was particularly sought after by Assyria due to its widespread use in the manufacture of weapons and military equipment, a fact attested by the Assyrian annals which meticulously document the vast quantities that had been purchased from Phoenician, Syrian and Cilician merchants. The discovery of 160 tons of iron in the ruins of the palace of Sargon II at Khorsabad offers further evidence of the metal's importance and the huge quantities in which it was being traded.

THE EASTERN MEDITERRANEAN

Anatolia

The Phoenician cultural and commercial expansion into the northern regions of the Levant and Anatolia can be securely traced as far back as the ninth century but is likely to have begun much earlier, possibly even as early as the eleventh century. The attractiveness of these regions was twofold: firstly, they contained a number of highly desirable natural resources, and, secondly, large profits could be made from trading with their indigenous populations.[9] Archaeology has shown that Cilicia, located in southern Anatolia, was one of the first regions in which the Phoenicians founded a number of small commercial settlements and trading posts. The primary appeal of Cilicia was its fir trees which were strong, supple, easily worked and devoid of resin, attributes which made them ideally suited for the construction of ships. The location of these early settlements, the Bay of Iskenderun, was chosen because it was located in close proximity to one of Cilicia's largest forests and because it was well supplied with rivers and streams that could be harnessed for transport.[10] According to Strabo (*Geography*, 14.5.3), once the logs had been felled and stripped of their branches, they would be floated seaward where they were loaded onto a merchant ship and transported to Phoenicia. This system is remarkably similar to the one utilised by the Phoenicians when harvesting cedars from Mount Lebanon. The Phoenicians also established a number of settlements in the southern foothills of the Tarsus mountain range. These mountains, which ran parallel to the Cilician coastal plains, were of particular interest due to the richness of their mineral deposits.

As they would when seeking to establish a commercial presence in more distant regions, the Phoenicians initially used commercial and political alliances in order to gain access to the commodities they desired. A possible example of one such commercial relationship can be found in the *Report of Wenamun*. In his speech to the protagonist, the king of Byblos, Zakar-Baal, refers to 50 Sidonian vessels that were in a trading association with an Anatolian man named Werket-El. Archaeology has shown that the Phoenicians supplied the Anatolian aristocracies and royal houses with prestige goods, such as gold and silver ornaments, decorated bronze utensils, carved ivory, precious and semi-precious stones, and luxury table-wares, in exchange for unprocessed bronze, iron and timber, and slaves. Significantly, all of these items are also mentioned in the Israelite prophet Ezekiel's invectives against Tyre. According to Ezekiel, the central Anatolian tribes of Cappadocia and Phrygia supplied Tyre with slaves and bronze utensils, whilst Adana and Tarsus, which were located close to the foothills of the Taurus Mountains, traded in iron ore and minerals. A number of the classical authors also suggest that the Phoenicians had longstanding, close economic and commercial relationships with the royal houses of Anatolia (e.g. Xenophon, *Anabasis* I, 4, 6, and Pseudo-Scylax, *Periplus*, 102).

The impact of the Phoenician presence in Anatolia went beyond just political and economic agreements. By the eighth century the Phoenician script had become the principal form of writing in Cilicia, both as a symbol of prestige in royal inscription (e.g. the Kilamuwa and Çineköy inscriptions) and as a lingua franca in business documents. Furthermore, it was Phoenician symbols, imagery and motifs which were widely incorporated into Anatolian artistic traditions, as is clearly evident on the Karatepe relief, rather than Hittite or Syrian as might be expected. Although in the mid-eighth century Anatolia was to lose its attractiveness as a source of iron and timber following the Syrio-Urartian alliance (which led to the kingdom of Urartu seizing control of the Anatolian trade routes and networks) and the extensive settlement of Iberia, there nevertheless continued to be regular political and commercial contact between the two regions. Significantly, the Phoenician penetration of Anatolia was not accomplished via a policy of military invasion or political subjugation but rather through political co-operation and coexistence, an approach which was to be replicated in regions throughout the Mediterranean.

Cyprus

The island of Cyprus, which lies approximately 250 kilometres to the west of modern Lebanon, was relatively easy to reach from the Levant (even in fairly primitive vessels) meaning that by the Iron Age there was already a long history of interactions between the island's indigenous inhabitants and the Phoenicians.[11] The discovery of Cypriot pottery at Sidon, Sarepta and Arqa, and small quantities of Cypriot fabrics at Tyre and Arqa, indicates that there was substantial and sustained contact between Cyprus and Phoenicia from at least the Middle Bronze Age (*c.*1700).[12] Despite these early contacts, however, it was not until the Early Iron Age that Phoenician merchants first began to visit Cyprus in large numbers. The recovery of a sizeable quantity of eleventh-century Phoenician pottery from Palaepaphos-Skales, near modern Paphos, provides the earliest evidence of these visits and reveals that Cyprus had now become a regular port-of-call for Phoenician merchants.[13] Significantly, Palaepaphos-Skales was located on the western coast of Cyprus and thus it appears to have been used as a staging post by Phoenician merchants travelling to or from western Anatolia, the Aegean and Italy.

Aside from being conveniently located for accessing the central Mediterranean, Cyprus's principal attraction for Phoenician merchants was its abundant supplies of copper. An analysis of the pottery recovered from Palaepaphos-Skales indicates that the Phoenicians traded oils, spices, perfumes and wines, all of which had important functions within Cypriot funerary rites, in order to acquire copper. Significantly, as Cyprus was heavily forested, there was no market for the Phoenician's primary export, cedar wood, perhaps explaining the sporadic nature of mercantile contact prior to the eleventh century. By the ninth century, manufactured luxury goods (such as jewellery, carved ivory, dyed cloth and bronze table vessels) had become the primary Phoenician exports to Cyprus and were being consumed in substantial quantities by the Cyprian royal houses, wealthy courtiers and important religious officials.

The Early Iron Age also witnessed the emergence of the first Phoenician settlements on Cyprus. As none of the pre-eighth-century epigraphic material, or the later Greek and Latin historical texts, provides any indication that the Phoenician cities had, or indeed sought, direct political control over any part of Cyprus, it is likely that this new influx of emigrants was the result of economic or commercial migration rather than colonialism (that is, the settlers established themselves on Cyprus as they sought to pursue business or trading opportunities that were not available to them in their homeland, rather than because they had been formally dispatched by a polity which wanted to assert its political control over the island).[14] This initial influx of settlers would therefore have been comprised of rival mercantile groups who settled on the island in order to secure, protect and expand their most important overseas markets and trade routes. The strength of this economic rivalry is perhaps attested by the emergence of two distinct commercial spheres of influence (a Tyrian one encompassing the west of the island and a Sidonian, Byblian and Arwadian one encompassing the east). Although the initial migrations to Cyprus were not the result of a deliberate colonialist policy, the Phoenicians nevertheless played an important role in the island's political and cultural affairs for the next 500 years.

One of the most important Phoenician settlements on Cyprus was Kition, located at the site of modern Larnaka. Kition was first occupied during the Early–Middle Bronze Age and is thought to have been founded by a group of indigenous prospectors seeking to exploit the copper deposits located 12 kilometres to the north of the city.[15] Excavations in the northernmost areas of Kition have shown that by the Late Bronze Age the original settlement had become an influential and powerful city that was robust and affluent enough to survive the turmoil of the thirteenth and twelfth centuries relatively unscathed. This may be in part due to the large influx of Mycenaean Greeks in the late thirteenth century, which irrevocably changed the city's culture and political outlook. This Mycenaean settlement thrived for two centuries before it was destroyed by a natural disaster, most probably a flood, and, although being quickly rebuilt, was re-abandoned less than 50 years later when the city's harbour became unusable due to heavy silting (the depositing of sedimentary materials such as sand and clay). The city remained semi-deserted until the arrival of a group of Tyrian settlers sometime during the early ninth century. One of the first priorities of these settlers was to construct an artificial harbour, or *cothon*, which could accommodate even the largest merchant vessels, and it was around this installation that the new town developed. Significantly, these settlers appear to have peacefully coexisted with the remaining indigenous and Mycenaean populations, a situation attested by the homogeneity of the material culture recovered from the city's temples and cemeteries.

Though it is impossible to identify the kind of control Tyre exercised over this settlement during its early years, by the end of the eighth century parts of western Cyprus, including Kition, appear to have been ruled by the Tyrian king, Luli. That Luli's sovereignty over Kition was unpopular is attested by the city's rebellion at the end of the eighth century, an event which is recorded in the annals of the Assyrian king Sargon II, and in a report that Josephus attributes to Menander of Ephesus. As Kition's rebellion was unsuccessful, and as neither the prism of Esarhaddon nor the cylinder of Ashurbanipal includes the king of Kition amongst the 10 independent Cypriot rulers, the city is thought to have been subject to Tyrian rule until the middle of the seventh century. Further evidence for Tyre's political control over parts of Cyprus is found on a pair of silver bowls that mention a governor named Ab/ḥiṭōb of Qartihadast (Carthage or New City) who is the servant of Hiram, king of the Sidonians (this is most likely Hiram II who ruled Tyre and Sidon from *c.*739 to *c.*730). Although the identity of Qartihadast is still debated, the most convincing hypothesis is that it equates with the Cypriot city of Amathus. Whether Ab/ḥiṭōb exercised full economic and political control over Qartihadast or kept a watchful eye on things is unclear, but what is certain is that his power was bestowed upon him by Hiram.

Significantly, aside from the stele of Sargon II, there is no evidence of an Assyrian political or military presence on the island. In fact, as soon as Assyria had assimilated the Phoenician coast into its provincial system and took control of the Levantine trading ports, the Cypriot leaders quickly and voluntarily submitted to Assyrian authority. This appears to be a pragmatic move designed to ensure that they were not cut off from the lucrative markets which were now under Assyrian control. After the fall of the Assyrian Empire in 609, Kition became increasingly autonomous as regards Tyrian control. Although the Phoenician inhabitants of the city appear to have remained, there is no evidence of direct governance by an external power until the late sixth century when the Persian king Cambyses added Egypt and Cyprus to the Persian Empire. Following Cypriot participation in the unsuccessful Ionian Revolt in 499/498–497, the Persian king Darius I (522–486) employed his Phoenician vassals to act as political intermediaries, charging them with overseeing the administration of the various Cypriot kingdoms and of ensuring their loyalty. The Phoenicians retained control of Kition until 312 when the Macedonian general, Ptolemy, seized control of the city and brought it into the Egyptian sphere of influence.

THE CENTRAL MEDITERRANEAN: GREECE AND THE AEGEAN

Rhodes

Rhodes is the most easterly of the Aegean islands and so, from at least the latter half of the second millennium, served as a gateway to the Levant for ships sailing eastwards from the Central Mediterranean.[16] Archaeological excavations at three of the oldest cities, Lindos, Ialysos (Trianda) and Kamiros, have provided evidence for commercial contact with Cyprus and the Levant that stretched back as far as the sixteenth century.[17] However, during the twelfth century Rhodian ties with the eastern Mediterranean appear to have been severed and were not re-established until the early decades of the tenth century.[18] The renewal of these ties is evinced by the discovery of large quantities of tenth-century Cypro-Geometric pottery at sites across Rhodes. By the middle of the eighth century, finds of Phoenician luxury items (including ivories, *tridacna* shells, and gold and silver jewellery) indicate that trade between Rhodes and the eastern Mediterranean was flourishing. During the succeeding centuries, the volume of trade flowing between Rhodes and Tyre was so great that the Israelite prophet Ezekiel (27:15) included the former in his list of the latter's most important commercial partners. Rhodian workshops also served as regional production centres for Levantine goods and thus, from 725 onwards, they can be identified manufacturing and exporting Cypro-Phoenician wares such as faience scarabs, anthropomorphic unguent vessels and incised vases decorated with Levantine motifs. Contact with Phoenicia is also attested by the votive objects found in temple warehouses and in cemeteries, especially those at Ialysos and Lindos.[19] That there was a small, permanent Phoenician community on Rhodes is indicated by the presence of infant burials in Phoenician 'torpedo jars' at the cemeteries of Kamiros and Ialysos, one of which was inscribed with three Phoenician letters. Although the Greek historiographers attribute the founding of several archaic settlements to the Phoenician hero Cadmus, there is no evidence of large-scale Phoenician settlements or enclaves on Rhodes prior to the Hellenistic period. During the third and second centuries, Rhodes significantly expanded its Levantine trade networks, thereby encouraging an influx of Phoenician settlers (a situation that is highlighted in a series of bilingual inscriptions which document the progressive assimilation of these newly arrived expatriates into the indigenous population).

Crete and Cythera

Crete, the largest island in the Aegean Sea and its natural southern boundary, was a vital stopping point for ships travelling between the eastern and western Mediterranean.[20] The importance of this role has been highlighted by the discovery of a large Phoenician-style rock-cut *cothon* at Phalasarna (Crete's most western port town) which served as the departure point for ships sailing north to Cythera and the south-eastern Peloponnese, or west across the open ocean to Malta or Sicily. Both the archaeological and the literary evidence show that, from the Middle Bronze Age onwards, Crete maintained close commercial links with a number of Levantine cities and states. Although these links appear to have been severed for a short period during the Late Bronze Age, they had been re-established by the end of the tenth century, and so, by the middle of the ninth century, Crete had once again become a crucial transit point for Phoenician merchants (a situation envisaged by Homer when describing the protagonist's journey from Crete to Ithaca aboard a Phoenician vessel in book 13 of the *Odyssey*). In addition to being located at the centre of one of the most important east–west trade routes, Crete was also an attractive destination due to its deposits of phosphorus-bearing iron ore. Crete's participation in the international trade in iron is clearly attested at Kommos, where a large iron-working centre and a considerable quantity of imported eastern pottery have been uncovered, and in the name Cape Sideros ('Iron Cape') which was assigned to the island's north eastern promontory.[21] To the south of Sideros lay the port of Itanos, a supposedly Phoenician settlement which coin deposits suggest had a close commercial connection with Arwad.

Lying just to the north-west of Crete is the island of Cythera which was also blessed with rich deposits of iron. The most easterly harbour on Cythera, which would have been the first landfall merchants encountered when sailing directly across the open ocean from Cyprus or the Levant, was known in antiquity as *Phoinikous*, perhaps alluding to the island's close association with Phoenician merchants (Xenophon, *Hellenica*, 4.8.7). Neither Crete nor Cythera appears to have been settled by the Phoenicians, although small enclaves of Phoenician merchants and craftsmen were established in some of the islands' coastal towns and cities. For example, an eighth-century tholos tomb discovered at the Cretan city of Tekke was found to contain the grave of a Levantine silversmith who appears to have been living and working in the town. Excavations at Fortetsa have also unearthed evidence of an eighth-century Phoenician unguent factory which was selling its perfumes in locally produced, imitation Cypro-Phoenician-style *aryballoi*. Despite never establishing large settlements on either island, the Phoenicians' cultural and commercial influence on Crete and Cythera was still considerable.

Athens

Although the Phoenicians first reached the Greek mainland in the Late Bronze Age, archaeology has shown that it is not until the mid- to late sixth century that a sizeable Phoenician enclave was established in

Athens. In fact, the city has yielded remarkably few eastern imports prior to the Archaic Period (even the Egyptianising faience trinkets which are found in large quantities at other sites around the Greek mainland are conspicuously absent from the material record of Athens). This must have been in part due to the relatively small size of Athens which made other, larger Greek cities, such as Argos and Corinth, more attractive commercial partners. The sudden increase in imported Phoenician and Levantine luxury goods at the end of the sixth century, as revealed by the excavations conducted at the Kerameikos and in Eleusis, as well as the appearance of grave markers adorned with Phoenician inscriptions, both suggest there was an increased Phoenician presence in Athens at this point. This early Phoenician enclave appears to have been concentrated at Phaleron, a small sheltered bay which served as Athens's main harbour until the construction of the Piraeus at the beginning of the fifth century (interestingly, despite the diminishing importance of Phaleron, this early Phoenician community does not appear to have relocated its homes or businesses to the Piraeus).

Although a small number of Phoenicians had settled in Athens following the cessation of hostilities at the end of the Persian Wars, it was during the fourth century that this community rapidly grew in size and significance; a situation that is reflected in the increased number of Greek-Phoenician bilingual funerary stelai and the widespread worship of Phoenician deities in and around the Piraeus (e.g. Aphrodite Ourania ('Ashtart), Ba'al [possibly Bel?], and Nergal).[22] A late fourth/early third-century bilingual epigram (*IG II*[2] 8388), in which the name of the deceased differs between the Phoenician and Greek texts (Shem/Antipatros) and in which the individual who has commissioned it, Domseleh, transliterates his Phoenician name and patronymic into Greek, provides evidence that at least some Phoenician emigrants resided in Athens long enough to become fully naturalised. By *c.*350, the number of Phoenician expatriates living in Athens had increased so much that Xenophon could plausibly represent them as a distinct multilingual and acculturated community (*Ways and Means*, 2.3–6). A situation which is also attested in the Athenian decrees honouring a group of Sidonian merchants in 367 (*IG* II–III[2] 141) and a group of Kition merchants in 333 (*IG* II–III[2] 337). This community included simple brokers like Pythodōros who was active in Athens in around 394 (Isocrates, 17.4), great money-lenders such as Therodōros (Demosthenes, 34.6), and renowned personalities like Zeno of Kition who founded the Stoic school of philosophy in 301 (Diogenes Laertius, *Xeno*, 16; 38).

Aegina, Argos and Corinth

The recovery of substantial quantities of Levantine goods and commodities from Aegina, Argos and Corinth indicate that these cities must also have been integrated into the Phoenicians' central Mediterranean trade network. For instance, from at least as early as the seventh century, Aegina, the ceramic traditions of which attest to a long and sustained exposure to Eastern culture, appears to have functioned as a receiving and redistribution centre for Levantine commodities entering mainland Greece. Although undocumented in the archaeological record, Herodotus (*Histories*, 1.1.1) suggests that the city of Argos also had a long history of contact with the Phoenicians. Recalling events that had occurred long before the Persian Wars, Herodotus claims that Argos's pre-eminence amongst the Greek cities meant that it was an attractive destination for Phoenician merchants (especially those dealing in Egyptian and Assyrian commodities). Excavations at Corinth, which unearthed large quantities of Phoenician amphorae and luxury items (such as jewellery and metalwork), indicate that the city was also regularly visited by Phoenician traders.

Corinth was a particularly attractive destination for Eastern merchants as it was located on the isthmus connecting the Peloponnese with the rest of mainland Greece. The city's two harbours (Kenchreai on the Saronic Gulf and Lechaion on the Corinthian Gulf), both of which housed vibrant markets, enabled it to function as a nexus between East and West. Corinth further enhanced its commercial attractiveness by constructing the Diolkos, a large canal connecting the Saronic and Corinthian gulfs which provided sailors with an alternative to navigating the treacherous seas located off the southern tip of the Peloponnese. Thucydides and Strabo provide a general picture of Corinth as a cosmopolitan city bustling with commerce and industry. Although neither author comments on the precise ethnic mix of the city's inhabitants, the archaeological evidence indicates that it housed a Phoenician community of similar size and composition to the one that was established in Athens during the sixth century. Further indications of a significant Phoenician presence in Corinth include: a hill which was known as *Phoinikon*; a temple dedicated to Athena Phoenice (who seems to have been worshipped by a guild of craftsmen specialising in the use of Phoenician dyeing techniques); and a local folktale recounting the bewitching of a young man by a Phoenician woman (Phillostratus, *Life of Apollonius of Tyana*, 4.24). Both the archaeological and literary evidence indicate that the Phoenician artisans and merchants who established communities in Aegina, Argos and Corinth did so in order to take advantage of the unique commercial opportunities offered by each city.

The Southern and Northern Aegean

The southern Aegean is dominated by the Cyclades, a group of islands situated between Turkey to the east and Greece to the west. The Cyclades comprise more than 200 small islands with the largest and most important being Naxos, Melos, Paros, Thera, Mykonos and Delos. Due to their isolation from the Greek mainland, the inhabitants of the Cyclades developed their own distinctive culture, retained a fierce sense of independence and were reliant on inter-regional trade to meet the subsistence needs of their populations. As many of the islands contained rich deposits of obsidian (volcanic glass), lead, copper and marble, they had little difficulty in attracting the attention of Eastern merchants.

According to classical traditions, the Phoenicians first arrived in the Cyclades during the Middle Bronze Age, whereupon they immediately began founding settlements on a number of the larger islands (including Melos, Naxos and Paros). However, these accounts are contested by the archaeological evidence which shows that the Phoenicians were not regular visitors to the Cyclades until the eighth century. Even Delos, a hub of Phoenician economic activity during the fourth to second centuries, did not maintain extensive cultural or commercial links with the Phoenicians prior to the late fifth century. In fact, the first incontrovertible evidence of Phoenician activity on Delos is an inscription dating to *c*.365 recording the gifts and envoys that had been sent to the island's Pan-Hellenic sanctuary by the Sidonian king Abd'ashtart I. The archaeological evidence therefore reveals that the Cyclades were not regularly visited by the Phoenicians until the Middle to Late Iron Age and, even then, these visitors did not deem it necessary to found a major colony or settlement in order to better exploit the commercial opportunities on offer.

Significantly, the same observations can also be drawn with regard to the Phoenicians' infiltration of the northern Aegean. For instance, both the archaeological and literary evidence (e.g. Homer, *Iliad*, 741–5) indicate that the Phoenicians first began to establish trade networks in the northern Aegean during the eighth century: however, although enticed to the region by its abundance of rich mineral deposits, they once again made no effort to establish any permanent settlements or colonies. Thus contrary to Herodotus's assertion that it was the Phoenicians who were responsible for opening the Ainyra and Koinyra mines on Thasos (*Histories*, 6.47), archaeology has now shown that these installations were actually established and governed by the indigenous population, as were the numerous mines and processing facilities discovered at the base of Mount Pangaeum and along the banks of the River Strymon on the Thracian mainland. Therefore, unlike their counterparts in Iberia, who deemed it necessary to establish a variety of commercial enclaves and settlements in order to fully exploit its natural wealth, the Phoenician merchants operating in the southern and northern Aegean relied on trade agreements to acquire the resources they desired.

THE CENTRAL MEDITERRANEAN: THE TYRRHENIN BASIN, MALTA AND GOZO

Sicily

Due to its position at the centre of the Mediterranean, Sicily was a vital port-of-call for ships traversing between the eastern and western Mediterranean, and between Southern Europe and North Africa, and so had immense strategic value. Although the island maintained particularly close links with Cyprus during the Middle and Late Bronze Age, thus highlighting its pivotal role in the interrelationships between East and West, it had no sustained contact with Phoenicia prior to the end of the ninth century (a time when the Phoenicians began establishing new markets and trade routes throughout North Africa and Italy).[23] This initial contact was sporadic, however, and so the earliest permanent Phoenician settlements on Sicily, all of which are located in the north-western regions of the island, were not founded until the eighth century. Thucydides (6.2.6) provides a brief but informative description of the Phoenicians' arrival on the island. According to his account, the Phoenicians, keen to foster commercial interactions with the indigenous populations, established a series of small *emporia* and trading posts all around the Sicilian coast (typically locating them on promontories or offshore islets). Although these settlements initially flourished, the arrival of the Greeks during the last quarter of the eighth century led many to be abandoned as the Phoenicians withdrew to the north-western regions of the island. If Thucydides is to be believed, and there is little reason to question the veracity of his account, the Phoenicians voluntarily evacuated their eastern settlements so they could invest all of their time, energy and resources into strengthening Motya, Panormo and Solunto. These three settlements were the most strategically and commercially valuable to the Phoenicians as they were: best positioned to profit from the trade with Carthage and North Africa; the closest points of departure for vessels sailing to or from the mineral-rich regions of southern Sardinia; and could trade with Campania and Etruria without having to sail through the Greek-controlled Straits of Messina.

Though little is known about Panormo and Solunto, the settlement at Motya, which was inhabited continuously from the end of the eighth to the fourth centuries, has been extensively excavated, thus enabling archaeologists to create a detailed picture of its history. Motya was situated on a small island (roughly 45 hectares in size) which lay at the centre of a large lagoon located just to the north of Lilybaum (modern Marsala).[24] Scholars have tentatively identified three distinct stages in the city's development: firstly, its founding at the end of the eighth century; secondly, a period of growth and transformation occurring in the latter half of the seventh century; and, thirdly, the emergence of urbanisation during the mid- to late sixth century. Initially, Motya appears to have been a moderately sized, unwalled trading post comprising a market, small natural harbour and a handful of houses; however, following a population boom during the middle decades of the seventh century, the original settlement was substantially enlarged. This period of rapid urban growth and development was marked by significant improvements to the main harbour, the creation of several new *emporia* and *agorae*, the renovation and extension of the main market, and the emergence of specialised industries (as attested by the construction of numerous warehouses and industrial complexes). This period of growth also witnessed the monumentalising of the so-called 'Cappiddazzu' shrine (an originally modest-sized temple that is thought to have been dedicated to Ba'al Hammon), and the reorganising and enlarging of the city's *tophet*.[25] It was upon the completion of a second programme of large-scale public works in the latter half of the sixth century that Motya first emerged as a true urban centre (these works included: the erection of monumental defensive walls; the enlarging and embellishing of the *temnos* of the Cappiddazzu shrine; the excavation of a new harbour near the southern tip of the island; and the construction of a large causeway linking Motya to the Sicilian mainland).

In contrast to the Greeks, who colonised Sicily in order to gain direct control of its agricultural land and resources, the Phoenicians settled on the island because its location allowed them to dominate the newly established markets and trade routes in North Africa, Italy and Iberia. By adopting a commercial, rather than colonial, strategy when dealing with their indigenous neighbours, the Phoenicians were able to acquire the agricultural resources needed by their settlements without having to seize control of large swathes of territory. Moreover, by establishing symbiotic relationships that were based on peaceful coexistence and trade, rather than on power and dominance, the Phoenicians successfully encouraged cultural tolerance, exchange and assimilation (a situation evinced by the blending of funerary rites and traditions, the prevalence of cross-cultural marriages, and the merging of artistic styles and traditions).

Sardinia

Phoenician interest in Sardinia appears to have been twofold: firstly, because it was rich in copper, bronze and silver-bearing lead ores, and, secondly, because of the island's close proximity to Carthage and the North African trade routes. Though Phoenician and Cypriot merchants first arrived on Sardinia in the Late Bronze Age, they did not become regular visitors to the island until the end of the twelfth century (as attested by the discovery of Cypriot-style bronze tripods, copper ingots adorned with Cypriot markings and the sudden adoption of the lost wax casting technique by local metalworkers). Having instigated more consistent contact, the Phoenicians found that they were able to increase their economic and political influence over the indigenous populations: a situation evinced by the Nora Stone, a monumental inscribed stele recovered from the south-western coastal site of Nora and which has been dated to around 850–825 (*TSSI* no. 25). Although there is currently no scholarly consensus regarding

191

its interpretation (suggestions include a military decree, political propaganda, war memorial, legal document or interstate alliance), the Nora stele is nevertheless evidence of the Phoenicians' expansion westwards and of their political and military interactions with the indigenous populations.

The Phoenicians maintained regular, albeit temporary, contact with Sardinia until the eighth century, at which point they established a number of small ports and market towns at regular intervals along the island's south-western coast. There appears to have been a commercial impetus for the founding of these early settlements as they were carefully positioned so as to help facilitate trade between Iberia, North Africa, Tyrrhenian Italy, Sardinia and the cities of mainland Phoenicia. However, many also appear to have been positioned according to a territorial strategy which sought to ensure that each settlement had access to a hinterland that was rich in agricultural or mineral resources (thus justifying the use of the term colony when discussing these settlements). Sulcis (*Slky*), one of the earliest colonies, was founded on an islet close to the cape of Sant' Antioco in the Gulf of Palmas. The city's position enabled it to exploit and profit from the mineral wealth of Iglesiente, a mountainous region lying just to the north on the Sardinian mainland. The city therefore became an important market for silver and lead, a situation attested by its two large commercial ports, both of which could provide safe anchorage to any type or size of merchant vessel, and by the extensive network of fortifications constructed during the seventh century. These fortifications, which marked out a vast defensive belt behind the colony, were positioned so as to ensure that the city was able to retain direct control over its mineral-rich hinterland. Sulcis's relationship with the territory under its control demonstrates that the founding of Phoenician settlements on Sardinia was a genuinely strategic venture aimed at securing and then defending a sizeable inland territory which encompassed both arable agricultural land and mineral deposits.

In addition to Sulcis, four other important Phoenician colonies were founded during the eighth century: Tharros, Cagliari (of which we know very little prior to the Roman Period), Nora and Bitia (Bithia). Tharros, situated on the isthmus of Capre San Marco in the Gulf of Oristano, was, like Sulcis, founded on a narrow promontory, served by multiple harbours, and had access to an agriculturally rich hinterland. The original colony started out as a modest trading post and appears to have been built on the remains of several abandoned indigenous villages. Although Tharros quickly assumed control of the agricultural land at its periphery, there is no evidence that it ever exercised sovereign control over a large hinterland during the eighth and seventh centuries. Nevertheless, archaeology shows that by the sixth century the city had become a flourishing urban centre which, due to its excellent harbour facilities and large market, attracted merchants from across the Mediterranean. In antiquity, Tharros was famed for its production of luxury gold items that were highly desired by Etruscan and Latin aristocratic customers on mainland Italy. It was also a regional production and distribution centre for a range of other commodities including: stone funerary reliefs and sculptures; terracotta wares; metal objects and implements; and faience jewellery.

The city of Nora, founded at Capo di Pula on an isthmus extending out into the Gulf of Cagliari, appears to have been founded in the mid- to late eighth century. The city remained unfortified and without a large temple until the late sixth or early fifth century, suggesting that it did not pursue a policy of rapid expansion into its hinterland. In fact, there is little evidence to suggest that Nora ever attempted to dominate and control its hinterland to the same extent as Bitia, Sulcis or Tharros. Bitia, constructed on the promontory of Torre di Chia at the end of the eighth century, was situated at the mouth of the River Chia and thus positioned so as to be able to take advantage of two inlets that were ideal natural harbours. The site was first occupied during the initial Phoenician drive to establish a series of landing stations and markets along Sardinia's south-western coastline. The city's position on Sardinia's southernmost tip meant that Bitia was able to integrate itself quickly into the most important east–west trade routes; this in turn led to a period of rapid and sustained growth throughout the seventh and sixth centuries. In fact, aside from at Nora, the seventh and sixth centuries marked a period of territorial consolidation during which many of the Phoenician colonies on Sardinia tightened their control over their hinterlands whilst simultaneously undertaking a programme of urban and civic development. These centuries also witnessed the founding of a number of new commercial or defensive settlements at major river arteries, both on the coast (e.g. Bosa and Villaputzu) and further inland (e.g. Othoca, Pani Lriga and Monte Sirai).

Though the Phoenician colonists on Sardinia clearly sought to gain sovereign control over large swathes of territory, they nevertheless interacted peacefully with the indigenous peoples via a process of aggregation and integration. This was a policy that was intended to ensure that, as far as possible, a state of harmonious coexistence was maintained between the two populations. Significantly, the regularity of intermarriages between the two groups and the syncretising of funerary rites and rituals (both of which are clearly attested in the composite funerary assemblages recovered from the *tophets* and necropoleis of Sulci, and in the shared burial sites at San Giorgio) indicate that this policy was relatively successful.[26] While research into the transformation of indigenous politico-territorial and economic organisation following the influx of Phoenician emigrants is still in its infancy, what is clear is that by the last few decades of the seventh century the Phoenician emigrants were not just peacefully coexisting with the autochthonous population but had in fact started to form composite communities. Thus, despite seeking to control the hinterlands around their settlements, the Phoenician colonisation of Sardinia was not accomplished via a policy of military invasion or harsh political subjugation but rather through peaceful co-operation and coexistence.

Italy

The discovery of Levantine commodities in the Late Bronze Age strata at Frattesina da Fratta Polesine in northern Italy and at Torre Galli in southern Italy, reveal that the Phoenicians first began trading with these settlements in around 1200. However, despite initiating sporadic commercial contact during the Late Bronze Age, archaeology has shown that Phoenician merchants did not begin regularly visiting Italy until the end of the ninth century, and it was not until the end of the eighth or start of the seventh century that these visits became annualised.[27] The large quantities of Phoenician manufactured goods recovered from eighth- and seventh-century cemeteries and cremation sites throughout Italy and Etruria, demonstrate that this contact was not only sustained but also widespread. This resulted in the strengthening of commercial and cultural ties and led to the indigenous population adopting a number of specifically Levantine customs, in particular a number of Eastern religious rites and rituals, and to the orientalising of local artistic traditions.

Although it was the desire to gain access to the Etruscan heartland with its ore-rich deposits of copper, lead, iron and silver which provided the initial impetus for the Phoenician presence in Italy; it was the highly profitable commercial opportunities created as a result of the social and economic changes that swept through the region during the Early and Middle Iron Age which were to sustain their interest.[28] The Phoenicians found Italy to be a land of opportunity on four counts: firstly, there was a substantial indigenous demand for Eastern commodities and prestige goods throughout the Iron Age; secondly, a number of the most important Mediterranean and Central European trade networks converged at the Italian peninsular, meaning that it became an important transit point through which the majority of trade between North Africa, Western and Central Europe, and the Levant flowed; thirdly, there was an abundance of agricultural and mineral resources which could be acquired easily and at a reasonable price; and, finally, the considerable wealth owned by the indigenous populations meant there were ample opportunities for entrepreneurial Phoenician artisans and craftsmen.

Malta and Gozo

Unlike Sicily and Sardinia, the Maltese archipelago (comprising the islands of Malta and Gozo) possessed little in the way of natural resources, either in terms of arable land or mineral deposits, and thus, as Diodorus clearly recognised (5:12.3–4), its importance was due to its position at the heart of the Mediterranean.[29] Blessed with an abundance of natural harbours, and situated midway between two of the most important Phoenician trade routes (one to the north along the southern coast of Sicily and the other to the south along the top of North Africa), the islands were of considerable strategic importance to the Phoenicians, especially following the loss of eastern Sicily in the seventh century. The Phoenicians first made contact with the Maltese archipelago at the end of the eleventh century and quickly established commercial relations with the indigenous populations. Although initially sporadic, the frequency and scale of these interactions increased during the tenth and ninth centuries, leading to the founding of the first permanent settlement in around the middle of the eighth century. By the end of the eighth century, the Phoenicians had spread throughout Malta and Gozo, settling at coastal sites or in locations that were easily defended. There appear to have been two main Phoenician enclaves on Gozo; one in the highlands close to modern Victoria and the other in the bay of Mgarr. Both enclaves were modest in size and were deliberately founded in close proximity to a larger, pre-existing indigenous settlement.

Malta also accommodated two main groups of Phoenician expatriates; one located in the northern hill city of Rabat-Mdina and the other in a large bay close to modern Marsaxlokk. In part, this must have been due to the initial decision to establish settlements in a region that was already densely populated by an indigenous people who were culturally and politically developed. Due to its position and profusion of safe natural anchorages, the region around Marsaxlokk, located on Malta's south-eastern coast, functioned as the island's commercial hub: a situation that is evinced both by the high number of emigrant and indigenous settlements, and by the presence of two large Phoenician sanctuaries, one consecrated to Melqart and the other to 'Ashtart. The temple of 'Ashtart, located at Tas-Silġ, provides an unrivalled insight into the relationship between the Phoenician settlers and the indigenous communities around Marsaxlokk. Although largely abandoned prior to the Phoenicians' arrival, the hill on which the temple was constructed nevertheless still housed an ancient cultic installation that held significance for the ingenious people. Accordingly, rather than completely levelling the site when re-consecrating it to 'Ashtart in the seventh century, the Phoenicians carefully incorporated the upstanding remains of the earlier sanctuary into their new temple. This sympathetic approach to indigenous spiritual beliefs and practices not only led to the shared use of the site, it also resulted in the gradual amalgamation of religious rites and rituals (a process which is attested by 'Ashtart's appropriation of some of the more chthonic features of her local counterpart).

That the two communities coexisted peacefully is also apparent from the blending of pottery types and the emergence of a new artistic style that drew inspiration from both native and emigrant traditions.[30] Despite a willingness to embrace indigenous customs, the Phoenicians who settled on the Maltese archipelago appear to have been remarkably resistant to the cultural sway of Carthage, Iberia and even the Levant (for instance, Phoenician architectural styles on Malta tend to retain an archaic vestige up until the fourth century). This conservatism was perhaps due to the isolated open-sea location of the Maltese archipelago and to its diminishing commercial importance during the sixth and fifth centuries. Though the Phoenician settlements on Malta and Gozo had initially played an important role in facilitating trade with the interior of Africa, by the middle of the fifth century they had been eclipsed by Carthage. The absence of any notable Carthaginian presence on either island reveals just how much of an irrelevance they had become to the principal Mediterranean trade circuits.

THE WESTERN MEDITERRANEAN: NORTH AFRICA

Although the Phoenicians founded a large number of settlements along the coastlines of present-day Libya, Tunisia, Morocco and Algeria, less is known about the migration to North Africa than for almost any other region of the Phoenician diaspora, an observation which holds particularly true for the western Maghreb (Algeria and Morocco).[31] With no Phoenician account of the migration, and with the majority of sites remaining partially or completely unexcavated, scholars are reliant on classical sources when reconstructing the settlement of North Africa. As the views presented are often one-sided and highly distorted due to the fierce competition between the Phoenicians and their Greek and Roman neighbours (particularly in places such as Spain, Italy, North Africa and Sicily), relying on these sources is far from ideal. Many of the Latin sources, for instance, demonstrate an almost instinctive hostility towards the Phoenicians as a result of the devastating and costly wars fought by Rome and Carthage during the latter half of the first millennium. Despite their biases and prejudices, the classical texts, as long as they are used cautiously and in conjunction with the available archaeological evidence, can still be of use when trying to reconstruct the motivations and timing of the Phoenician settlement of North Africa.

Libya
The city of Lepcis was founded close to the Lebda Wadi on a stretch of coastal land that was located between the Gulf of Syrtis to the west and the desert of Sytica to the east. The earliest traces of occupation at Lepcis date to the second half of the seventh century, a time when Carthage was already exerting commercial and political control over the region (which perhaps explains the confusion regarding the ethnic origins of the original settlers: Sallust = Sidonian; Pliny = Tyrian; Silius

Italicus and Pseudo-Scylax = Carthaginian). The earliest settlement is widely considered to have been a small port-of-call which provided safe anchorage for vessels traversing the North African coastline; however, its close proximity to a number of overland trade routes also enabled it to become the primary market for goods originating from the interior of the African continent. The importance and profitability of this commerce is clearly attested in the earliest remains at Lepcis which include extensive harbour facilities, a substantial *emporium* and a number of large warehouses. Like Lepcis, Oea and Sabratha were also founded as small ports-of-call which could provide safe anchorage to vessels traversing the coast of North Africa. The earliest occupation level at Oea dates to around the middle of the fifth century; however, as the site has only been partially excavated it is possible that the remains of an earlier settlement might still be discovered. The grave goods and funerary architecture found in the settlement's necropolis show that by the mid-third century the inhabitants of Oea were heavily influenced by Punic culture and religion, although whether the original settlers were Phoenician or Carthaginian remains to be determined. Sabratha, located about 65 kilometres to the west of Oea, is thought to have been founded in the early to mid-sixth century. The diminutive size of its harbour belies the fact that, due to an absence of natural anchorages along the stretch of coast on which it was founded, Oea was a vital stopping point for mariners. Like Lepcis, the earliest settlement included both a sizeable emporium and a number of modest-sized warehouses, thus indicating its commercial significance.

Tunisia
The city of Carthage, which is often referred to as the Phoenician colony *par excellence*, was founded on a pronounced headland overlooking the Gulf of Utica in present-day Tunisia. Recent radiocarbon dates acquired from the site's earliest occupation levels suggest that the initial settlement was founded sometime between 835 and 800. As it was founded on a hill, next to a large lagoon, and in close proximity to the coast, the settlement was ideally positioned to control the shipping routes which passed through the straits separating North Africa and Sicily. Unlike many of the other Phoenician trading posts and ports-of-call established in North Africa, Carthage was also blessed with an agricultural hinterland that was both extensive and

fertile, meaning that it could sustain a large population (although it must be noted that this hinterland was not systematically exploited prior to the sixth century).

The early settlement was constructed using methods and techniques that were commonly found in the ancient Near East (e.g. 'pier-and-rubble' walls), and adhered to a 'Hippodamic', or axial, grid plan. As with the cities of the Phoenician mainland, Carthage was divided into two distinct districts: an 'upper city' which would eventually accommodate a citadel, palace, temples, administrative buildings and the residences of the aristocracy, and a 'lower city' which housed the commercial and industrial zones, and the residential districts occupied by the less affluent. During the eighth to seventh centuries, Carthage's industrial zone, which lay on the city's outskirts, comprised workshops, large furnaces for metal working, industrial-sized kilns and factories devoted to the extraction of purple dye from murex.[32] The city's burial grounds, located just beyond the industrial zone, extended over an area of about 1,350 metres by 700 metres and formed a semi-arch that enclosed the northern half of the settlement. The discovery and excavation of these necropoleis have provided invaluable insights into the socio-economic and ethnic makeup of Carthage's early population. Contrary to expectation, the necropoleis of Carthage did not demonstrate homogeneity in funerary rites and customs: instead, they revealed a great diversity in tomb types, grave goods and methods for disposing of human remains. This indicates that Carthage's population was socially and ethnically diverse and likely included a significant number of indigenous peoples.

In the first 100 years of its history, Carthage differed little from any of the other Phoenician settlements in North Africa: however, by the end of the eighth century the city had emerged as an economic and political powerhouse. Four primary factors best account for the city's rise to prominence: firstly, its ability to control the central Mediterranean trade routes; secondly, its introduction of new and innovative political and civic institutions that other settlements would be slow to adopt; thirdly, its unique social make-up which encouraged a rapid transition to urban and state institutions; and, finally, it had been founded according to a different set of political and commercial objectives (i.e. it was always intended that Carthage would become a large urban centre capable of curtailing Greek commercial advances in the west). Carthage's emergence as a true political and military heavyweight is traditionally thought to have occurred in the mid-sixth century, when, under the auspices of the general Mago and his descendants (the Magonids), the city became a thalassocracy, assumed control over Sardinia and large parts of Sicily, and established several colonies along the coast of present-day Morocco.

Next to Carthage, both geographically and in terms of power and prestige, was the city of Utica. Founded in the mid-seventh century, the city was built on a small islet at the mouth of the Bagradas River, a position which allowed it to control the river's fertile alluvial plains that lay just to the south. Although the settlement now lies some 12 kilometres inland, modern geological surveys have shown that at the time of its foundation its northern section would have been directly adjacent to the coast. It is thought that the original Semitic name for the city, 'Utiq (meaning 'transit place'), was an allusion to the fact that the settlement had functioned as an *emporium* and way-station for ships travelling between the eastern and western Mediterranean. It is thus likely that the original settlement consisted of little more than a seasonal anchorage site and a temporary market. Significantly, neither of these facilities would have left much of a trace in the archaeological record which perhaps explains why so few vestiges of the early settlement have thus far been found. In fact, the only evidence pertaining to the original Phoenician settlement comes from two necropoleis – Ile (in use between the seventh and sixth centuries) and La Berge (in use between the seventh and fifth centuries). As the earliest burials in both necropoleis were closer in form and style to those of mainland Phoenicia rather than Carthage, scholars have concluded that the original settlers must have been Phoenician rather than Punic. The grandiose style of Utica's architecture and the lavishness of the grave goods (many of which were imported from disparate regions of the Mediterranean) are indicative of a highly wealthy society which had profited greatly from maritime trade. Despite its close ties with Carthage, Utica appears to have retained its political independence until the fourth century, a fact reflecting the power and prestige the city obtained through being positioned at the heart of a number of lucrative trade routes.

As Phoenician settlers in other regions (e.g. Iberia, Sardinia and Sicily) were highly tolerant of indigenous infiltration into the nuclei of their settlements, it was expected that the same would be true of those in Libya and Tunisia. However, contrary to expectations, an analysis of burial customs, religious rites and material culture has shown that, aside from in Carthage, there was little, if any, assimilation of either the indigenous populations or their culture. Significantly, the indigenous peoples also appear to have been remarkably resistant to the cultural sway of both the Phoenicians and the Carthaginians. The almost complete lack of evidence for social or cultural interactions between the two groups has been widely interpreted as the result of Phoenician disinterest in the agricultural hinterlands adjacent to their settlements. However, recent research has shown that the Phoenician settlers took a far greater interest in agricultural matters than was previously thought; consequently, the lack of cultural assimilation and infiltration cannot simply be attributed to lack of contact between the two groups but instead should be seen as the result of indigenous indifference towards Phoenician customs, traditions and material culture.

The Western Maghreb (Algeria and Morocco)
According to Strabo (*Geography*, 17.3.8), there were no fewer than 300 Phoenician colonies founded in the western Maghreb (all of which were apparently razed to the ground by the indigenous populations). Though this figure is thought to be highly exaggerated, even by many of Strabo's peers, it is clear that the Phoenicians did establish a significant presence in North-West Africa. Despite this high concentration of Phoenician settlements, however, Morocco and Algeria have received considerably less scholarly attention than the rest of North Africa.[33] This is partly due to the lack of coverage given to the region in the classical sources and partly due to a lack of archaeological investigation. Furthermore, even though archaeologists have identified a number of small settlements which are thought to have been Phoenician trading-posts or *emporia*, it is often impossible to determine whether a site is truly a Phoenician foundation or an indigenous settlement that had imported Phoenician goods. The two most important Phoenician settlements in the western Maghreb were Lixus and Mogador, both of which are situated in present-day Morocco.

According to the classical authors, Lixus was one of the first Phoenician settlements in the far West and was founded just after the Trojan War: however, this claim is not substantiated by the archaeological evidence which indicates that the settlement was established at some point during the first half of the eighth century. The original settlement was sited in a highly advantageous location which was: one of the few natural anchorages along the inhospitable Moroccan coastline; surrounded by an abundance of rich, highly fertile agricultural land; adjacent to the mouth of the River Loukkas, a large navigable river which provided good transport and communication links with the Moroccan interior from where the settlers could acquire gold and ivory; and in close proximity to the extensive mineral deposits of the Atlas Mountains. Consequently, Lixus quickly became an important commercial centre which prospered throughout the eighth and seventh centuries. The volume and types of pottery assemblages discovered at Lixus reveal that by the end of the eighth century the city had already established close and sustained commercial contact with a number of the Phoenician settlements in Iberia.

Lixus also functioned as an important waypoint for merchants travelling south to Mogador, a small, temporary trading post used by Phoenician merchants seeking to trade with the inhabitants of Morocco's interior. Mogador was founded on an island lying just off the Moroccan coast and appears to have been periodically inhabited between the seventh century and the mid-sixth century. The lack of permanent dwellings, defensive fortifications or cultic centres suggests that the site was only occupied during the annual trading season; thereafter it would be abandoned until the following year. It is thus likely that the temporary inhabitants of Mogador lived in lightweight huts or tents, as was the case with the Phoenician merchants who visited the Island of Cerne (Pseudo-Scylax, *Periplus*, 112). From the limited evidence pertaining to the Phoenician presence in the western Maghreb, it is possible to identify that the penetration of the region was not accomplished by force or power but rather by peaceful co-operation and coexistence, this approach, when combined with a willingness to allow elements of the indigenous peoples to assimilate into the new settlements, enabled the Phoenician settlements to prosper and flourish.

THE WESTERN MEDITERRANEAN: IBERIA

The Iberian Peninsula (the ancient name given to the region encompassing present-day Spain and Portugal) represents the westernmost point in the Phoenician migration across the Mediterranean.[34] Significantly, southern Iberia is also the region of the western Mediterranean for which the earliest period of Phoenician colonisation is best understood. Extensive excavations along the Mediterranean coast of Andalucia, in the bay of Cádiz and along the coast of Portugal have provided a substantial amount of archaeological data. The number of early Phoenician settlements in this region far exceeds that of any other in the central and western Mediterranean. For instance, 10 large Phoenician settlements have thus far been discovered in the region to the east of the Straits of Gibraltar. These include: Cádiz (Gadir), Cerro del Villar (Mainake), Málaga (Malaka), Toscanos, Morro de Mezquitilla, Chorreras, Almuñécar (Sexi) and Adra (Abdera). Although archaeology has shown that there was a substantial period of pre-colonial contact from the late tenth century, the foundation of the earliest settlements did not occur until the late ninth century (Morro de Mezquitilla, c.807–802; Toscanos, c.805–780).[35] During the eighth century, Phoenician settlements were also founded on both the Atlantic and Mediterranean coasts of southern Spain, on the island of Ibiza and at a number of sites on the western coast of Portugal. Contrary to expectation, there appears to be no correlation between the geographic location of a settlement and the date at which it was founded (thus, for example, the foundation dates of these settlements do not get progressively later the further north they were located). This indicates that the settlements, rather than being founded in a random or haphazard manner, were actually positioned in accordance with an agreed strategy that sought to maximise the sustainability and profitability of each. That the commercial aims of these settlements varied from region to region is strongly evinced by their diverse size and form.

As elsewhere in the Mediterranean, the Phoenician settlements in Iberia tended to be located on promontories or small islands in the mouth of rivers. Prominent examples include Abul and Santa Olaia in Portugal, Gadir and Huelva in south-western Spain, Cerro del Villar, Toscanos and Morro de Mezquitilla along the Andalucian coastline (i.e. the modern provinces of Cádiz, Málaga, Granada and Almería), and Fonteta on Spain's southeast coast (see Map 3). A number of these rivers, particularly those located in the Guadalquivir, Río Tinto, Tagus and Mondego regions, provided access to the mineral-rich regions of the Iberian interior, thus explaining their attractiveness to the Phoenicians. However, as will be seen, metals were by no means the only resources which were attractive to the Phoenicians, nor can the location of mineral deposits adequately explain all, or even most, of the Phoenician settlements in Iberia. Like the cities of the Phoenician mainland, the settlements in Iberia were generally modest in size, occupying between 2 and 10 hectares (Morro de Mezquitilla and Abdera = 2 ha, Gadir = 10 ha). Despite their diminutive size, these settlements had a relatively regular urban layout and contained a high density of buildings and dwellings. One of the most extensively excavated of these settlements, Cerro del Villar, covered an area of 8 hectares and is believed to have accommodated 30 large dwellings which housed approximately 200 inhabitants. Another characteristic feature of Phoenician city planning which is replicated in Iberia is the location of burial grounds (which, where feasible, were separated from the settlement by a body of water). Unfortunately, aside from Gadir, no traces of any public buildings of an administrative or religious nature have thus far been identified in any of the Phoenician settlements in Iberia. In fact, aside from harbours, the only example of a structure for which a public use has been attributed is the so-called 'storehouse' or Building C in Toscanos.

Although the character of these settlements is distinctly Eastern, especially in terms of their architecture and urban planning, there is compelling evidence to suggest that they were home to an ethnically diverse population. For instance, the settlement at Castillo de Doña Blanca, and the associated cemeteries at nearby Sierra de San Cristóbal, have revealed that there was a far closer relationship between the emigrant and indigenous populations than previously thought. The discovery of shared burial grounds and the syncretising of religious rites and rituals challenge the traditional view that the indigenous population was dominated and exploited by the Phoenician settlers (as suggested by Diodorus, 5.35.4–5). Instead, the archaeological record shows that the two groups lived in peaceful coexistence with one another and that their relationship was based on equity, tolerance, exchange and assimilation rather than on power and control.[36] The closeness of these relationships left a strong cultural imprint on native Iberian society and led to a period of cultural hybridisation and amalgamation known as the 'Orientalising Phase' – a period which was to witness the blending of funerary rites and traditions (e.g. the adoption of Phoenician tomb types and burial customs), an increase in the number of cross-cultural marriages, the sharing of technology (e.g. the introduction of iron, the potter's wheel, viticulture, distilling and irrigation), the merging of artistic and architectural styles and traditions (e.g. the use of ashlar stone and mudbrick construction), and the introduction of an alphabetic tradition into the native south-west Iberian script.[37] The Phoenician cultural imprint was particularly widespread in Huelva, the lower Guadalquivir and Portugal, a situation which perhaps indicates that these settlements were home to sizeable indigenous populations. Furthermore, recent archaeological excavations have shown that cultural syncretism and amalgamation also occurred as a result of the fact that, in addition to the assimilation of native families into the nuclei of Phoenician settlements, there were a considerable number of Phoenician emigrants living and working in indigenous towns and villages.

According to the classical sources, including Herodotus (*Histories*, 4.152), Strabo (*Geography*, 3.2.8–11), Diodorus (5.35.4–5) and Pseudo-Aristotle (*De Mirabilis auscult*, 135), the Phoenicians were primarily attracted to Iberia due to the quantity and purity of its metal deposits (principally silver but also gold, lead and tin). Although originally acquiring these metals through trade and barter, the Phoenicians recognised that they would incur fewer costs, and could do away with the need for Iberian middlemen, if they extracted the metals for themselves and so they began to found small mining settlements. Significantly, these accounts have been partially confirmed by the discovery of mineral and metallurgic processing facilities, all of which date to the eighth and seventh centuries, at sites throughout Spain (in particular in the Guadalquivir region). As is still true today, the richest deposits of silver, gold, iron, lead and copper were located in the mountains of Huelva, the western region of the present-day province of Seville, and the foothills of the Sierra Morena mountain range. Unsurprisingly, the Phoenicians, most notably those from Gadir and its dependents, established numerous mines and metallurgic processing facilities in all three regions.

Undoubtedly, it was the Rio Tinto mines in Huelva which contained the densest concentration of pyrites and so were subject to the greatest activity. The discovery of 6 million tons of silver slag spread over an area roughly one-and-a-half kilometres by half a kilometre, reveals that the Phoenicians were able to obtain huge quantities of silver which would need to be refined and purified before being traded. That the silver was processed locally is evinced by the founding of a mining settlement devoted entirely to the extraction and processing of metals at Cerro Salomón in the eighth century (a similar facility was also founded at the mines of Aznalcóllar in the province of Seville), the discovery of large furnaces and processing facilities in the nearby port-town of Huelva, and the discovery of processed silver ingots on Phoenician ships that had been wrecked off the coast of southern Spain. Although the Phoenicians appeared to have relied on indigenous labour to mine the silver, they nevertheless introduced their own technologies and methods of extraction to increase the overall efficiency of the process. In addition to silver, the Rio Tinto mines also yielded significant quantities of gold, copper, iron and lead.

Despite mineral and metallurgical deposits accounting for the dense clustering of Phoenician settlements situated beyond the Straits of Gibraltar (and to a certain extent on the Balearic archipelago – as evinced by the silver mines and processing facilities found at Santa Argentera on Ibiza),[38] the high number of emporia, market towns and villages located on the eastern Andalucian coastline cannot be so easily explained (in contrast to the sites in North Africa, for instance, which have an average of 30–40 kilometres between them, the settlements in south-western Spain are often situated just a few kilometres apart). For example, the only mineral that was both easily accessible and found in substantial quantities in eastern Andalucia was iron which could be obtained from the Penebetic mountain range. Even then, excavations at many of these mines have revealed that they were extremely small-scale operations and thus could only have served to meet the needs of the towns or cities that had established them. Consequently, the dense clustering of settlements along the south-eastern coast of Spain cannot simply be attributed to the trade in metals.

Over the past 20 years archaeological investigation has shown that, in addition to prospecting for metals, there were a number of other lucrative commercial and industrial opportunities which made Iberia attractive to the Phoenicians. These included: the cultivation and harvesting of natural resources (including grain, olives, grapes, timber and fish); the manufacture of prestige or luxury items (including ornate metal objects, carved ivories, purple dye and textiles); and the desirability of Eastern products and commodities amongst the indigenous aristocracies.[39] It is important to note, however, that the extent to which these alternate opportunities influenced the initial Phoenician migration to Iberia is still disputed. Consequently, there is currently no consensus as to whether a desire to harness the agricultural wealth of Iberia was a primary or secondary motivation for the founding of settlements (in particular those of eastern Andalucia). Nevertheless, what is certain is that those settlements which were founded in, or in close proximity to, large tracts of fertile agricultural land took full advantage of that fact. For instance, due to its rich and well-irrigated alluvial soil, the Guadalhorce Valley was ideally suited for intensive agriculture and thus a large number of farms and farming communities were established in the region during the eighth and seventh centuries. As all of these farms were attached to a coastal settlement and were generally founded within a few years of their mother-city, it is clear the initial settlers recognised the valley's agricultural potential.

Significantly, an analysis of the pollen record reveals that the majority of these farms were geared towards the intensive production of wheat, a crop that was notoriously difficult to grow in large quantities in mainland Phoenicia. Therefore, although it has been impossible to determine conclusively whether these farms solely met the subsistence needs of the local population or produced a significant surplus that could be exported, the enormous agricultural possibilities of the Guadalhorce Valley, combined with the diminutive size of the Phoenician settlements in this region, suggest the latter is most likely. Moreover, it is probable that some, if not all, of this surplus would have been exported to the cities of the Phoenician mainland.[40] The substantial quantity of animal remains found at these sites indicates that horticulture and cereal production were undertaken alongside the rearing of cattle, sheep and goats. In fact, the presence of such large numbers of animals can only be explained by intensive agricultural production (as is clearly evinced at Toscanos and El Villar). There is also evidence for the widespread production of olive oil and wine, two highly desirable and easily trafficked commodities. Importantly, the trade in these commodities was not just profitable in and of itself, but also because it provided a boost to the local economy as the transportation of liquids required massive quantities of amphorae and the pitch needed to line and seal them (a situation which is perhaps evinced by the discovery of specialist amphorae production centres at sites such as La Peña Negra).

Some regions of Iberia appear to have been attractive to the Phoenicians as they contained an abundance of other highly desirable natural resources. Of these, timber (which was widely employed in the construction of buildings, ships and furniture) and its by-products, pitch and resin (which were used as a waterproof varnish to caulk the joints and hull of ships, as a lining on the inside of wine amphorae, as an ingredient in medicinal balms and salves, and as a protective polish for wooden objects) were perhaps the most important and most valuable. At the time of the Phoenicians' arrival, large areas of southern Iberia were covered by extensive forests which were not only easily accessible but which also contained several species of evergreen and deciduous oaks, and numerous types of coniferous trees (including both pine and fir). The widespread deforestation that followed the arrival of the Phoenicians highlights the importance and profitability of the trade in timber, pitch and resin, as does the emergence during the sixth century of specialised industries focused on harvesting and processing the raw materials needed for shipbuilding, the production of pitch and the manufacturing of ornate luxury furniture.[41] As these industries were highly specialised, they were also extremely lucrative and so became equally as profitable as the exploitation of metallurgical resources.

The rich marine resources found in the oceans surrounding Iberia (including murex, numerous varieties of edible fish and salt) are also likely to have attracted Phoenician interest. The presence of considerable quantities of crushed murex shells at Almuñécar, Toscanos and Morro de Mezquitilla are indicative of the large-scale manufacture of purple dye and textiles. With purple dye being worth more than its equivalent weight in gold, any region that could sustain this type of industry would have been of great interest to the Phoenicians. Classical authors, such as Strabo (*Geography*, 3.2.7) and Pliny (*Natural Histories*, 32.15), also describe the seas around the straits of Gibraltar as being rich in fish (to this day huge shoals of tuna migrate through the straits during the summer months). Although fishing was originally a strategy for self-sufficiency, by the sixth century there is evidence for the large-scale production of garum, an expensive fish sauce that had become a must-have for aristocratic dinner parties throughout the Mediterranean. Finally, a number of the coastal settlements were also in a position to mine or harvest salt, a valuable commodity which was not only used in the preservation of various foods but is also a vital part of the human diet.

Epilogue

Following Alexander the Great's death in 323, which marked the beginning of the Hellenistic Period, his empire was divided between his most powerful generals (who became known as the *diadochi* or 'successors'). During the next 125 years, control of Phoenicia passed backwards and forwards between the Seleucid and Egyptian empires, before finally becoming a Seleucid province in 198. In general, the Phoenician cities welcomed their integration into the Seleucid kingdom which not only ensured stability but also brought with it many privileges. For instance, with the consent of the Seleucid king, the Phoenician cities were allowed to issue their own coins.[1] The large influx of Greek emigrants that arrived in Phoenicia during the final years of the Seleucid kingdom meant that many of the Phoenician cities became Hellenised (i.e. adopted aspects of Greek culture and language).[2] A Greek inscription found at Byblos, and which is believed to date to the late Hellenistic period, provides evidence for the spread of Hellenisation as it documents that Dionysodoros and his son Aspasios held the office of *gymnasiarchos* (director of the gymnasium). The gymnasium was one of the indispensable features of Greek culture and education and thus the presence of this type of facility in Byblos indicates just how Hellenised the city had become – as do the names Dionysodoros and Aspasios which are both Greek in origin. By the end of the first century, Phoenicia had become so Hellenised that its inhabitants could be referred to as 'Hellenes' (Plutarch, *Life of Lucullus*, 21.3).

The political and economic weaknesses of the Seleucid kingdom eventually caused its collapse in 83. Following a period marked by civil wars between rival claimants to the throne and a number

Mark Woolmer

of internal revolts and uprisings, the states forming the Seleucid kingdom invited the Armenian king Tigranes II (95–55) to govern the country. Phoenicia was to be ruled by Tigranes between 83 and 69 before Roman intervention in the Near East forced him to retreat back to Armenia; he was succeeded by the last of the Seleucid kings, Antiochus XIII Asiaticus (69–65). The campaigns of the Roman general Pompey in 64 BCE subdued the last remains of the Seleucid Empire, leading Phoenicia to be incorporated into the Roman province of Syria. This heralded the end of Phoenician autonomy and the start of a period of Romanisation in the region. With their increasing adoption of western ways the Phoenicians lost much of their ethnic distinctiveness (including their language) and thus, by the end of the first century CE, there were very few remnants of the unique and vibrant culture that had existed before the arrival of the Greeks and Romans.

Further Reading

GENERAL INTRODUCTIONS AND HISTORIES

Acquaro, E. and De Vita, P., *The Phoenicians: History and Treasures of an Ancient Civilisation* (Vercelli: White Star, 2010).

Elayi, J., 'The Phoenician cities in the Persian Period', *Journal of the Ancient Near Eastern Society* 12 (1980), pp. 13–28.

Grainger, J., *Hellenistic Phoenicia* (Oxford: Oxford Clarendon Press, 1991).

Katzenstein, H.J., *The History of Tyre from the Beginning of the Second Millennium* BCE *until the Fall of the Neo-Babylonian Empire in 538* BCE (Jerusalem: Shocken Institute for Jewish Research, 1973).

Markoe, G.E., *The Phoenicians* (London: British Museum Press, 2000).

Marston, E., *The Phoenicians* (New York, NY: Benchmark Books, 2002).

Moscati, S., *The Phoenicians* (London: I.B.Tauris, 2001).

Peckham, B., *Phoenicia: Episodes and Anecdotes from the Ancient Mediterranean* (Winona Lake, IN: Eisenbrauns, 2014).

Woolmer, M., *Ancient Phoenicia: An Introduction* (London: Duckworth, 2011).

ARCHAEOLOGY

Bietak, M. and Czerny, E. (eds), *The Bronze Age in the Lebanon: Studies on the Archaeology and Chronology of Lebanon, Syria, and Egypt* (Vienna: Verlag der Österreichischen Akademie der Wissenschaften, 2008).

Doumet-Serhal, C. (ed.), *Decade: A Decade of Archaeology and History in the Lebanon* (Beirut: Lebanese British Friends of the National Museum, 2004).

Meyers M. (ed.), *The Oxford Encyclopaedia of Archaeology in the Near East*, vols. 1–5 (Oxford: Oxford University Press, 1995).

Pritchard, J.B., *Recovering Sarepta, A Phoenician City* (Princeton, NJ: Princeton University Press, 1978).

Richard, S. (ed.), *Near Eastern Archaeology: A Reader* (Winona Lake, IN: Eisenbrauns, 2003).

Steiner, M. and Killebrew, A. (eds), *The Oxford Handbook of the Archaeology of the Levant* (Oxford: Oxford University Press, 2014).

LANGUAGE AND LITERATURE

Gibson, J., *Textbook of Syrian-Semitic Inscriptions: Volume III Phoenician Inscriptions* (Oxford: Clarendon Press, 1982).
Hackett, J.A., 'Phoenician and Punic', in *The Ancient Languages of Syria-Palestine and Arabia*, ed. R.D. Woodard (Oxford: Oxford University Press, 2008), pp. 82–6.
Krahmalkov, C.R., *A Phoenician and Punic Grammar* (Leiden: Brill, 2001).
Lemaire, A., *Levantine Epigraphy and History in the Achaemenid Period: 539–322 BCE* (Oxford: Oxford University Press, 2015).
Pritchard, J.B. (ed.), *Ancient Near Eastern Texts Relating to the Old Testament* (Princeton, NJ: Princeton University Press, 1969).
Schmitz, P., *The Phoenicia Diaspora: Epigraphic and Historical Studies* (Winona Lake, IN: Eisenbrauns, 2012).

ECONOMY

Elayi, J. and Elayi, A.G., *The Coinage of the Phoenician City of Tyre in the Persian Period: 5th–4th Century BCE* (Leuven: Peeters, 2009).
—— *A Monetary and Political History of the Phoenician City of Byblos* (Winona Lake, IN: Eisenbrauns, 2014).
—— *Phoenician Coinages* (Pendé: Gabalda, 2014).
Fletcher, R.N., 'Opening the Mediterranean: Assyria, the Levant and the transformation of Early Iron Age trade', *Antiquity* 86 (2012), pp. 211–20.
Master, D.M., 'Economy and exchange in the Iron Age kingdoms of the southern Levant', *Bulletin of the American Schools of Oriental Research* 372 (2014), pp 81–97.
Moore, K.J. and Lewis, D.C., 'Multinational enterprise in ancient Phoenicia', *Business History* 42/2 (2000), pp. 17–42.
Sommer, M., 'Networks of commerce and knowledge in the Iron Age: the case of the Phoenicians', *Mediterranean Historical Review* 22/1 (2007), pp. 97–111.

RELIGION

Ackerman, S., 'The mother of Eshmunazor, priest of Astarte: a study of her cultic role', *Die Welt des Orients* 43/2 (2013), pp. 158–78.
Aubet, M.E. (ed.), *The Phoenician Cemetery of Tyre-Al Bass: Excavations, 1997–1999* (Beirut: Ministère de la Culture, Direction Générale des Antiquités, 2004).
—— 'The Phoenician cemetery of Tyre', *Near Eastern Archaeology* 73 (2010), pp. 2–3.
Bonnet, C. and Niehr, H., *Religionen in der Umwelt des Alten Testaments II: Phönizier, Punier, Aramäer* (Stuttgart: Kohlhammer, 2010).
Brody, A., *'Each Man Cried Out to His God': The Specialized Religion of Canaanite and Phoenician Seafarers* (Atlanta, GA: Scholars Press, 1998).

Clifford, R.J., 'Phoenician religion', *Bulletin of the American Schools of Oriental Research* 279 (1990), pp. 55–64.

Escacena-Carrasco, J.L., 'Orientation of Phoenician temples', in *Handbook of Archaeoastronomy and Ethnoastronomy*, ed. C.L.N. Ruggles (New York, NY: Springer Science Business Media, 2014), pp. 1793–9.

Gras, M., Rouillard, P. and Teixidor, J., 'The Phoenicians and death', *Berytus* 39/3 (1991), pp. 127–76.

Groenewoud, E.M., 'Use of water in Phoenician sanctuaries', *Journal of Ancient Near Eastern Studies* 38 (2001), pp. 139–59.

Tubb, J., 'Phoenician dance', *Near Eastern Archaeology* 66/3 (2003), pp. 122–5).

ART AND MATERIAL CULTURE

Brown, S., 'Perspectives on Phoenician art', *The Biblical Archaeologist* 55 (1992), pp. 6–24.

Doumet, J., 'Purple dye', in *Decade: A Decade of Archaeology and History in the Lebanon*, ed. C. Doumet-Serhal (Beirut: Lebanese British Friends of the National Museum, 2004), pp. 38–49.

Gubel E., 'Multicultural and multimedial aspects of early Phoenician art, c. 1200–675 BCE', in *Images as Media: Sources for the Cultural History of the Near East and the Eastern Mediterranean – 1st Millennium BCE*, ed. C. Uehlinger (Fribourg: Fribourg University Press, 2000), pp. 185–214.

Herrmann, G. and Laidlaw, S., 'Assyrian Nimrud and the Phoenicians', *Archaeology International* 16 (2013), pp. 84–95.

Koren Z.C., 'The first optimal all-murex all-natural purple dyeing in the eastern Mediterranean in a millennium and a half', *Dyes in History and Archaeology* 20 (2005), pp. 136–49.

Markoe, G., *Phoenician Bronze and Silver Bowls from Cyprus and the Mediterranean* (Berkeley, CA: University of California Press, 1985).

——— 'The emergence of Phoenician art', *Bulletin of the American Schools of Oriental Research* 279 (1990), pp. 13–26.

Markoe, G. and McGovern, P.E., 'A nation of artisans', *Archaeology* 43/2 (1990), pp. 31–5.

Sader, H., *Iron Age Funerary Stelae from Lebanon* (Barcelona: Edicions Bellaterra, 2005).

——— 'Phoenician "popular art": transmission, transformation, and adaptation of foreign motifs in the light of recent archaeological evidence from Lebanon', in *Interkulturalität id der Alten Welt: Vorderasien, Hellas, Ägypten und die vielfältigen Ebenen des Kontakts*, ed. R. Rollinger et al. (Wiesbaden: Harrassowitz, 2010), pp. 23–39.

OVERSEAS EXPANSION

Aubet, M.E., *The Phoenicians in the West: Politics, Colonies, and Trade*, 2nd ed. (Cambridge: Cambridge University Press, 2001).

Bierling, M.R. (ed.), *The Phoenicians in Spain* (Winona Lake, IN: Eisenbrauns, 2002).

Dietler, M. and López-Ruiz, C. (eds), *Colonial Encounters in Ancient Iberia: Phoenician, Greek, and Indigenous Relations* (Chicago, IL: University of Chicago Press, 2009).

Hodos, T., *Local Responses to Colonization in the Iron Age Mediterranean* (London: Routledge, 2006).

Hoyos, D., *The Carthaginians* (New York, NY: Routledge, 2010).

Lipiński, E., *Itineraria Phoenicia* (Leuven: Peeters, 2004).

Maïla-Afeiche, A.-M. (ed.), *Interconnections in the Eastern Mediterranean Lebanon in the Bronze and Iron Ages: Proceedings of the International Symposium of Beirut 2008* (Beirut: Ministère de la Culture, Direction Générale des Antiquités, 2008).

Pappa, E., *Early Iron Age Exchange in the West: Phoenicians in the Mediterranean and the Atlantic* (Leuven: Peeters, 2013).

Sagona, C. (ed.), *Beyond the Homeland: Markers in Phoenician Chronology* (Leuven: Peeters, 2008).

Notes

INTRODUCTION

1 For example, E. van Dongen, '"Phoenicia": naming and defining a region in Syria-Palestine', in R. Rollinger et al. (eds), *Interkulturalitätin der Alten Welt: Vorderasien, Hellas, Ägyptenund die vielfältigen Ebenen des Kontakts* (Wiesbaden: Harrassowitz, 2010), vol. 34, pp. 471–88.

2 For a comprehensive discussion of this issue see J. Quinn, *In Search of the Phoenicians* (Princeton, NJ: Princeton University Press, forthcoming 2017).

3 O. Tammuz, 'Canaan – a land without limits', *Ugarit-Forschungen* 33 (2001), pp. 501–43; N. Na'Aman, 'Four notes on the size of Late Bronze Age Canaan', *Bulletin of the American Schools of Oriental Research* 313 (1999), pp. 31–7; N. Na'Aman, 'The Canaanites and their land: A rejoinder', *Ugarit-Forschungen* 26 (1994), pp. 397–418.

4 I. Finkelstein, 'Pots and people revised: Ethnic boundaries in the Iron Age I', in N.A. Silberman and D.B. Smalls (eds), *The Archaeology of Israel: Constructing the Past, Interpreting the Present* (Sheffield: Sheffield Academic Press, 1997), pp. 216–37.

5 W. Röllig, 'On the origins of the Phoenicians', *Berytus* 31 (1983), pp. 79–93.

6 S. Moscati, 'Who were the Phoenicians?', in S. Moscati (ed.), *The Phoenicians* (London: I.B.Taurus, 2001), pp. 17–19.

7 Cedar Lake Ventures: available at https://weatherspark.com/averages/32849/Beirut-Mt-Lebanon (accessed 12 January 2017).

8 M. Suriano 'Historical geography of the Ancient Levant', in M. Steiner and A. Killebrew, (eds), *The Oxford Handbook of the Archaeology of the Levant* (Oxford: Oxford University Press, pp. 9–23; C.N. Raphael, 'Geography and the Bible' (Palestine), in D.N. Freeman (ed.), *The Anchor Bible Dictionary*, vol. 2 (New York, NY: Doubleday, 1992), pp. 964–77.

9 J. Elayi and J. Sapin, *Beyond the River: New Perspectives on Trans-euphratene* (Sheffield: Sheffield Academic Press, 1998), pp. 97–109; N. Morley, *Writing Ancient History* (New York: Cornell University Press, 1999), pp. 53–96; K.L. Noll, *Canaan and Israel in Antiquity: A Textbook on History and Religion* (London: Bloomsbury, 2013), pp. 23–33.

10 The standard, and still most accessible, collection of mainland Phoenician inscriptions is: J. Gibson, *Textbook of Syrian-Semitic Inscriptions: Volume III Phoenician Inscriptions* (Oxford: Clarendon Press, 1982).

11 Elayi and Sapin, *Beyond the River*, pp. 85–96; P. Schmitz, *The Phoenicia Diaspora: Epigraphic and Historical Studies* (Winona Lake, IN: Eisenbrauns, 2012).

12 W. Bukert, *The Orientalizing Revolution: Near Eastern Influences on Greek Culture in the Early Archaic Age* (Cambridge, MA: Harvard University Press, 1995), pp. 33–40.

13 E. Renan, *Mission de Phénicie* (Paris: Imprimerie Impériale, 1864).

14 H. Sader, 'Archaeology in Lebanon today: its politics and its problems', *The Ancient Near East Today* 4 (2013), available at http://asorblog.org/archaeology-in-lebanon-today-its-politics-and-its-problems/ (accessed 12 January 2017).

CHAPTER 1: HISTORICAL OVERVIEW

1 R.R. Stieglitz, 'Early Iron Age geopolitics', *Archaeology* 43.2 (1990), pp. 9–12; D.B. Redford, *Egypt, Canaan, and Israel in Ancient Times* (Princeton, NJ: Princeton University Press), pp. 297–9; M. Yon, 'The end of the Kingdom of Ugarit', in W. Ward, M. Joukowsky, P. Aström et al. (eds), *The Crisis Years: The 12th Century B.C.: From Beyond the Danube to the Tigris* (Dubuque, IA: Kendall/Hunt Publishing, 1992), pp. 111–22; W.T. Ward, 'Phoenicians', in A. Hoerth, G. Mattingly and E. Yamauchi (eds), *Peoples of the Old Testament World* (Grand Rapids, MI: Baker Academic Press, 1994), pp. 183–206.

2 L. Stager, 'The impact of the Sea Peoples in Canaan (1185–1050 B.C.E.),' in T.E. Levy, (ed.), *The Archaeology of Society in the Holy Land* (London: Continuum, 1995), pp. 332–48; W.G. Dever, 'The Late Bronze–Early Iron I horizon in Syria-Palestine: Egyptians, Canaanites, "Sea People", and Proto-Israelites', in Ward et al. (eds), *The Crisis Years*, pp. 99–110; I. Singer, 'The origin of the Sea Peoples and their settlement on the coast of Canaan', in M. Lipinski and E. Lipinski (eds), *Society and Economy in the Eastern Mediterranean (c. 1500–1000 B.C.)* (Leuven: Peeters, 1988), pp. 239–50.

3 H. Genz and H. Sader, 'Bronze Age funerary practices in Lebanon', *Archaeology and History in Lebanon* (2007–8), pp. 26–7 and 258–83.

4 C. Pulak, 'The Uluburun shipwreck: an overview', *International Journal of Nautical Archaeology* 27/3 (1998), pp. 236–54.

5 H.J. Katzenstein, *The History of Tyre* (Jerusalem: Shocken Institute for Jewish Research, 1973), p. 59; E. Stern 'New evidence from Dor for the first appearance of the Phoenicians along the northern coast of Israel', *Bulletin of the America Schools of Oriental Research* 279 (1990), pp. 27–34; P.M. Bikai, 'The Phoenicians', in Ward et al. (eds), *The Crisis Years*, pp. 132–41. D.B. Redford, *Egypt, Canaan, and Israel in Ancient Times* (Princeton, NJ: Princeton University Press, 1992), p. 229; Stager, 'The impact of the Sea Peoples', pp. 332–48.

6   V. Jigoulov, 'The Phoenician city-states of Tyre and Sidon in ancient Jewish texts', *Scandinavian Journal of the Old Testament: An International Journal of Nordic Theology* 21/1 (2007), pp. 73–105; E. Nyirimana, 'Hiram's relations with Solomon', *Old Testament Essays* 26/1 (2013), pp. 172–95.

7   P. Boyes, '"The King of the Sidonians": Phoenician ideologies and the myth of the Kingdom of Tyre-Sidon', *Bulletin of the American Schools of Oriental Research* 365 (2012), pp. 33–44.

8   See letters 12 and 13 in H.W.F. Saggs, 'The Nimrud Letters, Part II', *Iraq* 17.2 (1955), pp. 126–60.

9   J. Elayi, 'The Phoenician cities and the Assyrian Empire in the time of Sargon II', *Sumer* 42 (1986), pp. 129–32.

10 E. Lipiński, 'The Kingdom of Sidon in the early seventh century B.C.', in E. Lipiński, *Itineraria Phoenicia*, Orientalia Lovaniensia Analecta 127 (2004), pp. 17–37.

11 N. Na'aman 'Esarhaddon's treaty with Baal and Assyrian provinces along the Phoenician coast', *Rivista di Studi Fenici* 22 (1994), pp. 3–8.

12 P. Briant, *From Cyrus to Alexander: A History of the Persian Empire* (Winona Lake, IN: Eisenbrauns, 2002), pp. 55–9.

13 M.A. Dandamaev, *A Political History of Achaemenid Empire* (New York, NY: Brill, 1989), pp. 60–5.

14 J. Elayi, 'The Phoenician cities in the Persian Period', *Journal of the Ancient Near Eastern Society* 12 (1980), pp. 13–28; J. Elayi, 'The Phoenician cities in the Achaemenid Period: remarks on the present state and prospects of research', *Achaemenid History IV* (1990), pp. 227–37.

15 V. Jigoulov, *The Social History of the Achaemenid Phoenicia: Being a Phoenician, Negotiating Empires* (London: Equinox, 2010), pp. 71–112.

16 A.K. Grayson, *Assyrian and Babylonian Chronicles* (New York, NY: J.J. Augustine, 1985), p. 114.

CHAPTER 2: GOVERNMENT AND SOCIETY

1   M.E. Aubet, *The Phoenicians in the West: Politics, Colonies, and Trade* (Cambridge: Cambridge University Press, 2001), pp. 144–58.

2   J. Elayi, 'The role of the Phoenician kings at the battle of Salamis (480 B.C.E.)', *Journal of the American Oriental Society* 126/3 (2006), pp. 411–18.

3   S. Garfinkle, 'Ancient Near Eastern city-states', in P.F. Bang and W. Scheidel (eds), *The Oxford Handbook of the State in the Ancient Near East and Mediterranean* (Oxford: Oxford University Press, 2013), pp. 259–78.

4   S. Stockwell, 'Before Athens: early popular government in Phoenician and Greek city states', *Geopolitics, History, and International Relations* 2/2 (2010), pp. 123–35.

5   C. Meyers, '"Eves" of everyday ancient Israel', *Biblical Archaeology Review* 40/6 (2014), pp. 50–4 and 66–8; C. Meyers, *Rediscovering Eve: Ancient Israelite Women in Context* (Oxford: Oxford University Press, 2013).

6 K.R. Nemet-Nejat, 'Women in ancient Mesopotamia', in B. Vivante (ed.), *Women's Roles in Ancient Civilisations: A Reference Guide* (London: Greenwood Press, 1999), pp. 85–114.

7 G. Abousamra and A. Lemaire, 'Astarte in Tyre according to New Iron Age funerary stelae', *Die Welt des Orients* 43/2 (2013), pp. 153–7.

8 S. Ackerman, 'The mother of Eshmunazor, priest of Astarte: a study of her cultic role', *Die Welt des Orients* 43/2 (2013), pp. 158–78.

9 G. Markoe, *Phoenician Bronze and Silver Bowls from Cyprus and the Mediterranean*, Classical Studies 26 (Berkeley CA: University of California Press, 1985); N. Vella, '"Phoenician" metal bowls: boundary objects in the archaic period', *Bollettino di Archeologia Online*, volume speciale A/A2/5 (2010), pp. 22–37, available at www.archeologia.beniculturali.it (accessed 3 May 2015).

10 A.S. Giammellaro, 'The Phoenicians and the Carthaginians: the early Mediterranean diet', in J.-L. Flandrin and M. Montanari (eds), *Food: A Culinary History* (New York, NY: Columbia University Press, 2013), pp. 55–65.

11 M. Botto, 'The Phoenicians and the spread of wine in the central west Mediterranean', in S. Celestino, J. Pérez and P. Blánquez (eds), *Vine and Wine Cultural Heritage* (Madrid: Universidad Autónoma de Madrid, 2013), pp. 103–31.

12 M. Heltzer, 'Olive oil and wine production in Phoenicia and in the Mediterranean trade', in M.C. Amouretti and J.P. Brun (eds), *La production du vin et de l'huile en Méditerranée* (Toulon: Caisse D'épargne de Toulon, 1993), pp. 49–54.

13 C. Doumet-Serhal, *Sidon: 15 Years of Excavations* (Beirut: Lebanese British Friends of the National Museum, 2013), pp. 81–4; J.B. Pritchard, *Recovering Sarepta, A Phoenician City* (Princeton, NJ: Princeton University Press, 1978), pp. 88–9.

14 H. Gzella, 'North-west Semitic in general', in S. Weninger (ed.), *The Semitic Languages: An International Handbook* (Berlin: De Gruyter, 2011), pp. 425–51.

15 G.E. Markoe, *The Phoenicians* (London: British Museum Press, 2000), pp. 108–15.

16 W. Röllig, 'Phoenician and Punic', in W. Stefan (ed.), *The Semitic Languages: An International Handbook* (Berlin: De Gruyter, 2011), pp. 472–9.

17 C.R. Krahmalkov, *A Phoenician and Punic Grammar* (Boston: Brill, 2001), pp. 5–7.

18 J.A. Hackett, 'Phoenician and Punic', in R.D. Woodard (ed.), *The Ancient Languages of Syria-Palestine and Arabia* (Oxford: Oxford University Press, 2008), pp. 82–6.

19 H. Gzella, 'Phoenician', in H. Gzella (ed.), *Languages from the World of the Bible* (Berlin: De Gruyter, 2011), pp. 55–75.

20 M. Sommer, 'Networks of commerce and knowledge in the Iron Age: the case of the Phoenicians', *Mediterranean Historical Review* 22/1 (2007), pp. 97–111; T. Brughmans, 'Thinking through networks: a review of formal network methods', *Journal of Archaeological Method and Theory* 20 (2013), pp. 623–62.

21 V. Krings, 'Re-reading Punic agriculture: representation, analogy, and ideology in the classical sources', in P. van Dommelen and C.G. Bellard (eds), *Rural Landscapes of the Punic World* (London: Equinox, 2008), pp. 22–43.

22 D.C. Hopkins, *The Highlands of Canaan: Agricultural Life in the Early Iron Age* (Sheffield: Almond Press, 1985), pp. 171–87.

23 Heltzer, 'Olive oil and wine production', pp. 49–54.

24 B. Isserlin, 'Phoenician and Punic rural settlement and agriculture: some archaeological considerations', in P. Bartoloni et al. (eds), *Atti del I congresso int. di studi fenici e punici, 1979* (Rome: Consiglio Nazionale delle Ricerche, 1983), pp. 157–63.

25 R. Ballard et al., 'Iron Age shipwrecks in deep water off Ashkelon, Israel', *American Journal of Archaeology* 106 (2002), pp. 151–68.

26 P.G. van Alfen, *Pant'agatha: Commodities in Levantine-Aegean Trade During the Persian Period*, PhD dissertation, University of Texas at Austin, 2002; J. Aruz, S. Graff and Y. Rakic, *Assyria to Iberia: At the Dawn of the Classical Age* (New Haven, CT: Yale University Press, 2014).

27 K.J. Moore and D.C. Lewis, 'Multinational enterprise in ancient Phoenicia', *Business History* 42/2 (2000), pp. 17–42; M.E. Aubet, *The Phoenicians in the West: Politics, Colonies, and Trade* (Cambridge: Cambridge University Press, 2001), pp. 159–93.

28 D.M. Master, 'Economy and exchange in the Iron Age kingdoms of the southern Levant', *Bulletin of the American Schools of Oriental Research* 372 (2014), pp. 81–97.

29 R.N. Fletcher, 'Opening the Mediterranean: Assyria, the Levant and the transformation of Early Iron Age trade', *Antiquity* 86 (2012), pp. 211–20.

30 M. Elat, 'Phoenician overland trade within the Mesopotamian empires', in M. Cogan and I. Eph'al (eds), *Ah Assyria … Historiography Presented to Hayim Tadmor, Scripta Hierosolymitana*, vol. 33, pp. 21–35.

31 H.J. Katzenstein, 'The Phoenician term *hubur* in the report of Wen-Amon', *Atti del I Congresso Internazionale di Studi Penici e Punici. Roma 5–10 novembre 1979* II, Consiglio Nazionale delle Ricerche (1983), pp. 599–602.

32 K. Radner, 'Traders in the Neo-Assyrian Period', in J.G. Dercksen (ed.), *Trade and Finance in Ancient Mesopotamia*, MOS Studies 1, pp. 101–26.

33 M.E. Aubet, *The Phoenicians in the West: Politics, Colonies, and Trade* (Cambridge: Cambridge University Press, 2001), pp. 97–143.

34 J. Elayi and A.G. Elayi, *A Monetary and Political History of the Phoenician City of Byblos* (Winona Lake, IN: Eisenbrauns, 2014); J. Elayi and A.G. Elayi, *The Coinage of the Phoenician City of Tyre in the Persian Period (5th–4th cent. BCE)* (Leuven: Peeters, 2009); J. Elayi and A.G. Elayi, *Phoenician Coinages* (Pendé: Gabalda, 2014).

35 F.S. Frick, 'Cities', in E.M. Meyers (ed.), *The Oxford Encyclopaedia of Archaeology in the Near East*, Volume II (Oxford: Oxford University Press, 1997), pp. 14–18.

36 Y. Shalev and S.R. Martin, 'Crisis as opportunity: Phoenician urban renewal after the Babylonians', *Transeuphraténe* 41 (2012), pp. 81–100.

37 A. Faust, 'Domestic architecture, Bronze and Iron Ages', in D. Master, B. Alpert-Nakhai and A. Faust et al. (eds), *Oxford Encyclopedia of Bible and Archaeology* (Oxford: Oxford University Press, 2013), pp. 302–10.

38 G.R. Wright, *Ancient Building in South Syria and Palestine* (2 vols) (Boston, MA: Brill, 1985), pp. 332–72.

39 S. Dunham, 'Ancient Near Eastern architecture', in D.C. Snell (ed.), *A Companion to the Ancient Near East* (Oxford: Blackwell Publishing, 2005), pp. 219–28.

40 I. Sharon, 'Phoenician and Greek Ashlar construction techniques at Tel Dor, Israel', *Bulletin of the American Schools of Oriental Research* 267 (August 1987), pp. 21–42.

CHAPTER 3: RELIGION

1 D. Schwemer, 'The storm-gods of the ancient Near East: summary, synthesis, recent studies Part II', *Journal of Ancient Near Eastern Religions* 8/1, pp. 1–44.

2 C. Bonnet, *Astarté. Dossier documentaire et perspectives historiques*, Collezione di Studi Fenici 37 (1996); R.C. Steiner, 'Northwest Semitic incantations in an Egyptian medical papyrus of the fourteenth century BCE', *Journal of Near Eastern Studies* 51 (1992), pp. 191–200.

3 H.W. Attridge and R.A. Oden, Jr., *The Syrian Goddess (de Dea Syria) Attributed to Lucian* (Missoula, MT: Scholars Press, 1976); R.A. Oden, Jr., *Studies in Lucian's De Syria dea* (Missoula, MT: Scholars Press, 1977); L. Lightfoot, *Lucian, On the Syrian Goddess* (Oxford: Oxford University Press, 2003) (especially pp. 12–16).

4 R.J. Clifford, 'Phoenician religion', *Bulletin of the American Schools of Oriental Research* 279 (1990), pp. 55–64.

5 A.E. Zernecke, 'The Lady of the Titles: the Lady of Byblos and the search for her "true name"', *Die Welt des Orients* 43/2 (2013), pp. 226–42.

6 C. Bonnet and H. Niehr, *Religionen in der Umwelt des Alten Testaments II: Phönizier, Punier, Aramäer. Studienbücher Theologie*, Bd 4.2 (Stuttgart: Verlag W. Kohlhammer, 2010), pp. 50–5.

7 E. Lipiński, *Reseph: A Syro-Canaanite Deity* (Leuven: Peeters, 2009); K. Ulanowski, 'The god Reshef in the Mediterranean', in L. Bombardieri, A. D'Agostino and V. Orsi (eds), *Identity and Connectivity: Proceedings of the 16th Symposium on Mediterranean Archaeology* (Oxford: Archaeopress, 2013), pp. 157–64.

8 A. Brody, *'Each Man Cried out to His God': The Specialized Religion of Canaanite and Phoenician Seafarers* (Atlanta, GA: Scholars Press, 1998), pp. 22–6; A. Brody, 'The specialized religions of ancient Mediterranean seafarers', *Religion Compass* 2 (1998), pp. 444–54.

9 J.B. Pritchard, *Recovering Sarepta, A Phoenician City* (Princeton, NJ: Princeton University Press, 1978), pp. 105–8 and 131–48.

10 B. Strawn, *What Is Stronger than a Lion?: Leonine Image and Metaphor in the Hebrew Bible and the Ancient Near East* (Fribourg: Academic Press, 2005), pp. 189–90.

11 T.N.D. Mettinger, *The Riddle of Resurrection: 'Dying and Rising Gods' in the Ancient Near East* (Stockholm: Almqvist and Wiksell International, 2001).

12 J.L. Escacena-Carrasco, 'The Melqart Égersis: a hypothesis on a Cananean sun theology', *Complutum* 20/2 (2009), pp. 95–120; J.L. Escacena-Carrasco, 'Orientation of Phoenician temples', in C.L.N. Ruggles (ed.), *Handbook of Archaeoastronomy and Ethnoastronomy* (New York, NY: Springer Science Business Media, 2015), pp. 1793–9.

13 H. Sader, 'The stelae', in M.E. Aubet (ed.), *The Phoenician Cemetery of Tyre al-Bass: Excavations 1997–1999* (Beirut: Ministère de la Culture, Direction Générale des Antiquités, 2004), BAAL – Hors-Série I, pp. 383–94; H. Sader, 'Iron Age funerary stelae from Lebanon', *Cuadernos de arqueologia Mediterranea* 11 (2005).

14 E. Lipiński, *Itineraria Phoenicia* (Leuven: Peeters, 2004), p. 106.

15 A.D. Kilner, 'Music and dance in ancient Western Asia', in J.M. Sasson (ed.), *Civilisations of the Ancient Near East: Volume Four* (New York, NY: Charles Scribner's Sons, 1995), pp. 2601–13; Y. Garfinkel, *Dancing at the Dawn of Agriculture* (Austin, TX: University of Texas Press, 2003).

16 J.D. Seger, 'Limping about the altar', *Eretz Israel* 23 (1992), pp. 120–7.

17 G. Markoe, *Phoenician Bronze and Silver Bowls from Cyprus and the Mediterranean* (Berkeley, CA: University of California Press, pp. 348–9; J. Tubb, 'Phoenician dance', *Near Eastern Archaeology* 66/3, pp. 122–5.

18 M. López-Bertran and A. Garcia-Ventura, 'Sound in some Phoenician and Punic contexts', *SAGVNTVM* (P.L.A.V.) 40 (2011), pp. 27–36.

19 S. Iwry, 'New evidence for belomancy in ancient Palestine and Phoenicia', *Journal of the American Oriental Society* 81/1 (1961), pp. 27–34.

20 E.M. Groenewoud, 'Use of water in Phoenician sanctuaries', *Journal of Ancient Near Eastern Studies* 38 (2001), pp. 139–59.

21 P. Xella, 'Death and afterlife in Canaanite and Hebrew thought', in M. Sasson et al. (eds), *Civilizations of the Ancient Near East* (New York, NY: Charles Scribner's Sons, 1995), pp. 2059–70.

22 M. Pope, 'The cult of the dead at Ugarit', in G.D. Young (ed.), *Ugarit in Retrospect: Fifty Years of Ugarit and Ugaritic* (Winona Lake, IN: Eisenbrauns, 1981), pp. 159–82.

23 M. Gras, P. Rouillard and J. Teixidor, 'The Phoenicians and death', *Berytus* 39/3 (1991), pp. 127–76 (especially 173–4).

24 P. Metcalf and R. Huntington, *Celebrations of Death: The Anthropology of Mortuary Ritual* (Cambridge: Cambridge University Press, 1991); S. Campbell and A. Green (eds), *The Archaeology of Death in the Ancient Near East* (Oxford: Oxbow, 1995).

25 Aubet (ed.), *The Phoenician Cemetery*; M.E. Aubet, 'The Phoenician cemetery of Tyre', *Near Eastern Archaeology* 73 (2010), pp. 2–3.

CHAPTER 4: ART AND MATERIAL CULTURE

1 G. Markoe, 'Phoenician metalwork abroad: a question of export or on-site production', in N.C. Stampolidis and V. Karageorghis (eds), *Sea Routes ... Interconnections in the Mediterranean 16th–6th Centuries* BC (Athens: University of Crete and the A.G. Leventis Foundation, 2003), pp. 209–16.

2 S. Brown, 'Perspectives on Phoenician art', *The Biblical Archaeologist* 55 (1992), pp. 6–24; G.E. Markoe, *The Phoenicians* (London: British Museum Press, 2000), pp. 143–69.

3 G. Markoe, 'The emergence of Phoenician art', *Bulletin of the American Schools of Oriental Research* 279 (1990), pp. 13–26.

4 E. Gubel, 'Multicultural and multimedial aspects of early Phoenician art, *c.* 1200–675 BCE', in C. Uehlinger (ed.), *Images as Media: Sources for the Cultural History of the Near East and the Eastern Mediterranean (1st Millennium BCE)* (Fribourg: University Press, 2000), pp. 185–214; E. Gubel, 'Notes on the Phoenician component of the Orientalizing horizon', in C. Riva and N.C. Vella (eds), *Debating Orientalization: Multidisciplinary Approaches to Change in the Ancient Mediterranean* (London: Equinox, 2006), pp. 85–93.

5 H. Frankfort, *The Art and Architecture of the Ancient Orient* (New Haven, CN: Yale University Press, 1996), pp. 310, 316–18, 331.

6 G. Markoe and P.E. McGovern, 'A nation of artisans', *Archaeology* 43/2 (1990), pp. 31–5, 76.

7 G. Herrmann and S. Laidlaw, 'Assyrian Nimrud and the Phoenicians', *Archaeology International* 16 (2013), pp. 84–95, available at http://dx.doi.org/10.5334/ai.1611 (accessed 9 November 2016). See also R.D. Barnett, *A Catalogue of the Nimrud Ivories in the British Museum* (London: British Museum Publications, 1957, reprinted 1975).

8 N.C. Vella, '"Phoenician" metal bowls: boundary objects in the Archaic Period', in Proceedings of the XVIIth International Congress of Classical Archaeology, 22–6 September 2008, Rome, *Bollettino di Archeologica on line* (2010), pp. 22–37.

9 G. Markoe, *Phoenician Bronze and Silver Bowls from Cyprus and the Mediterranean* (Berkeley, CA: University of California Press, 1992); H. Matthäus, 'Phoenician metal-work up-to-date: Phoenician metal bowls with figural decoration in the eastern Mediterranean, Near East, and North Africa', in A.-M. Maïla-Afeiche (ed.), *Interconnections in the Eastern Mediterranean Lebanon in the Bronze and Iron Ages: Proceedings of the International Symposium of Beirut 2008*, Ministère de la Culture: Direction Générale des Antiquités (2009), pp. 439–52.

10 F. Onnis, 'Levantine iconography: was there a conscious figurative programme in the decoration of the "Phoenician Metal Bowls"?', in Maïla-Afeiche (ed.), *Interconnections*, pp. 499–514.

11 K. Ulanowski, 'God Reshef in the Mediterranean', in L. Bombardieri et al. (eds), *SOMA 2012: Identity and Connectivity: Proceedings of the 16th Symposium on Mediterranean Archaeology, Florence, Italy, 1–3 March 2012* (Oxford: Archaeopress, 2013), pp. 157–63.

12 H. Sader, *Iron Age Funerary Stelae from Lebanon*. Cuadernos de arqueologia Mediterranea 11 (2005); H. Sader, 'The stelae', in M.E. Aubet (ed.), *The Phoenician Cemetery of Tyre al-Bass: Excavations 1997–1999* (Beirut: Ministère de la Culture, Direction Générale des Antiquités, 2004), BAAL – Hors-Série I, pp. 383–94; G. Abousamra and A. Lemaire, *New Funerary Phoenician Stelae – Private Collection* (Beirut: Kutub, 2014).

13 H. Sader, 'Phoenician "popular art": transmission, transformation, and adaptation of foreign motifs in the light of recent archaeological evidence from Lebanon', in R. Rollinger et al. (eds), *Interkulturalität id der Alten Welt: Vorderasien, Hellas, Ägypten und die vielfältigen Ebenen des Kontakts* (Wiesbaden: Harrassowitz Verlag, 2010), pp. 23–39.

14 B. Mustafa and N. Abbas, 'New marble sarcophagus from the Syrian Coast', *Scientific Culture* 1/1 (2015), pp. 17–26.

15 M. O'Shea, 'Another look at the origins of Iron Age II cast glass vessels in the Levant', *Levant* 43/2 (2011), pp. 153–72.

16 J. Henderson, *Ancient Glass: An Interdisciplinary Exploration* (Cambridge: Cambridge University Press, 2011), especially chaps 6 (pp. 158–202), 7 (pp. 203–34), and 8 (pp. 235–51).

17 J.B. Pritchard, *Recovering Sarepta, A Phoenician City* (Princeton, NJ: Princeton University Press, 1978), pp. 111–26.

18 W.P. Anderson, 'The beginnings of Phoenician pottery: vessel shape, style, and ceramic technology in the early phases of the Phoenician Iron Age', *Bulletin of the American Schools of Oriental Research* 279 (1990), pp. 35–54.

19 A. Gilboa, 'The dynamics of Phoenician bichrome pottery: a view from Tel Dor', *Bulletin of the American Schools of Oriental Research* 316 (1999), pp. 1–22.

20 M.M. Homan, 'Beer and its drinkers: an ancient Eastern love story', *Journal of Near Eastern Archaeology* 67 (2004), pp. 84–95.

21 D. Regev, 'Phoenician transport amphorae', in J. Eiring and J. Lund (eds), *Transport Amphorae and Trade in the Eastern Mediterranean: Acts of the International Colloquium at the Danish Institute at Athens, September 26–29, 2002* (Athens: The Danish Institute at Athens, 2004), pp. 337–52; P.M. Bikai, 'The late Phoenician pottery complex and chronology', *Bulletin of the American Schools of Oriental Research* 229 (1978), pp. 47–56.

22 D.S. Reese, 'Shells from Sarepta (Lebanon) and east Mediterranean purple-dye production', *Mediterranean Archaeology and Archaeometry* 10/1 (2010), pp. 113–41.

23 D. Frangié-Joly, 'Perfumes, aromatics, and purple dye: Phoenician trade and production in the Greco-Roman Period', *Journal of Eastern Mediterranean Archaeology & Heritage Studies* 4/1 (2016), pp. 36–56.

24 I. Ziderman, '"BA" guide to artefacts: seashells and ancient purple dyeing', *The Biblical Archaeologist* 53/2 (1990), pp. 98–101.

25 Z.C. Koren, 'The first optimal all-murex all-natural purple dyeing in the eastern Mediterranean in a millennium and a half ', *Dyes in History and Archaeology* 20 (2005), pp. 136–49.

26 For example, J. Doumet, 'Purple dye', in C. Doumet-Serhal (ed.), *Decade: A Decade of Archaeology and History in the Lebanon* (Beirut: Lebanese British Friends of the National Museum, 2004), pp. 38–49.

CHAPTER 5: OVERSEAS EXPANSION

1 H.G. Niemeyer, 'Trade before the flag? On the principles of Phoenician expansion in the Mediterranean', in A. Biran and J. Aviram (eds), *Biblical*

Archaeology Today 1990 (Jerusalem: Israel Exploration Society, 1993), pp. 335–44; H.G. Niemeyer, 'The Phoenicians in the Mediterranean: between expansion and colonization: a non-Greek model of overseas settlement and presence', in G.R. Tsetskhldze (ed.), *Greek Colonization: An Account of Greek Colonies and Other Settlements Overseas* (Boston: Brill, 2006), pp. 143–68.

2 M.E. Aubet, *The Phoenicians in the West: Politics, Colonies, and Trade* (Cambridge: Cambridge University Press, 2001), pp. 194–211.

3 M.E. Aubet, 'Political and economic implications of the new Phoenician chronologies', in C. Sagona (ed.), *Beyond the Homeland: Markers in Phoenician Chronology* (Leuven: Peeters, 2008), pp. 247–60.

4 R. Osborne, 'Early Greek colonization? The nature of Greek settlement in the West', in N. Fisher and H. van Wees (eds), *Archaic Greece: New Approaches and New Evidence* (London: Duckworth, 1998), pp. 251–69; C. Gosden, *Archaeology and Colonialism* (Cambridge: Cambridge University Press, 2004); P. van Dommelen, 'Colonial interactions and hybrid practices', in G.J. Stein (ed.), *The Archaeology of Colonial Encounters* (Santa Fe, NM: School of American Research Press, 2005), pp. 109–41.

5 T. Hodos, *Local Responses to Colonization in the Iron Age Mediterranean* (Abingdon: Routledge, 2006).

6 S. Frankenstein, 'The Phoenicians in the Far West: a function of Neo-Assyrian imperialism', in M.T. Larson (ed.), *Power and Propaganda. A Symposium on Ancient Empires*, Mesopotamia 7 (Copenhagen: Akademisk Forlag, 1979), pp. 263–94.

7 Aubet, 'Political and economic implications', pp. 179–91.

8 Aubet, *The Phoenicians in the West*, pp. 70–96.

9 E. Lipiński, *Studia Phoenicia XVIII: Itineraria Phoenicia* (Leuven: Peeters, 2004); B. Peckham, 'Phoenicians and Aramaeans: the literary and epigraphic evidence', in M.M. Michèle Daviau, J.W. Wevers, M. Weigl et al. (eds), *The World of the Aramaeans: Studies in Honour of Eugène Dion* (Sheffield: Sheffield Academic Press, 2001), pp. 19–44.

10 B. Watkins Treumann, 'Beyond the cedars of Lebanon: Phoenician timber merchants and trees from the "Black Mountain"', *Die Welt des Orients* 31 (2000–1), pp. 75–83.

11 V. Karageorghis, 'Phoenicians in Cyprus', in S.C. Pérez and J.J. Ávila (eds), *Actas del III Simposio Internacional de Arqueología de Mérida: Protohistoria del Mediterráneo Ocidental – El Periodo Orienalizante (Volumen I)*, Anejos de AEspA XXXV, pp. 31–46.

12 V. Karageorghis, 'Interconnections between Cyprus and Lebanon from the Bronze Age to the end of the Archaic Period', in A.-M. Maïla-Afeiche (ed.), *Interconnections in the Eastern Mediterranean Lebanon in the Bronze and Iron Ages: Proceedings of the International Symposium of Beirut 2008*, Ministère de la Culture, Direction Générale des Antiquités (2009), pp. 325–37.

13 P.M. Bikai, 'Cyprus and the Phoenicians', *The Biblical Archaeologist* 42/4 (1989), pp. 203–9.

14 M. Iacovou, 'External and internal migrations during the 12th century BC: setting the stage for an economically successful Iron Age', in M. Iacovou

(ed.), *Cyprus in Cyprus and the Aegean in the Early Iron Age: The Legacy of Nicolas Coldstream* (Nicosia: Bank of Cyprus Cultural Foundation, 2012), pp. 207–27.

15 V. Kassianidou, 'The exploitation of the landscape: metal resources and the copper trade during the age of the Cypriot city-kingdoms', *Bulletin of the American Schools of Oriental Research* 370 (2013), pp. 49–82.

16 N. Kourou, 'Rhodes: the Phoenician issues revisited – Phoenicians at Vroulia?', in N.C. Stampolidis and V. Karageorghis (eds), *Sea Routes ... Interconnections in the Mediterranean 16th-6th Centuries* BC (Athens: University of Crete and the A.G. Leventis Foundation, 2003), pp. 249–62.

17 O. Negbi, 'The Phoenician presence in the Mediterranean islands', *American Journal of Archaeology* 96 (1992), pp. 599–615.

18 C. Mee, *Rhodes in the Bronze Age: An Archaeological Survey* (Warminster: Aris and Philips, 1989).

19 N. Coldstream, 'Phoenicians at Ialyssos', *Bulletin of the Institute of Classical Studies* 16 (1969), pp. 1–8.

20 N. Chr. Stampolidis and A. Kotsonas, 'Phoenicians in Crete', in S. Deger-Jalkotzy and I.S. Lemos (eds), *Ancient Greece from Mycenaean Palaces to the Age of Homer* (Edinburgh: Edinburgh University Press, 2006), pp. 337–60; G. Hoffman, *Imports and Immigrants: Near Eastern Contacts with Iron Age Crete* (Ann Arbor, MI: University of Michigan Press, 1997).

21 J.W. Shaw and M.C. Shaw, 'Excavations at Kommos (Crete) during 1986–1992', *Hesperia* 62 (1993), pp. 129–90.

22 R. Garland, *The Piraeus: From the Fifth to the First Century B.C.* (Bristol: Bristol Classical Press, 1987), pp. 62–7.

23 R.M. Albanese-Procelli, 'Sicily', in C. Sagona (ed.), *Beyond the Homeland: Markers in Phoenician Chronology* (Leuven: Peeters, 2008), pp. 461–86.

24 Aubet, *The Phoenicians in the West*, pp. 231–5.

25 V. Tusa 'Sicily', in S. Moscati (ed.), *The Phoenicians* (London: I.B.Tauris, 2001), pp. 231–50.

26 R. Bernardini, 'Sardinia: the chronology of the Phoenician and Punic presence from the ninth to fifth centuries B.C.', in Sagona (ed.), *Beyond the Homeland*, pp. 537–96; Aubet, *The Phoenicians in the West*, pp. 235–46.

27 A.J. Niboer, 'Italy and the Levant during the late Bronze and Iron Age', in Sagona (ed.), *Beyond the Homeland*, pp. 423–60.

28 G. Markoe, 'In pursuit of metal: Phoenicians and Greeks in Italy', in G. Kopcke and I. Tokumaru (eds), *Greece Between East and West: 10th-8th centuries* BC – *Papers of the Meeting at the Institute of Fine Arts, New York University March 15th-16th, 1990* (Mainz am Rhein: von Zabern, 1992), pp. 61–84.

29 C. Sagona, 'Phoenician settlement: how it unfolded in Malta', in A. Lemaire (ed.), *Phéniciens d'orient et d'occident: Mélanges Josette Elayi* (Paris: Librarie d'Amérique et d'Orient, 2014), pp. 351–72; S. Moscati, 'Some reflections on Malta in the Phoenician world', *Journal of Mediterranean Studies* 3/2 (1993), pp. 286–90; A. Ciasca, 'Malta', in Moscati (ed.), *The Phoenicians*, pp. 254–8.

30 C. Sagona, 'Malta between a rock and a hard place', in Sagona (ed.), *Beyond the Homeland*, pp. 487–536.

31 E. Pappa, *Early Iron Age Exchange in the West: Phoenicians in the Mediterranean and the Atlantic* (Leuven: Peeters, 2013); Lipiński, *Studia Phoenicia XVIII*, chap. IX.

32 R.F. Docter, 'The topography of archaic Carthage: preliminary results of recent excavations and some prospects', *Talanta – Proceedings of the Dutch Archaeological and Historical Society* 34–5 (2002–3), pp. 113–33.

33 E. Pappa, 'Reflections on the earliest Phoenician presence in North-West Africa', *Talanta – Proceedings of the Dutch Archaeological and Historical Society* 40–1 (2008–9), pp. 53–72.

34 A. Neville, *Mountains of Silver and Rivers of Gold: The Phoenicians in Iberia* (Oxford: Oxbow, 2007); Aubet, *The Phoenicians in the West*, especially chaps 9 and 10 (pp. 257–346); B. Treumann-Watkins, 'Phoenicians in Spain', *The Biblical Archaeologist* 55/1 (1992), pp. 28–35.

35 E. Pappa, 'Phoenicians in the West: remarks on some Western Phoenician ceramic assemblages from Atlantic Iberia', in Maïla-Afeiche (ed.), *Interconnections in the Eastern Mediterranean*, pp. 489–98.

36 Pappa, *Early Iron Age Exchange in the West*, pp. 49–82; M.E. Aubet, 'Phoenician trade in the West: balance and perspectives', in M.R. Bierling (ed.), *The Phoenicians in Spain* (Winona Lake, IN: Eisenbrauns, 2002), pp. 97–112.

37 M.E. Aubet, 'On the organization of the Phoenician colonial systems in Iberia', in N.C. Vella and C. Riva (eds), *Debating Orientalization: Multidisciplinary Approaches to Changes in the Ancient Mediterranean* (London: Equinox, 2006), pp. 94–109.

38 V.M. Guerro Ayuso and M. Clavo, 'Models of commercial exchange between the indigenous population and colonists in the proto-history of the Balearic Islands', *Rivista di Studia Fenici* 30/1 (2003), pp. 1–30.

39 J.F. Jurado, 'The Tartessian economy: mining and metallurgy', in Bierling (ed.), *The Phoenicians in Spain*, pp. 241–62.

40 M.E. Aubet, 'Notes on the economy of the Phoenician settlements in Southern Spain', in Bierling (ed.), *The Phoenicians in Spain*, pp. 79–95.

41 B. Truemann, 'Lumbermen and shipwrights: Phoenicians on the Mediterranean coast of Southern Spain', in M. Dietler and C. López-Ruiz (eds), *Colonial Encounters in Ancient Iberia: Phoenician, Greek, and Indigenous Relations* (Chicago, IL: University of Chicago Press, 2009), pp. 169–92.

EPILOGUE

1 J. Grainger, *Hellenistic Phoenicia* (Oxford: Oxford Clarendon Press, 1991).

2 F. Millar, 'The Phoenician cities: a case-study of Hellenisation', *The Cambridge Classical Journal* 29 (1983), pp. 55–71.

Index

Index